D1557263

THE AIROLA DIET

&

COOKBOOK

Including: Dr. Airola's Weight Loss Program

Other Books by Dr. Paavo Airola

How To Get Well
Everywoman's Book
Are You Confused?
Hypoglycemia: A Better Approach
How To Keep Slim, Healthy And Young
With Juice Fasting
Cancer: Causes, Prevention, And Treatment —
The Total Approach
Worldwide Secrets For Staying Young And Healthy
(Original title: Rejuvenation Secrets From Around
The World — That "Work")
Stop Hair Loss
Swedish Beauty Secrets
The Miracle Of Garlic
There ***Is*** A Cure For Arthritis
Sex And Nutrition
Health Secrets From Europe

World Famous Diet of Supernutrition for Superhealth

The Airola Diet & Cookbook

INCLUDING

Dr. Airola's
Weight Loss Program
the only reducing program that results in safe and successful weight loss while improving your health.

by Paavo Airola, Ph.D.

Recipes compiled, edited, and tested by

Anni M. Lines, R.D.

HEALTH PLUS PUBLISHERS, Phoenix, Arizona

THE AIROLA DIET AND COOKBOOK
Copyright © 1981 by
Health Plus Publishers

All rights reserved. No part of this publication may be reproduced, stored in a retrieval system, or transmitted in any form or by any means, electronic, mechanical, photocopying, recording, or otherwise without the prior written permission of the publisher.

World Rights Reserved

First Printing, Nov., 1981

Drawings by Karen Lyman and the Author
Cover photograph of Dr. Airola by Diane Padys, 1979
Typography by Citigraphics, Scottsdale, Arizona

Published by
HEALTH PLUS, Publishers
P.O. Box 22001, Phoenix, AZ 85028

ISBN #0-932090-11-7

Printed in the United States of America

DEDICATION

This book is dedicated to all those who are confused and bewildered by the deluge of extreme and bizarre diets and nutritional fads, and are earnestly searching for a down-to-earth, common-sense super-nutritious diet with scientifically confirmed potential for superior health, greater vitality, optimal resistance to disease, and long life; and to millions of faithful Airola Diet adherents worldwide, who attest that it, indeed, holds that potential.

ACKNOWLEDGEMENTS

I wish to thank all my readers and students who, throughout the years, have admonished me to write the Airola Diet Cookbook — their appeals motivated me to finally sit down and do it.

My grateful acknowledgement goes to all those who so generously contributed recipes, especially to the members of my family: Evi Wiltbank, Karen Lyman, Becky Airola, and Paula Clure. They also performed the invaluable service of testing many of the recipes. My warm and very special appreciation goes to my dedicated wife, Marsha, who worked tirelessly in assisting me to make this book possible — a formidable task for someone whose basic tenet is the same as mine: That natural foods are best eaten as they are, and need only minimal preparation to be enjoyed!

I also wish to thank my secretary, Karen Jensen, for her much appreciated editorial and secretarial assistance in the preparation of the manuscript.

Lastly, and mostly, I wish to express my deepest gratitude to my daughter and co-author of this book, Anni M. Lines, R.D., who performed the mammoth task of compiling, editing, and testing all the recipes in the book. Her contribution is especially valuable because of her extensive professional background as a Registered Dietician and clinical nutritionist.

TABLE OF CONTENTS

SECTION II

RECIPES

SECTION III

CHARTS AND TABLES

Publisher's Preface

With his earlier works, especially the international best-sellers, HOW TO GET WELL, ARE YOU CONFUSED?, and EVERYWOMAN'S BOOK, Dr. Paavo Airola established his well-earned position as a leading authority on holistic medicine, and one of the most reputable and knowledgeable nutritionists of our time. A courageous pioneer, Dr. Airola almost single-handedly shook the foundation of the high-protein craze in this country; restored the reputation of grains as the nutritional "staff of life"; awakened his world-wide readership (his books are translated into seven languages) to the danger of rancid oils and foods; revolutionized the treatment of hypoglycemia; and introduced the concept of Biological Medicine in the United States.

Perhaps Dr. Airola's most significant contribution to the welfare of humanity is his discovery and formulation of the Optimum Diet. The Airola Optimum Diet has become a distinctive nutrition concept recognized world-wide. In this age of unprecedented nutrition awareness, there are almost as many nutrition philosophies and dietary programs as there are nutrition "experts" and writers. Yet, today, more nutrition-conscious people in the United States and around the world adhere to the Airola Diet than to any other nutrition system. Millions of people read Dr. Airola's books and millions of people follow his sound, common-sense advice — changing their diets, optimizing their nutrition, and reaping the wonderful rewards of better health, greater vitality, and longer life.

A question is often asked: How and why has Dr. Airola become the world's best-known and most respected nutritionist in such a short span of time? Certainly, his encyclopedic knowledge of the subject, his sincerity, his dynamic, honest, charismatic, and down-to-earth style of writing, as well as lecturing, hits the right note in the minds of confused health-seekers. After suffering disappointment and harm at the hands of all kinds of self-styled experts and charlatans whose books and lectures are often nothing more than sales gimmicks for their products, people are pleasantly surprised to discover that Dr. Airola never sells any of the vitamins and health products that he so highly recommends! This is one of the reasons Dr. Airola enjoys such massive respect and admiration from thousands of his readers, students, and colleagues.

But his expertise and integrity may not be the main reasons for Dr. Airola's meteoric rise to the top position in the field of nutrition and holistic health. As publishers of his books, we receive thousands of unsolicited letters each month from grateful readers who claim to have benefitted greatly from the information in his books. Two specific kinds of comments — one from doctors, and one from laymen — illustrate, we think, more than anything else the reason for Dr. Airola's phenomenal popularity. Here is a typical example of a response from laymen readers: "I have been into health and nutrition for 25 years; I have heard them all and read all the books — Dr. Airola has more common sense than any of them. He has it all together!" And, from doctors: "Dr. Airola's are the first so-called 'health books' that don't turn me off!" As renowned medical educator and author, Robert S. Mendelsohn, M.D. recently wrote, "Invaluable qualities of judgement, assessment, evaluation, and selectivity . . . and the analytical deliberation, ethical standards, and mature wisdom distinguish Dr. Airola as a giant in the field."

The reason Dr. Airola's message seems to reach both critical laymen and skeptical professionals is that his nutritional conclusions are based not only on common sense, but also on a solid scientific foundation. His research is painstaking and thorough, his documentation and references impeccable, and his conclusions logical and scientific. Dr. Airola is a rare combination of a highly trained scientist (his Ph.D. being in biochemistry and N.D. in Naturopathic Medicine) and a down-to-earth empiricist, visionary, philosopher, and original thinker.

The universal appeal of the Airola Diet is also linked to the fact that it is not based on current fads or unproven theories. In this age when man-made nutrition fads abound, it is reassuring to find a diet that is not concocted in the mind of an ambitious self-styled nutritionist, but is based on well-established traditions and is empirically proven by thousands of years of actual application. In fact, Dr. Airola refuses to take all the credit for inventing his famous Optimum Diet. He says that he discovered the diet by traveling around the world and studying the eating habits of various people known for their exceptional health, absence of disease, and long life: Abhkasians in Caucasus, Hunzas in Pakistan, Yuccatan Indians in Mexico, Bulgarians, Russians, etc. He found many common denominators in the diets of all of these people, which formed the structural basis for his Optimum Diet. In Dr. Airola's *Introduction* to this book you will find the empirical and scientific basis for the Airola Diet outlined in detail.

Although Dr. Paavo Airola has authored fourteen books, most of which are dealing with various aspects of his Diet, this is the first time that he has agreed to and authorized the publication of a book of Airola Diet Recipes. The reasons for this delay and for the final decision to publish the Recipe Book, according to Dr. Airola, are as follows:

1. The ultimate Airola Diet is so simple that ideally the daily menu should consist of only a few main selections, the same day after day. He felt, therefore, that everyone would be able to prepare the Airola Diet menu by following a very few simple recipes and instructions which are included in most of his earlier books. And millions of Airola Diet adherents are doing just that.

2. In the past, most converts to the Airola Diet came from veteran health-foodists who became disenchanted with

whatever nutrition system they had followed previously (such as a high-protein diet, macrobiotic diet, natural hygiene diet, mucusless diet, fruitarian diet, etc.). They were experienced enough in health-oriented eating that they could switch to the Airola Diet easily and without requiring a transition-type diet. Now, however, millions of new readers are exposed to Airola's teachings every year. Many of these readers are recent converts to health-oriented nutrition and they require a gradual transition from the typical American diet of canned, over-processed, and denatured foods to a more natural diet of whole, unrefined, made-from-scratch-type of foods. These newcomers seem to have a need for a greater variety of choices rather than a few well-planned super-nutritious courses, which the ultimate Airola Diet consists of. Consequently, this book is aimed at helping these new converts to healthful eating and to making a painless transition to the ultimate, pure, and simple Airola Optimum Diet.

We take great pride in presenting this new book by Dr. Paavo Airola. We are confident that it will be just as helpful as his other books to those who are sincerely searching for ways to improve their health.

To your health! And, Bon Appetit!

Health Plus Publishers

INTRODUCTION

Why the Airola Optimum Diet?

Although most people agree that nutrition is a very important factor affecting one's health, almost everyone, including doctors and nutritionists — or, should I say, *especially* doctors and nutritionists — disagree as to *WHAT* constitutes ideal or optimal nutrition for optimum health.

There are those who believe that the so-called "Basic Four" food groups will assure optimum nutrition. There are those who advocate a high-animal-protein diet, with lots of meat. There are those who condemn all seeds and grains ("seeds are for the birds") and those who would eat seeds, but not grains. There are those who advocate eating only raw foods, and those who consider the discovery of fire to be the greatest boon to man's nutrition. There are those who eat only vegetables that grow above the ground, and those who consider tomatoes, garlic and onions to be poisonous. Then there are nutritionists and health writers who wish to please everyone (just like the politicians) and advise eating anything that you like, or "what agrees with you," as long as it is natural and unprocessed. There are those who feel that you should supplement your diet with vitamins — and there are those who claim that all added vitamins are harmful and/or unnecessary and that you will get all your vitamins from the foods you eat.

Lately, we seem to have more and more extreme and bizarre diets and nutrition fads. Fruitarians advise eating nothing but fruits. Raw foodists claim that cooked food is "dead" food and cannot produce anything but death — consequently, they advocate eating everything raw, even grains. Mucusless diet proponents attribute all disease to mucus-producing foods, such as milk, grains, and meats, and claim that avoidance of them can ensure optimum health. Sproutarians claim that the secret of health is in eating sprouts, especially wheat sprouts and wheat grass. Even among those who adhere to vegetarian dietary philosophies there are strict vegetarians or vegans who avoid all animal products, including milk and eggs, lacto-vegetarians who use milk, and lacto-ovo-vegetarians who use milk and eggs. Then there is the macrobiotic diet of Japanese culinary flavor with emphasis on rice and soy products, all heavily salted, cooked, and fried. There are even those who suggest that we quit eating completely, and replace it with drinking, claiming that by drinking copious amounts of juices we will solve all of our health problems. Some of the newest fads put all the blame on fats and claim that by eliminating from the diet not only butter, vegetable oils, and other concentrated fats, but also all fat-containing foods such as milk, cheese, nuts, seeds, and avocados, we can eliminate all of our degenerative diseases.

The proponents of each of the above-mentioned diets claim in their books or lectures that *theirs* is the diet that is the perfect one — and, what's more, they have "wonderful results" to prove it! No wonder the average person is confused! The more books he reads, the more lectures he hears, the more confused and bewildered he becomes. Who is right? Whom can you believe? Why is there so much confusion and disagreement among experts?

In my book, *Are You Confused?*, I have answered these questions quite thoroughly, so I will not go into detail here, except to mention that commercialism (most nutritionists are selling the products or services that they so highly recommend), scholastic dogmatism, outdated and obsolete information (many still-popular nutrition books were written 20-30-40 years ago when many of the vitamins had not even been discovered and nutrition science was in its infancy), and personal likes and dislikes (for examples, one late leading nutritionist extolled the value of eating lots of meat because he "personally liked the taste of meat"), are at the root of so much nutrition misinformation, confusion, and disagreement.

But the main reason there is so much confusion on nutrition is that creators of some of these obviously deficient diets have overlooked the extremely important difference between a *therapeutic diet* and a *preventive diet.* Let me explain.

The crucial difference between therapeutic and preventive nutrition

Example: Arnold Ehret was a very sick man. After trying a long line of conventional doctors and drugs for years, his health went from bad to worse and nothing seemed to help. Finally, in desperation, he started to experiment with his own diet and he discovered that by eliminating bread, cereals, milk, cheese, meat, fowl, and fish from his diet, he miraculously became well. Since all the above-mentioned foods are mucus-producing, Ehret concluded that excess mucus is the cause of all illness, and by eliminating all mucus-forming foods from our diet, not only will we all get well, but such a diet will prevent disease if we remain on it continuously. Consequently, he wrote books, lectured, and proclaimed to his enthusiastic followers that he had discovered the ideal diet, the *mucusless* diet, and he advocated that all should adhere to such a diet to optimize their health and prevent disease.

Another example: In the past few decades, several sincere seekers of better health have discovered that eating nothing but fresh fruits for several months (often nothing but oranges and tomatoes) helped dramatically to restore their health. They drew the erroneous conclusion that because a fruit diet made them feel so good, and because it had such a healing effect, it must be the ultimate, divinely-designed diet for man. Consequently, they recommended that all those concerned with preserving their health become fruitarians.

One more example: Nathan Pritikin discovered that by eliminating all fats from the diet, including such foods as milk, cheese, butter, vegetable oils, eggs, nuts, seeds, and avocados, patients at his health center were miraculously cured from such degenerative cardiovascular disorders as angina, atherosclerosis, high blood pressure, and heart disease. After a few weeks on this diet, heart patients scheduled for by-pass surgery no longer needed surgery. Angina patients, who previously could not walk ten feet without pain, could walk miles and climb mountains. Impressed by the tremendous *therapeutic* effect of his diet, Pritikin concluded that the prime reason we Americans are so sick and suffer from so many degenerative diseases is that we eat too much protein and too much fat. By eliminating excess protein and all the fat from our diet, we can get rid of all the degenerative diseases.

What *all* the above-mentioned writers overlooked is that although their diets, and many others, such as sproutarian, juice, grape, or other limited diets, are obviously remarkably *therapeutic* — i.e., they are able to cure disease and restore health — they are also, nutritionally speaking, *far too deficient to maintain health and prevent disease* once health has been restored. A therapeutic diet doesn't have to be an *optimal* diet in terms of its nutritional adequacy. For the best therapeutic effect, it can be, *in fact often must be,* inadequate or deficient in certain nutritive elements. Eating nothing but fresh fruit for a period of time obviously has such a thorough cleansing effect on the body that many ailments, especially those related to overeating, constipation, intestinal sluggishness, poor digestion and assimilation, and a slowed down metabolism, are miraculously corrected, and the functions of all organs and glands normalized. But, *if, after health has been restored on such a deficient but therapeutic diet, the patient continues to adhere to it, it will eventually create even more serious health disorders than the ones it corrected.* With an excess of mineral-binding fruit acids and the lack of sufficient fat and protein in an exclusive fruitarian diet, severe deficiencies and imbalances, which may lead to serious health disorders, will eventually manifest themselves.

The same applies to a fat-free diet. Because we Americans eat far too much fat (45 percent or more of the calories in our average diet come from fat), we have an epidemic of diseases related to, or caused by, excess fat in our diet, notably cardiovascular diseases, heart disease, high blood pressure, diabetes, liver and gallbladder disorders, and obesity. By eliminating all fats from the diet, these disorders respond dramatically, especially in combination with vigorous exercise. Not able to get any fat from dietary supplies, the body is forced to burn its own fatty deposits, including those in arteries, tissues, and organs — which results in a speedy improvement of all ailments related to excess dietary fat, overeating, obesity and lack of exercise. But, if the patient stays on such a diet *after* health has been restored, he will eventually suffer from other severe health disorders which the dietary lack of saturated and unsaturated fatty acids and fat-soluble vitamins can cause, such as multiple sclerosis, diseases of the nervous system, senility, sexual dysfunction, and mental disorders. In order to arrive at a ratio of 10 percent fat in the diet (calorie-wise), as, for example, Pritikin recommends, some indispensable and nutritionally-superior foods, such as many grains, nuts, seeds, avocados, milk, and cheese, must be totally eliminated from the diet. Such a diet, just like a fruitarian, sproutarian, or exclusive juice diet, will have a tremendous therapeutic effect, *but it is too deficient to be an optimal preventive diet, a diet that can build and maintain health and prevent disease.*

An optimal *preventive* diet must be adequate in all the essential nutrients necessary for the maintenance of the highest level of health and prevention of disease, not only for a few weeks or months, but for a lifetime, while the *therapeutic* diet can be deficient in one or more vital nutrients and yet produce remarkable therapeutic results. The best example of this is *juice fasting.* Drinking nothing but fresh fruit and vegetable juices for several weeks is the safest, fastest, and most effective therapeutic method known. Practically every condition of ill health can be corrected by juice fasting. Yet, if you continue a juice fast indefinitely, it will eventually kill you. So it is with the various fad diets mentioned previously. They are all excellent *therapeutic* diets and are able to correct specific diseases and restore health. But as soon as health is restored, you must discontinue them, and go on an optimum *preventive* diet.

Once you understand this crucial difference between the *therapeutic* diet and the *preventive* diet, it will enable you to orient yourself in the growing maze of nutrition misinformation and dietary fads, and avoid confusion. Next time a persuasive and eloquent lecturer tries to convert you to his diet by the usual appeal, "If you don't believe me, just try my diet for three weeks and see for yourself how great you feel," you respond: "I am not interested in how I feel in *three weeks* — I would like to know what kind of diet will make me feel great and help me avoid disease *for a lifetime.*" In other words, what you are looking for is not just a therapeutic diet (although therapeutic diets are valuable in the treatment of disease) but an *optimal health-building and disease-preventing diet,* a diet that can assure you of the greatest potential for building and maintaining health and preventing disease.

The Airola Optimum Diet is such a diet. It is not based on my subjective beliefs or wishful thinking, but on reliable empirical evidence. I have traveled around the world studying the eating and living habits of people known for their exceptional health, absence of disease, and long life. The eating habits and lifestyles of these people are strikingly similar in terms of the relationship to their superior health and extended longevity.

The Airola Diet, outlined in the next chapter, is based on my above-mentioned empirical studies as well as the latest scientific discoveries in the field of nutrition and health. It is an optimal health-building and disease-preventive diet that will supply optimal nutrition for any person of any age who is interested in a high level of wellness and a long, vigorous, disease-free life.

Section I

Airola Diet

I

Airola Diet: Basic Principles

The basic Airola Optimum Diet for Optimum Health should be made up of these three food groups (in this order of importance):

1. Grains, Legumes, Beans, Seeds, and Nuts
2. Vegetables
3. Fruits

A diet composed of a variety of fresh — raw and cooked — foods from these three food groups, properly balanced and conscientiously prepared, will supply adequate amounts of all the nutrients required for the maintenance of Optimum Health, including sufficient amounts of high-quality proteins (see "Vitamins and Supplements in the Airola Diet"). An addition of animal foods, such as meat, fowl, fish, and eggs, is not necessary for nutritional reasons. If the inclusion of animal foods is desired, especially during a transition period, they can be added in small amounts in this order of desirability (least desirable food mentioned last): eggs, preferably free-range, fertile eggs; fish, preferably deep-water ocean fish; fowl, preferably white skinless meat; and red meats. Pork and processed meats in any form should never be used.

Since millions of people in many different parts of the world, including Japan, Scandinavia, Europe, Canada, Australia, Pacific and Atlantic Islands, and far-northern regions live on the Airola Optimum Diet, it may be that people in some areas would wish to include in their diet certain foods indigenous to their location or traditional dietary habits. For example, the inclusion of fish may be desirable in coastal areas where fish has long been a traditional dietary staple, or meat in countries with long winters where there is almost a total unavailability of fresh fruits and vegetables for much of the year. A moderate amount of such animal foods may be added to the three basic food groups of the Airola Diet without substantially altering its Optimum Diet identity. However, in temperate, sub-tropical, and tropical climates, the highest level of wellness and extended longevity can be best achieved and maintained without meat.

The Universal Nature of the Airola Diet

One of the most distinctive characteristics of the Airola Optimum Diet is that it is universally adaptable. This fact may be responsible for its tremendous popularity around the world. Most nutrition systems advocate a strict menu of carefully selected foods. For example, the faithful followers of the macrobiotic diet eat rice, tofu, Aduki beans, miso, tamari, seaweeds, umeboshi, and other typically and traditionally Oriental foods, no matter where in the world they live, even if they happen to live in regions where none of these foods are grown or produced — actually they are continually eating foods that are imported from far-away areas or countries and are, thus, almost always stale and rancid, with much of the nutritional value lost in the process of transportation and storage. The Waerland Diet, for example, advocates a strict menu in which kruska (whole wheat porridge) is eaten daily — it doesn't matter what part of the world you live in, even if you happen to live in Central America, where corn and beans are the only major foods that are produced. Natural Hygienists are very much anti-grain and prohibit the eating of any form of grain foods, such as breads or cereals, even though you would happen to live in Northern Canada or Scandinavia where such a diet would be nothing less than suicidal. Raw food advocates and fruitarians are equally dogmatic and limiting.

The Airola Diet, on the other hand, is so universally applicable that it can be successfully adhered to in any part of the world. You build your daily menu from foods of the three basic food groups (grains, seeds, legumes, and nuts; vegetables; and fruits) that are indigenous to the area in which you live and are available locally. Thus, Waerland kruska (which represents the grain group) will be great if you live in Sweden or Canada. But, if you live in Finland, rye porridge will be better, since it has been used there as a staple for centuries. If you live in Scotland, oatmeal will be a typical grain meal. If you live in China or Japan, whole rice will be a natural daily staple representing the grain group. If you live in the Middle East, millet is a superb cereal. And, if you live in Mexico, corn and beans will be ideal. This principle applies to the other food groups, too. You build your menu of vegetables and fruits that grow in your own environment and locality. Mangoes, avocados, bananas, pineapple, cherimoyas, and guavas are terrific Airola Diet components if you live in Mexico, the Caribbean islands, or Central America. But, if you live in Canada or Scandinavia, or even in the northern parts of the United States, you will be better off eating potatoes, rutabagas, carrots, beets, cabbage, onions, and a variety of locally-grown apples, strawberries, blueberries, black or red currants, blackberries, cranberries, and such, rather than imported fruits or vegetables grown in far-away places which have much of their nutritive value lost by the time they reach your table. Not only are foods from your own area fresher — and freshness *IS* important: for example, lettuce loses up to 50% of its vitamin C content in 24 hours after it is harvested — but if you live in or near the place of your birth, foods grown in your own environment are more compatible with your own biological and physiological needs, since, being literally made from dust, you are a part and product of your own bio-chemo-cosmo-physical and electro-magnetical environment. The vital life-giving, vibratory energies present in foods grown in your own environment are more compatible with your bio-receptors and energy needs than those present in foods grown in other geographical, geological, and climatic environments. The transference of these energies from foods is just as important for your well-being as the tangible proteins, fats, minerals, and other chemical substances in foods.

This Principle of Universality of the Airola Optimum Diet explains why two persons living in different ends of the world and eating diets that are apparently as different as night and day, are both claiming that they adhere to the Airola Diet philosophy. Although the diet of one may not include any of the actual foods in the diet of the other, several unifying principles qualify both diets as optimum diets:

- Locally-grown grains, legumes, seeds, and nuts form the nutritional basis of both diets.
- Vegetables and fruits in both diets are grown in the immediate environment.
- Both diets are low-protein, low-fat, high-natural-carbohydrate diets.
- Both diets are composed of foods indigenous to the area, which are fresh, unprocessed, unadulterated, whole, and natural.

Recognize Your Nutritional Roots

Which brings us to another central principle of the Airola Optimum Diet: The importance of recognizing and respecting our nutritional roots — traditional ethnic dietary patterns and habits of our ancestors — and taking them into consideration when planning our own personalized Airola Diet.

The human body has an enormous capacity to adapt itself to a variety of nutritional patterns and adjust its metabolic processes to cope remarkably well, even when subjected to severe nutritional abuses. The Eskimo diet is an illustrative example. If an average American would be forced to eat a typical Eskimo diet, he would perish in no time at all. Yet, Eskimos survive relatively well (although their life expectancy is the lowest in the world). The reason they survive at all is that their bodies, through centuries of gradual adaptation and natural selection (the weaker perished, and the stronger survived, gradually increasing the survival rate), have developed a metabolic system that is specifically adapted to their unique dietary patterns; so much so that if Eskimos are suddenly given a more adequate and nutritionally superior diet, they suffer and become ill. Their bodies have become biologically, metabolically, and genetically programmed to function on an inferior diet. An analogy: If your car is set and tuned to run on diesel fuel, it will not run as well on high-test ethyl gasoline, and vice-versa. To develop such metabolic programming took centuries, even milleniums, and countless generations. To *change* such metabolic programming would likewise take centuries; by some estimates, as long as six to eight hundred years or more.

What does all this mean to you?

To enjoy optimal health and well-being it would be extremely helpful to know your nutritional roots and choose foods that are indigenous to the country of your origin and foods that were staples in the dietary patterns of your ancestors. Contrarywise, by avoiding foods that your body is not metabolically programmed to process effectively you can spare yourself lots of digestive and other health problems.

For example, almost half of all Blacks who reside in the United States cannot digest milk effectively because they are intolerant to milk. Why? Because, as Dr. Robert D. McCracken, anthropologist at the University of California School of Public Health, so ably explained, people whose ancestors historically herded dairy animals and traditionally lived on a lactose-rich diet of milk, cheese, etc., have plenty of the lactose-digesting enzyme, lactase, in their intestines, which makes digestion and utilization of milk easy. But those whose ancestors never or seldom used milk as a major element of their diet, such as the ancestors of most American Blacks, do not have this milk-digesting enzyme in sufficient quantities and are, thus, intolerant to milk; i.e., they cannot digest milk effectively. This is true also if your ancestry is Chinese, Filipino, Japanese, or American Indian. It will be better for you to exclude milk and milk products completely from your diet. On the other hand, if your nutritional roots are in the traditionally milk-eating countries, then milk and milk products will most likely be well-tolerated by your body, and effectively digested.

This principle applies to other foods as well. Many are troubled by eating wheat and cannot digest it well. Perhaps you came from a background where wheat was never or seldom eaten. You will be better off, in such cases, if you make other grains the staple of your diet. For example, if you are of Mexican ancestry, use corn and beans, or tortillas and beans. This is one of the best food combinations possible, with improved nutritional benefits, especially in terms of protein. If you are from the Far East, put the emphasis in your diet on whole rice. If you are from Finland or Russia, use rye in preference to wheat. And so on. Some people cannot tolerate cabbage or sauerkraut, yet I've never seen a German or a Russian who complained of not being able to digest cabbage effectively — they are programmed by century-long adaptation to digest this food well.

Why No Meat in the Optimum Diet

Some have asked me: "My ancestors were heavy meat eaters; shouldn't I eat lots of meat?" Don't try to justify your meat-eating habit by making up your nutritional roots! Unless your roots are in the Polar Regions, your ancestors were *not* heavy meat-eaters. Excessive meat-eating is a very recent phenomenon, both in the United States and elsewhere in the world. Until just a few generations ago, meat was eaten only occasionally, mostly on weekends and holidays. This was true in European countries as well as in the United States. It is safe to say that 98 percent of all Americans have nutritional roots in low-animal-protein backgrounds, and, thus, will achieve better health on such a diet. Remember, it takes perhaps a thousand years to re-program the body's metabolic system. That's why most American Blacks, even after living on this continent for over 200 years, still cannot digest milk effectively.

But, my conclusions in regard to the undesirability of meat as a regular part of a diet are not based on your possible nutritional roots alone. Economic reasons are also important. Meat, as a protein source, is one of the most wasteful and expensive ways to feed the growing world population. Twenty to thirty times more people can be fed by the grains produced on one acre of land than by beef produced on the same acre. If Americans would cut their meat-eating in half, and obtain the other half of their protein from grains and beans, we could feed 200 million additional people in this country. As the world's supply of food is diminishing catastrophically, while the population is increasing at an alarming rate, the economic significance of moving towards a more vegetarian diet becomes evident.

My main objection to meat as a part of the Airola Optimum Diet is, however, medical. A high-animal-protein diet, especially an excess of meat, is definitely detrimental to the health and may be a contributing or a direct cause of the development of many of our most common diseases, as shown by recent massive research. It is well-documented (see the scientific references in *Everywoman's Book*) by reliable studies that the metabolism of proteins consumed in excess of the actual need leaves toxic residues of metabolic wastes in tissues, causes autotoxemia, over-acidity, and nutritional deficiencies, accumulation of uric acid and purines in the tissues, intestinal putrefaction, and contributes to the development of many of our most common and serious diseases, such as arthritis, kidney damage, pyorrhea, schizophrenia, osteoporosis, atherosclerosis, heart disease, and cancer. A high-protein diet also causes premature aging, and lowers life expectancy.

Recent American research done under the direction of Dr. Lennart Krook, shows that overindulgence in meat leads to a mineral imbalance in the system — too much phosphorus and too little calcium (meat has 22 times more phosphorus than calcium) — which in turn leads to severe calcium and magnesium deficiencies and resultant loss of teeth through decay or pyorrhea, and osteoporosis.

A study made at the U.S. Army Medical Research and Nutrition Laboratory in Denver, Colorado, demonstrated that the more meat you eat, the more deficient in vitamin B_6

you become. A high protein diet can cause severe deficiencies of B_6, magnesium, calcium, and niacin (vitamin B_3). Schizophrenia and other mental illness can be caused by a niacin deficiency and have been recently successfully treated with high doses of niacin. Russian researcher, Dr. Yuri Nikolayev, has been extremely successful in treating schizophrenia patients with a low-protein diet.

Extensive studies made in England showed a clear connection between a high-protein diet and osteoporosis. And doctors at the Vascular Research Laboratory in Brooklyn, New York, conducted research which indicates that excessive meat eating may be a contributing cause of widespread arteriosclerosis and heart disease. Researchers Dr. C.D. Langen, from Holland, and Dr. A. Hoygaard, from Denmark, came to the same conclusion.

Dr. Ph. Schwarz, of Frankfort University, in Germany, and Dr. Ralph Bircher, a famous biochemist in Zurich, Switzerland, report that the aging process is triggered by *amyloid*, a by-product of protein metabolism, which is deposited in all the connective tissues and causes tissue and organ degeneration — thus leading to premature aging. This explains why people who traditionally eat low-protein diets — Hunzakuts, Pakistanis, Bulgarians, Russian Caucasians, Yucatan Indians, East Indian Todas — also have the highest average life expectancy in the world — up to 90 years! And, why the people who live on high-animal-protein diets, such as Eskimos, Greenlanders, and Laplanders, have the lowest life expectancy in the world — 30-40 years. Americans lead the industrialized world in per capita meat consumption — and we are also in 27th place in life expectancy among industrialized nations!

Recently, Dr. Willard J. Visek, of Cornell University, implicated high-protein diets in the development of cancer. *Ammonia*, which is produced in great amounts as a by-product of meat metabolism, is highly carcinogenic and can trigger cancer development. A high-protein diet also breaks down the pancreas and lowers resistance to cancer, as well as contributes to the development of diabetes and/or hypoglycemia.

These are just a few examples of recent research and overwhelming scientific evidence which show that a high-animal-protein diet is *a very dangerous course to follow.*

Not only animal proteins, but *all* proteins should be consumed in moderation. Excessive protein consumption, no matter what the source, can be dangerous.

A good rule regarding proteins is: *Enough, but not too much.* By eating foods from the three basic food groups of the Airola Diet — seeds, nuts, and grains; vegetables; and fruits — you can be assured of obtaining all the vital nutrients you need for vigorous and vibrant health and prevention of disease, *including adequate amounts of complete proteins,* in a natural balance and in proper combination with all the other vital nutrients.

How Much Protein Do You Need?

In this era of the "high-protein cult", you have been brought up to believe that a high-protein diet is a *must* if you wish to attain a high level of health and prevent disease. Health writers and "experts" who have *advocated* a high-protein diet have been misled by slanted research financed by the dairy and meat industries, or by insufficient and outdated information. Most recent research, world-wide, shows more and more convincingly *that the past beliefs in regard to high requirements of protein are outdated and incorrect, and that the actual daily need for protein in human nutrition is far below that which has long been considered necessary.* Researchers, working independently in many parts of the world, arrived at the conclusion that our actual daily need of protein is only 30-40 grams (30 grams more for pregnant and lactating women) — *even less if raw proteins from milk and vegetable sources are used* (raw protein being utilized more efficiently than cooked). Independent researchers, not associated with or paid by dairy or meat industries, also point out that, contrary to past beliefs and claims of meat cultists, proteins from many vegetable sources are equal or superior to animal proteins in their biological value. Almonds, sesame seeds, soybeans, buckwheat, peanuts, sunflower seeds, pumpkin seeds, potatoes, and all leafy green vegetables contain *complete proteins*, which are comparable in quality (biological value) to animal proteins. This revealing information comes from the most reliable and respected nutrition research organization in the world, the Max Planck Institute of Nutritional Research, in Germany. This was also stressed by recent recommendations of the U.S. Senate Select Committee on Nutrition, which in the *Nutrition Guidelines*, published in 1977, the purpose of which was to help Americans improve their health by improving their nutrition, advised Americans to cut down on meat and eat more grains and vegetables — actually, in verbatim, advocating the Airola Diet as recommended in this book.

Why Grains, Beans, Seeds, and Nuts Should Form the Basis of the Airola Diet

Grains, seeds, beans, and nuts are the most important and potent health-building foods of all. Their nutritional value is unsurpassed. They contain all the nutrients essential for human growth, sustenance of health, and prevention of disease in the most perfect combination and balance. In addition, they contain the secret of life itself — the *germ*, the reproductive power that assures the perpetuation of the species. This reproductive power, the spark of life in all seeds, is of extreme importance for the life, health, and reproductive ability of human beings, too.

All seeds and grains are beneficial, but you should eat predominantly those which are grown in your own geographic area, and/or those which have been traditionally eaten by your ancestors.

Contrary to the common nutrition myth that all vegetable proteins are incomplete and of poor quality, the fact is that buckwheat, sesame seeds, pumpkin seeds, sunflower seeds, almonds, and peanuts all contain complete proteins of high biological value. But the proteins in all seeds and grains, even those which do not contain *all* the essential amino acids, are extremely useful if the foods are combined and eaten together.

Seeds, grains, and nuts are not only excellent sources of protein, but also the best natural sources of essential *unsaturated fatty acids* without which health cannot be maintained. They are also nature's best source of lecithin, a substance which is of extreme importance to the health of the brain, nerves, glands (especially sex glands), and arteries.

The *vitamin* content, especially vitamin E and the B-complex vitamins, of grains, seeds, and nuts is unsurpassed. Vitamin E is extremely important for the preservation of health and prevention of premature aging. Vitamin E can also help to increase fertility in both men and women, and can be helpful in preventing miscarriages and stillbirths. B-complex vitamins are absolutely essential for practically all body functions.

Grains, seeds, and nuts are also gold mines of *minerals and trace elements*. It is becoming increasingly apparent that minerals are even more important to health than the more glamourized vitamins. A balanced body chemistry, especially in terms of acidity and alkalinity, is dependent on minerals. Biochemical imbalance in the system is the basic underlying cause of most disease. Grains and seeds are the best sources of such trace elements and important minerals as magnesium, manganese, iron, zinc, copper, molybdenum, selenium, chromium, fluorine, silicon, potassium, and phosphorus. Molybdenum, which is still a very much ignored mineral, is present in many whole grains, especially in brown rice, millet, and buckwheat, and is involved with proper carbohydrate metabolism.

Grains, seeds, and nuts also contain *pacifarins*, an antibiotic resistance factor that increases natural resistance to disease. They also contain *auxones*, natural substances that help produce vitamins in the body and play a part in the rejuvenation of cells, preventing premature aging.

The importance of whole grains and seeds in the diet has recently been emphasized, stressing their fiber and roughage content. After several decades of eating refined and processed foods, from which the outer coating — the fiber — has been processed out, we have become a nation of people plagued by constipation, diverticulitis, colitis, and cancer of the colon and intestinal tract. Current studies show that we must go back to whole, unprocessed grains, legumes, and seeds, which provide enough bulk to help prevent these disorders.

The best seeds are: flax seeds, sesame seeds, chia seeds, and pumpkin seeds. Sesame seeds must always be hulled. Halva, tahini, and other sesame butters can also be used.

Flax seeds are an excellent food, largely neglected in the American diet. The extraordinary nutritional value of flax seeds is based on the fact that they contain a great amount of the highest quality essential fatty acids, such as *linoleic* and *linolenic* acids, or vitamin F factors. Flax seeds are also a highly mucilaginous food and are very beneficial for the healthy workings of the alimentary canal and eliminative system. They are an excellent food to help prevent and/or remedy constipation. Keep in mind, however, that flax seeds and sesame seeds contain 45-50 percent fat; so do not overeat — they can be fattening!

The best nuts are almonds and hazelnuts (filberts). Almonds are, in terms of rancidity, the most durable of all nuts, even when they are shelled. They, too, like sesame and flax seeds, supply complete high-quality proteins.

All seeds and nuts must be eaten *fresh* and **raw**, never roasted. Roasting of oil-rich seeds renders them carcinogenic. This means that seeds and nuts should never be heated to the excessively high temperatures which develop in roasting, frying, or baking; not even for making granola. Nuts can be eaten raw as they are, provided they are chewed well. Seeds and nuts can also be coarsely or finely ground in your own seed grinder just before eating, and sprinkled over other foods. Remember, ground flax seeds are especially vulnerable to rancidity and will become harmful and unsuitable for eating within a few days, so it is better to grind them fresh and eat them at once.

I have not mentioned another popular seed food, sunflower seeds, because it becomes increasingly difficult to get sunflower seeds that are not rancid. They are extremely vulnerable to rancidity, turning rancid quickly after they are shelled because the shelling process scratches and breaks the seeds, exposing the oil to oxygen. How can you tell if your seeds are rancid? Spread them on a white piece of paper and notice all the seeds that are not evenly gray, but are, in whole or in part, brown, yellow, white, black — these are all rancid. Even small quantities of rancid seeds can be extremely toxic and harmful, even carcinogenic, if consumed often. It would be, therefore, wise to sort them carefully before consuming.

Nuts and seeds combine beautifully with fresh fruits for breakfast, which can also include yogurt or other cultured milks.

The best grains for a daily cereal or porridge are buckwheat, oats, millet, and rice, although most other grains are also beneficial. Since wheat is one of the most common allergens (foods that cause allergic reactions) be sure you are not allergic to wheat before you incorporate it as part of your daily diet. If eating wheat in any form (even wheat germ) gives you any trouble, such as gas, indigestion, excessive mucus, stomach pain, or increased pulse rate, leave it out of your diet completely.

In the Airola Diet, buckwheat is preferred over all other cereals, especially if milk and milk products are not used in the diet. According to the U.S. Department of Agriculture, the proteins in buckwheat are complete and are of such high biological value that they are comparable to the proteins in meat. Buckwheat is also an excellent source of magnesium, manganese, and zinc. The best way to eat buckwheat is in the form of kasha (cooked buckwheat cereal) and buckwheat pancakes (see Index).

There are several very popular nutrition fads today which not only minimize the importance of grains, but actually are militantly anti-grain. In my world-wide studies of the eating habits of all people known for their exceptional health and long life, I have found that grains form a substantial basis in the diets of all of them. Grains, in the form of various kinds of breads, chappati, tortillas, or pita, or in the form of porridges (cooked cereals) and soups, are eaten at virtually every meal. There is a united consensus among experts who have studied the role of grains in human nutrition that grains should form a staple of any optimal nutrition program. Therefore, I am compelled to warn you against any nutrition fad that excludes grains as a major part of the diet. Even the U.S. Senate Select Committee on Nutrition, mentioned previously, has recently recognized the great importance of grains in the human diet, advising Americans to "eat more grains . . ."

Vegetables: A Daily Must

Vegetables are the next most important food group in the Airola Diet. Vegetables are extraordinary sources of minerals, enzymes, and vitamins. Most green leafy vegetables contain complete proteins of the highest quality. The proteins in alfalfa, parsley, and potatoes are comparable to the proteins in milk in their biological value.

Most vegetables should be eaten raw in the form of a salad. In fact, one meal of the day, lunch or dinner, should consist largely of vegetables. Some vegetables, such as potatoes, yams, squashes, and green beans, can be boiled, steamed, or baked.

The general rule of the Airola Diet — most vegetables should be eaten raw — has several notable exceptions. Some vegetables, such as spinach and chard, contain too much oxalic acid, and, therefore, should not be eaten raw in any appreciable quantities. A few leaves of spinach in a salad occasionally would not do much harm, but if raw spinach would be consumed often and in large quantities, and especially in the form of spinach juice, the damage could be considerable. Oxalic acid is very toxic. It can damage the liver and kidneys and cause formation of kindey stones. If you are fond of these vegetables, you must prepare them in the following manner before consuming: bring water to a boil, place the vegetables in the pan and boil for three to five minutes, strain the vegetables and discard the water. Thus prepared, these vegetables can be used in soup, stews, or other courses.

Asparagus is another vegetable that should not be eaten raw. It contains organic toxins that must be removed by boiling in water, using the method described above.

Vegetables of the cabbage family, including cauliflower, Brussels sprouts, savoy, kale, broccoli, etc., contain a factor that can contribute to the development of goiter. This factor is destroyed by heat, or by lactic acid that develops during the process of natural fermentation, as in sauerkraut or pickles. Therefore, vegetables of the cabbage family should be used mostly in cooked form or in lactic-acid-fermented form (see Index).

Garlic and onions are excellent health-promoting as well as medicinal foods and should form an important part of the diet. They contain sulfur and selenium — very important trace elements. Garlic and onions, complemented by a large assortment of natural herbs and spices, can help to improve your health as well as turn ordinary vegetable dishes into delectable gourmet foods.

Other excellent vegetables, often neglected in the American diet, are black radish, horse radish, parsley, celery root, and Jerusalem artichokes. Jerusalem artichokes are especially beneficial for diabetics, hypoglycemics, and arthritics.

There has been some controversy recently regarding possible undesirable qualities in vegetables from the nightshade plant family: potatoes, green and red peppers, eggplant, and tomatoes. Although it is true that the foliage (leaves, flowers, and stems) of nightshade plants are toxic, the vegetables, *if they are ripe*, are not. Make sure that the tomatoes which you eat are vine-ripened, and peppers and eggplants fully developed and ripe. Potatoes also should be fully grown — small, so-called new potatoes, although highly regarded as a delicacy, can be harmful and should be avoided.

Important Warning Re: Potatoes

Potatoes, along with a variety of other root vegetables, such as carrots, beets, turnips, yams, and parsnips, should constitute an important part of the Airola Diet. Especially for those who live in the Northern potato-growing parts of the world, potatoes are a convenient and super-nutritious staple food. Rich in important potassium, vitamin C (excellent orange substitute for those who live in the far North; cabbage is another vitamin-C rich citrus substitute for northern regions), and highest quality proteins (which are comparable in biological value to protein in eggs), potatoes provide maximum nutrition at minimum cost.

Potatoes are best boiled or baked with skins on. They can also be used in soups and stews. Potatoes are even edible raw — and very therapeutic as such, especially for rheumatic diseases, scurvy, and stomach ulcers.

But, there is an important catch! Watch out for *solanine*, a highly toxic chemical which develops in potatoes when they are exposed to light. I am sure you have seen potatoes that are partially or totally green. This is a sign that they have been exposed to the light, and as a result of excessive exposure, either to sunlight or even to regular daylight or artificial light, a large quantity of solanine has developed. Solanine is located in the skin and right under the skin of the potato.

The importance of protecting potatoes from exposure to light was well-known to farmers before the development of the present-day highly-mechanized potato harvesting processes. In the past, farmers dug potatoes by hand, quickly placing them in dark sacks or other light-tight containers, and stored them in dark cellars. With modern machine harvesting, transparent plastic-bag storage, and open display in supermarkets, potatoes are now exposed to light constantly.

Unless you grow your own potatoes, there is no guarantee that the potatoes you get today in your store are solanine-free. Solanine can be present in harmful quantities long before the development of a detectable tell-tale green color. Even most health food stores seem to be unaware of the danger of solanine in potatoes. If you cannot be sure that the potatoes you are getting are solanine-free, you will be better off to leave them out of your diet. And, believe me, I am giving this advice with a heavy heart, having grown up in a country where potatoes comprise a large part of the daily diet.

Solanine is also present in the "eyes" of the potato, the sprouts that begin to grow on the potatoes after prolonged storage. They should always be removed before cooking.

The Role of Fruits in the Airola Diet

Like vegetables, fruits are excellent sources of minerals, trace elements, and vitamins, plus easily digestible fruit sugars. They should, however, be eaten in moderation. Fruits are a good choice for between-meal snacks for children. They are also excellent cleansing breakfast foods. Fruits are best eaten fresh, *in season.* They lose their vitamin content quickly. Although with modern cold-storage technology it is possible to buy apples in May that were harvested nine months earlier and still look as fresh as when picked from the tree, such apples have lost up to 90 percent of their vitamin C content. The same thing happens to all fruits and berries after prolonged storage. These examples illustrate how important it is to eat all vegetables and fruits fresh, *in season,* while they are loaded with vital nutrients.

In northern regions, where fresh fruits are unavailable during a large part of the year, the Airola Optimum Diet can include sun-dried fruits. They must be unsulfured, and preferably organically grown. Such fruits are available in health food stores, or, better yet, dry your own. The best are raisins, currants, apricots, and figs. Dried fruits should be soaked before eating and the soaking water consumed as well.

The role of fruits in the Airola Diet (third place in importance, after grains and vegetables) contrasts dramatically with some of the popular nutrition fads, especially fruitarianism, which claims that fresh fruits are truly an original diet for man, and that the highest level of wellness as well as long life can best be achieved by eating nothing but fruits, or fruits and fruit juices. I will not dispute the originality of such a diet, but I also know that ever since man discovered fire several thousands of years ago and incorporated cooked grains into his diet, grains in various forms have formed the bulk and the staple of his diet. Thus, man has become dependent on grains as his major source of nutrition, and is now metabolically and genetically programmed to function at an optimal level of wellness on a diet which largely consists of grains. To ignore this biological reality is to take serious health risks, since reprogramming cannot be accomplished in a short period of time, not even in a generation or two. This is why those who live on a fruitarian diet for any length of time find that they become devitalized — girls stop menstruating (a sure sign that the body is too weak and/or unhealthy to ovulate and give life to a healthy offspring), and men become impotent or lose interest in the opposite sex (which is often mistakenly construed to be the result of enhanced spiritual awareness). After several years on such a deficient diet, a progressive physical and mental deterioration becomes evident.

My conviction that an optimal level of health and well-being is impossible unless grains and seeds form the bulk of the diet on a daily basis has been slowly developing and growing during my forty-five years of research and study of nutrition. The final "empirical" evidence that led to the irrefutable conviction of this all-important truth (and a fundamental doctrine in my nutrition philosophy) was my study of the dietary patterns and lifestyles of native tribes that are fortunate enough to live on some Pacific and Caribbean islands and in the coastal areas of Mexico and Central America — areas that resemble, as closely as I can imagine, a paradisiacal environment. A great variety of delicious fruits are growing wild and are free for the picking: mangoes, bananas, coconuts, breadfruit, papaya, guavas, etc. You would think that if fruits were the ideal and fully-sustaining foods for man, these natives would have an easy and leisurely life: eat of plentiful and delicious fruits and spend leisurely days on the beach, since no clothing or shoes, and only minimal housing, are required in this ideal climate. Yet, to my surprise, I found that these natives were eating hardly any fruits at all; instead they worked long and hard cultivating the stony hills or swampy paddies, planting corn, beans, and rice, and *making them the staples of their diet!* And, they have been doing this for generations. What other than inherent instincts could have told them that if health and life were to be preserved and continuation of the tribe assured, they must not fall for a lazy life of fruitarianism, but work hard and make grains and beans a daily staple in their diet?!

The Role of Lactic Acid Foods in the Airola Diet

All people known for their exceptionally good health and long life use fermented lactic acid foods in their diet — Hunzakuts, Bulgarians, Japanese, Germans, and Russians. Bulgarians eat soured milk, yogurt, kefir, pickled vegetables, and sourdough breads. Japanese eat fermented miso and tofu. Sauerkraut is an important part of the German and Russian diet. Black sourbread is a Russian, Finnish, and East European staple.

Fermented lactic acid foods have been used not only as a food but also as a medicine. Miraculous improvements in and/or cures from arthritis, scurvy, ulcers, colds, digestive disorders, and even cancer have been attributed to the regular use of fermented foods. People have eaten these foods for centuries without knowing why they had such a curative effect. German cancer researcher, Dr. Johannes Kuhl, shed some light on this question. He explains the health-giving properties of fermented foods thus:

"Natural lactic acids and fermentive enzymes which are produced during the fermentation process, have a beneficial normalizing effect on the metabolism and a curative effect on disease."

Lactic acid destroys harmful, putrefactive intestinal bacteria and contributes to the better digestion and assimilation of nutrients. Fermented foods can be considered "pre-digested" foods, which are very easily digested and assimilated, even by persons with weak digestive organs. Fermented foods improve intestinal hygiene and provide a proper environment for the body's own vitamin production within the intestines. They are also excellent foods for prevention of constipation.

In this book, you will find many recipes and instructions for making your own lactic-acid foods. In the section on breads, there is a recipe for sourdough rye bread. In the section on soups, there are several varieties of borsch, in which sauerkraut and/or sour pickles and pickled vegetables are used. In the section on lactic acid foods, you will find instructions on homemade cottage cheese. quark, and homemade yogurt, kefir, piima, and apple cider. The section also contains instructions on how to make sauerkraut, sour pickles, and pickled vegetables. These are all very beneficial foods and beverages, and should be included in your Airola Diet as frequently as possible, on a regular basis.

If you, at least in the beginning, are not going to make these foods yourself, you can buy them in most natural food stores. When you buy lactic-acid foods, make sure they are packaged in glass jars rather than metal or plastic containers. Also, *read the labels.* Lactic-acid vegetables must not contain anything but vegetables, water, salt, and natural spices. No vinegar, no alum, no preservatives or any other chemical additives. Remember, sauerkraut or sour pickles made with vinegar are not true lactic-acid foods. The beneficial lactic acid and naturally-delicious sour taste develops by normal fermentation if no vinegar is used.

The Three Main Meals in the Airola Diet

Of the three main food groups in the Airola Diet, one food group should supply the bulk of each of three main meals. Fruits are best eaten for breakfast, and also as snacks between meals. Grains and legumes, in the form of cooked cereal or porridge, or bean, pea, or lentil soup, are best eaten at lunch. Vegetables should form the major portion of dinner: always a large raw vegetable salad, plus potatoes, yams, squash, or any of your favorite raw or steamed vegetables, soups, stews, or other dishes.

As you'll recall, I said "the bulk." Some seeds and/or nuts can be eaten with fresh fruit at breakfast, along with a glass of yogurt or kefir. Cooked vegetables can be used with the cereal meal at lunch — vegetables and rice, for example.

And bread, beans, rice, or corn can be used with a predominantly vegetable dinner at night.

If you have heard the old and very unscientific advice that "You should breakfast like a king, lunch like a queen, and dine like a pauper" — meaning that breakfast should be the heaviest meal of the day — you will be wise to change it to read: "You should breakfast like a pauper, lunch like a king, and dine like a queen." There are several valid scientific reasons why the morning meal should be light. Morning is a cleansing period as far as your body workings are concerned. During the night, from about 11:00 P.M. to 5:00 A.M., your digestive, assimilative, and restorative systems are busy at work, while your eliminative system is at rest. The morning hours, from about 5:00 A.M. to 11:00 A.M., constitute a period of elimination, when the blood stream is heavily charged with the waste products from metabolism carried out during the night, and the eliminative organs are doing their jobs of cleansing the system of impurities and toxins — through the skin, through the lungs, and through the kidneys and alimentary canal. "Morning breath" is just one indication of such elimination. Lack of appetite in the morning is another. Eating a large breakfast as soon as you get up will disrupt this cleansing process and interrupt the elimination. What your body needs in the early morning is plenty of fresh air, lots of liquids, fresh juicy fruits, and vigorous physical work or exercise to help your body complete its cleansing and eliminating process. Then, but not before, you are ready for breakfast.

Paul Bragg, a veteran health writer, had a good way of putting it. He said, "You must earn your breakfast." In the morning, you should go for a long walk, swim, or do heavy exercise or other physical exertion and work, before your body is ready for food. This is how all "natural" people — the natives known for their excellent health — always do it. They get up early in the morning, normally "with the sun," and immediately go to their heavy chores: feeding the animals, milking the cows, preparing food, cleaning and washing, working the gardens and fields, fishing or hunting, or whatever their particular work or lifestyle is. Then, several hours later, after hard work and plenty of perspiration, they are ready for breakfast. To eat a large protein-rich breakfast right after you have just gotten out of bed and when you are really not hungry, is to do yourself a great disservice. It may contribute to premature aging, impaired health, and disease.

If you live in a very cold climate, and/or have children that go to school, the lunch meal can be interchanged with breakfast, and a cooked cereal meal, preferably of such cereals as millet, oatmeal, or rice, can be eaten for breakfast.

Will Cooked Foods Really Kill You?

If you have read even a minimal amount of popular health and nutrition literature, you must be aware that there are experts who recommend eating all foods in their natural raw state. In fact, some of them use pretty scary language. Like, "cooked food is dead food, and cannot produce anything but death." Or, "man is the only animal that destroys his food before he eats it."

Raw-foodism is a very popular nutrition fad and, I must admit, for valid reasons. Cooking does destroy some of the nutritive value in foods. It also damages some fats and proteins and renders them more difficult to digest. Frying foods at high temperatures can be especially harmful; more so if vegetable oil is used, since vegetable fats become carcinogenic if heated to high temperatures. Some of the vitamins and minerals can be leached out if food is cooked in water and the nutritive value lost unless the cooking water is consumed. Any way you look at it, the general rule of healthful eating seems to be that raw foods are preferable to cooked foods.

But, there are some very important exceptions to this rule, as there are to any rule. Fanaticism in nutrition can be dangerous. Unfortunately, some uncompromising fanatics who are "into" raw foods, refuse to recognize that in the science of nutrition (which, like medicine, is not an exact science, but rather an art) there are always exceptions, compromises, and special considerations. This is only natural since there are great physiological, biochemical, and structural differences between individuals, and because our present nutrition has evolved through thousands of years of search, selection, and environmental adaptation. An example: man has long been eating a great variety of initially wild, then cultivated, plants (vegetables). Many of these plants are excellent and edible in their raw state. But some plants contain too many harmful substances, such as oxalic acid, for example; early man, therefore, avoided them. However, with the discovery of fire, he learned to use even these plants by destroying or leaching out the harmful elements through cooking. Thus, spinach, rhubarb, asparagus, cauliflower, cabbage, and other vegetables of the cabbage family, have become a regular part of man's diet. In a raw state, especially if consumed in large quantities, they can be quite harmful, as I stated earlier in this chapter.

The story of beans is somewhat similar. Many beans, especially soybeans, contain enzymes that inhibit the body's protein utilization. It was discovered very early that eating raw beans led to digestive discomforts and disorders, and mineral and protein deficiencies. These foods become more useful if cooked. Cooking destroys the enzyme-inhibitors and makes digestion and assimilation of these foods better. Thus, cooked soybeans became an essential part of man's diet in the Orient. Soybeans can also be eaten raw after having been soaked for 24 hours in water which is changed every 6 hours. The enzyme-inhibitors are thus leached out from the beans.

There is another important factor — *the most* important in fact — that must be taken into consideration when dealing with the question of cooked or raw foods. Minerals in all *dry* grains and most *dry* beans, peas, and other legumes, are chemically bound with phytic acid, or phytins. If grains or legumes, such as raw corn on the cob, or raw soft peas or beans, are eaten very fresh, they can be digested fairly well and the mineral content in them can be sufficiently utilized. But dry grains or beans, if eaten raw, or if just soaked overnight, cannot be digested properly and the minerals in them will be largely wasted and excreted with the phytins to which they are chemically bound. Cooking grains, as in baking bread or making porridge or cereals, helps to break down this chemical bond and releases all the vital minerals and trace elements such as zinc, iron, copper, manganese, magnesium, molybdenum, etc., making them easily available and assimilable in the intestinal tract.

To avoid misunderstanding and confusion, let me summarize: *All seeds and nuts, all fruits, and most vegetables* should be eaten in their natural state — raw. Some vegetables, like those mentioned earlier, should be cooked, preferably boiled in water, discarding the water. And *all grains* should be either cooked, as in bread or cereals, or sprouted. Sprouting also breaks down the mineral-phytin bond and releases the minerals.

Perhaps I should mention for the benefit of those who are totally and inconvertibly "into" raw foods, that I, too, was a strong believer in "living foods" after I read the book, *Living Foods*, by one of my early teachers, Kristine Nolfi, in 1948. My "affliction" was cured when in the course of my travels and studies, I found that 60 to 80 percent of the diet of Hunzakuts, considered to be the healthiest people in the world, is cooked. The same percentage of cooked food can be found in the diet of Abhkasians, Vilcabambas, and other people known for their exceptional health and long life. Of course, the true believer may argue that these people would have been even healthier and would live even longer if they ate only "living foods." But, since this cannot be proven, and since we have no other example to follow — no known people or tribe on this planet eat only raw foods — I am content to follow the traditional way of Hunzakuts and Abhkasians, as well as my own and your ancestry's thousands of years of traditions, and incorporate into my Optimum Diet some cooked foods, without suffering terrible guilt over it — especially considering the valid scientific reasons for doing so mentioned earlier in the sections on grains and vegetables.

But, if you are a diehard raw-foodist and have fears that "dead" food may kill you, by all means continue with 100 percent living foods. For *it is better to eat a nutritionally-*

inferior diet believing that it is good for you, than to eat a nutritionally-superior diet, but have fears that it will harm you! The harm from inferior foods eaten with faith and thanksgiving may be a much lesser evil than the serious harmful and detrimental effects on the digestion, metabolism, and general mental and physical health that anxiety, fear, and guilt can cause.

Complementary Foods in the Airola Diet

The following foods, used in moderation, can be used to complement the three basic health-building food groups in the Airola Diet.

1. MILK. The value of milk in human nutrition has been highly disputed in the United States. Some authorities claim that milk is an excellent and indispensable food for man. Others insist that milk is food for calves and poison for man, that man cannot digest milk properly, that milk causes mucus, allergies, etc.

The answer to the milk controversy is simple: both sides are right! Milk is an excellent food for those who are milk tolerant, and poison for those who are not, as I explained in the section on nutritional roots earlier in this chapter.

Needless to say, when I recommend supplementing the diet with milk, I mean *only the highest quality, uncontaminated, raw milk from healthy animals.* Today's pasteurized supermarket-sold milk is loaded with toxic and dangerous drugs, chemicals, and residues of pesticides, herbicides, and detergents — such milk is not suitable for human consumption. If you are fortunate enough to get *real* milk —fresh, raw, "farmer's" milk from healthy animals fed organic food — then you can add milk to your diet. Note that many people we associate with remarkable health — Scandinavians, Bulgarians, Russians — are traditionally heavy dairy food consumers.

The best way to use milk is in its soured (cultured) form: as yogurt, kefir, acidophilus milk, or regular buttermilk or clabbered milk. Homemade cottage cheese can be made from any of these soured milks (see Index). Soured milk is superior to sweet milk, as it is in a *predigested* form and very easily assimilated. It also helps to maintain a healthy intestinal flora and prevents intestinal putrefaction and constipation.

Goat's milk is better than cow's milk for people of all ages. It is especially preferred for babies and young children after they have been weaned, goat's milk being closer than cow's milk to the nutritional composition of mother's milk.

2. COLD-PRESSED VEGETABLE OILS. High quality, fresh, cold-pressed, crude, unrefined, unheated, and unprocessed vegetable oil is recommended as an addition to the Airola Diet, *but only in a very moderate quantity.* Please reread the foregoing sentence, and notice all the specifications and requirements that I place on vegetable oils before I can recommend them for human consumption. Such oils are possible to obtain today, but it takes careful shopping. All commercially-produced, supermarket-sold oils are a complete no-no. They are all produced either with the use of extremely high temperatures, up to 400 degrees F, or with the process known as chemical extraction (cold-processed). Both methods result in a final product which has no resemblance to anything "natural." It is processed, filtered, refined, bleached, and deodorized. Beneficial lecithin, which normally clouds the natural unrefined oils, has been removed. Toxic chemical antioxidants, such as BHT, have been added. Margarines, made from such vegetable oils, have, in addition, been saturated with hydrogen and are even worse than the original processed oils from which they are made.

Even many oils sold in health food stores are not actually cold-pressed. Some manufacturers use a misleading term, "cold-processed," which really means that the oils were extracted with the help of chemical solvents, such as carcinogenic hexane. There are only a very few oils that can be made by hydraulic pressure, and, thus, can be truthfully labeled as cold-pressed. Sesame seed oil and olive oil are among these few oils. Most oils are extracted by a screw-type press. This method leads to development of extremely high temperatures, 300-350 degrees F. (Remember, vegetable oils should never be used in cooking, frying or baking, as there is evidence that high temperatures make them carcinogenic.)

In addition to these hazardous manufacturing and processing methods, there is another danger connected with edible oils. All natural foods are extremely perishable, and vegetable oils are no exception. Natural oils turn rancid very rapidly. It is difficult to keep them for any length of time without the use of preservatives. Storing them in metal cans or dark bottles helps. Also, constant refrigeration is essential. Even then, most oils will turn rancid within a few weeks or months after they are made.

So, now what? Should we leave all oils completely out of our diet? How can we get truly safe edible oils?

Since my book, *Are You Confused?*, which pioneered the information on the dangers of eating rancid foods and oils, was published a decade ago, many changes have taken place in the American health-oriented segment of the edible oil industries. Spurred by my research, an effort is being made to produce better oils. There are now several brands of better quality natural oils available. A couple of brands of high quality cold-pressed olive oil are produced in California. Ask for these oils in your health food store. If your store does not have them, they will get them for you. Some stores sell good imported brands of virgin olive oil from France, Italy, or Spain. The best oils are olive oil and sesame seed oil. These are also the two oils most likely to be non-rancid. Since most other vegetable oils are of dubious quality, I recommend using these two oils only. Actually, you will be even better off if you limit your oil use to olive oil. Use sesame oil only if you object to the flavor of olive oil. Most recipes in this book call for olive oil, and even that only occasionally and in small amounts.

My insistence upon using vegetable oils in the Airola Diet in strict moderation (one to two teaspoons a day in salad dressings) is based on recent research which shows that excessive use of polyunsaturated oils can lead to the deficiency of vitamins E, A, D, and K by leaching them out of the body, as well as to other serious health problems, such as cancer and cardiovascular disorders. Some research also indicates that excessive consumption of polyunsaturated oils can accelerate the aging processes, causing wrinkles, crow's feet, and other visible signs of premature aging. The best way of getting needed saturated and unsaturated fats in the diet is by eating natural fat-containing foods such as whole milk, nuts, seeds, grains, avocados, etc.

3. HONEY. Raw, unheated, unfiltered, natural, and unprocessed pollen-rich honey is the only sweetener that is allowed in the Airola Diet. Since the health-damaging properties of refined white sugar as well as that of artificial sweeteners such as saccharin and cyclamates are now widely recognized, several new "natural" sweeteners such as bran and rice syrups, maple syrup, and fructose have been developed. I have made a careful study of all these sweeteners and have found that none of them measures up to the ancient natural sweetener — honey. Honey possesses miraculous nutritional and medicinal properties, and has been used in the diets of virtually all people known for their superior health. For example: most centenarians in Russia and Bulgaria use honey as their only sweetener.

However, even honey must be used judiciously. Since it is so concentrated, too much honey may adversely affect the pancreas, liver, and adrenals and contribute to such disorders of sugar-metabolism as diabetes and hypoglycemia. One to two teaspoons a day is sufficient.

What About Juices?

Although I am one of the most avid advocates of drinking fresh fruit and vegetable juices *for therapeutic purposes*, as for example during juice fasting, I will probably shock many readers when I say that *I do not advocate drinking large amounts of juices on a regular basis, as a part of the daily diet.* A current vogue among many well-meaning health faddists is to drink large amounts of sweet fruit and vegetable juices, such as grape, pineapple, apple, or carrot juice. This practice can have a disastrous effect on sugar metabolism and can contribute to the development of hypoglycemia, as well as diabetes.

I dare to say that many cases of hypoglycemia, which is so prevalent among young health-food oriented people today, can be linked to copious amounts of sweet juices, albeit natural, drunk by these well-meaning but misguided people.

They subscribe to the idea of eating whole natural foods; they object to sugar and white flour on the grounds that they are refined, fragmented, concentrated substances. At the same time they gulp huge amounts of juices on a regular daily basis without realizing that juices are not *whole* and natural foods. They are fragmented, isolated, concentrated, sugar-laden liquids which the human body's metabolism is not equipped nor programmed to handle. I have seen some people who drink half a gallon, sometimes even a full gallon, of carrot juice a day. Not only do the palms of their hands turn yellow, but the large amount of sugar in this highly concentrated food puts a very real strain on the liver and pancreas. Our bodies are designed to handle efficiently only foods that are *eaten*. When we eat carrots or grapes, chewing them thoroughly, the carbohydrates and sugars in these foods are gradually and slowly digested and absorbed, supplying an even flow of sugar. But when we drink the sweet juices, an excessive amount of sugar that doesn't need elaborate digestion but is absorbed quickly through the membranes of the stomach and even the mouth, is suddenly flooding the bloodstream with the demanding strain on the pancreas and liver to quickly neutralize it and restore proper sugar levels. There is a certain maximum level of dietary sugar, even natural sugar, that our organs can handle without damage. This level was set by maximum dietary sugar that was obtained by *eating* foods. It has been determined during thousands of years of metabolic and genetic adaptation to the natural environment.

There is another factor to consider regarding the practice of copious juice drinking. Juices are extremely alkalizing foods, containing large amounts of highly alkaline minerals, especially potassium. For this reason, juices play a very important role in practically every therapeutic program, especially during fasting when they help cleanse and de-acidify tissues affected by acidosis (excessive meat-eating, among other things, leads to over-acidity). However, if juices are used in large amounts, on a prolonged basis, by relatively *healthy* people, they tend to alkalify the body excessively and cause a condition known as alkalosis. This, again, puts an extra strain on the adrenal glands which must synthesize large amounts of special hormones to restore and maintain a normal pH in the body. Most readers are probably aware of the fact that an overly-acid system (too many grains and/or too much meat in the diet) is not a desirable condition and may lead to metabolic disorders, contributing specifically to the development of arthritis and rheumatic diseases. But an overly-alkaline body (too many alkalizing vegetables and fruits, especially in concentrated juice form) is just as undesirable. It may make the body susceptible to many metabolic disorders, especially digestive and assimilative problems as well as an increased suscepti-bility to infections. Not too acid, but not too alkaline either, is the ideal. Normal pH should be about 6.4 on a urine test, which means slightly acid. Neutral pH is considered to be 7.0.

Now, after this warning about the indiscriminate drinking of sweet juices, especially by hypoglycemics or those prone to hypoglycemia or diabetes, I must hurry to clarify myself before I am misunderstood or misquoted. I am against the *excessive drinking* of juices. *Generally speaking, foods should be eaten, not drunk.* A small amount of juice, 2-3 oz. at a time, can be taken, either diluted 50-50 with water one hour before a meal, or undiluted with meals, provided it is not drunk rapidly, but sipped slowly and salivated well — as with any other food.

(For information on how to use juices therapeutically, and which juices to use for specific conditions, please see my book, *HOW TO KEEP SLIM, HEALTHY AND YOUNG WITH JUICE FASTING.* It also deals with fasting for losing weight.)

Highest Quality Foodstuffs — A Must in the Airola Diet

That your health and longevity are in direct relationship to the naturalness of the foods you eat is a well-established scientific fact. Where natives eat a diet of natural, whole, unprocessed, and unrefined foods, they enjoy excellent health, absence of disease, and long life. When denatured, refined, processed, man-made foods, such as white sugar and white flour, and canned and processed foods enter their lives, disease becomes rampant among them.

Natural foods are foods that are grown in fertile soils without the use of chemical fertilizers and sprays and are consumed in their *natural* state with all the nutrients nature put in them intact, *nothing removed and nothing added.* White bread is, for example, a denatured food from which most vital nutrients have been removed; the so-called "enrichment" is a joke — over 20 vital nutrients are removed in refining the flour, while only 4 nutrients are returned. Breakfast cereals are denatured foods with some "added features" — toxic preservatives and health-destroying white sugar. Supermarket-sold eggs are not natural food; they are produced by chickens deprived of natural food and a free-range environment, cooped-up without a rooster (thus infertile), and fed chemicalized commercial mash. Such eggs have a lower nutritional value, less vitamins, and more cholesterol than natural eggs.

Organically grown fruits and vegetables contain more vitamins, minerals, and trace elements than produce grown on depleted, chemically fertilized soils, as has been shown in many tests. Such foods have a greater health-building and disease-preventing potential. Researchers reported recently that anti-malignancy factors are apparently present in organically grown foods.

Synthetic, denatured, and devitalized foods will not sustain health, but will inevitably bring about a gradual degeneration of normal body functions and, ultimately, disease. Almost all foods sold at supermarkets today contain some chemicals used either in food producing, or added during food processing or packaging. Many of the poisons in fruits and vegetables are systemic; that is, they cannot be washed off or peeled off, as they penetrate the whole plant.

Speaking of highest quality, natural, unadulterated foods, I must mention granola, a currently-popular cereal among the health food crowd. There is nothing natural or wholesome about the kind of granola that is sold commercially. There is nothing wrong with the original individual ingredients in the mixture (with the exception of sugar, and the possible exception of blackstrap molasses, which used to be an excellent mineral supplement but now contains too many harmful chemical residues). But, by the time the initially healthful ingredients are all mixed together, then *roasted* or *baked*, the concoction becomes a nutritional perversion at the best and a carcinogenic product at the worst. Let me re-emphasize that oil and oil-rich nuts and seeds, when baked or roasted to 350 degrees F or more, become carcinogenic. Nuts and seeds should never be roasted, but eaten only in their natural raw state. The only healthful way to eat grains is in the form of bread and low-heat cooked cereals and porridges. Recipes can be found in Section II, *Whole Grains, Cereals, and Legumes, and Breads.* You will also find a recipe for "Granola", but you will notice that there is no oil or fat in it, and the nuts and seeds and wheat germ are never heated. This is the only kind of granola I recommend.

Vitamins and Supplements in the Airola Diet

Ideally, you should obtain all your required nutrients from the foods you eat, without the addition of any food supplements. A hundred, or even fifty years ago such advice would have been both sound and workable. Your grandparents didn't take any vitamin pills, yet they probably enjoyed better health than you do. They ate wholesome foods which were organically grown on their own farms, without the aid of chemical fertilizers. They ate fresh fruits and vegetables from their own gardens, grown without the use of poisonous sprays. They obtained meat, eggs, and dairy products from their own healthy farm animals. They ate no processed or refined foods.

The grains, vegetables, meat, and dairy products your grandparents ate had a higher vitamin, mineral, and protein content; and they were free from DDT, hormones, preservatives, insecticides, and other chemicals and drugs. For example: American wheat grown one hundred years ago contained 18-24 percent protein. Today's wheat, grown on depleted soils with the help of powerful artificial fertilizers, contains only 9-14 percent protein — only *half* of what it once was! This is true in regard to minerals as well.

Those who now advocate eating natural foods as the only source of vitamins and other nutrients live in a dream world of yesterday. What was yesterday's law is today's folly. It is a sad fact that due to vitamin-, protein-, and life-destroying practices of the food-producing and food-processing industries our *modern-day foods, not only those you buy at your supermarket or health food store, but even those grown in your own garden, are nutritionally inferior to the food your grandparents ate two or three generations ago.* Even those so-called organically grown foods are grown in a polluted atmosphere, are watered by polluted water, and contain residues of toxins from fallout, etc. Also, if you buy your organic foods from your health food store, they are probably delivered there from California or Florida, may be many days old, and their vitamin content thus dangerously reduced. So it really doesn't matter how well you balance your meals, or if you are a meat-eater, vegetarian, or a raw-foodist, *you still run the risk of malnutrition if you try to get all your vitamins exclusively from the foods you eat.*

It is a medically well-known fact that even minor deficiencies of one or more of the vital nutritive factors will result in deranged chemistry in the human system and lower the body's resistance to disease.

Thus, food supplements are necessary as nutritional insurance against disease. Well chosen food supplements are an easy, inexpensive way to improve your diet and ensure optimum health for you and your family.

The prime purpose of food supplements is to fill in the nutritional gaps produced by faulty eating habits and by nutritionally-inferior foods. Food supplements will replace in your diet the nutrients missing in food grown on depleted soils, lost in storage, or removed by food processing.

There is another good reason to supplement the diet with an extra supply of vitamins, minerals, and other nutrients. Many of these substances have protective properties against some of today's most toxic environmental factors. They can help protect you from the harmful effects of poisonous additives and residues in your food, water, and air. In this polluted world of ours, where lethal poisons are lurking everywhere — the air, water, food, clothing, cosmetics, household items, etc. — food supplements are virtually your only available protection against their harmful effects.

If you are convinced that vitamins and supplements should be an integral part of the Airola Optimum Diet for you and your family, I suggest you read my books, *Everywoman's Book*, and *How To Get Well*, where the complete vitamin and supplement story is presented in detail and where both therapeutic and preventive (maintenance) dosages of vitamins and supplements are outlined for all ages. *Everywoman's Book* lists dosages for children from the age of three months and up. See also the *Complete Vitamin-Mineral Guides, Recommended Daily Dietary Allowances*, and *Composition of Foods Chart* in Section III of this book.

Herbs and Herb Teas in the Airola Diet

Coffee, black tea, chocolate, and caffein-containing cola beverages have no place in the Airola Diet. Neither do other carbonated commercially-sold so-called refreshments, sugar-laden or sugarless (which are even worse because they are sweetened with carcinogenic artificial sweeteners).

What about herb teas?

Currently, herbs are very popular; in fact, we are witnessing an herbal renaissance. Younger people, especially, are "into" herbs in droves. Not only are herbs used several times a day in the form of herb teas, but they are also consumed in capsule form as food supplements, in alcohol extracts, in essential oils, and along with vitamin preparations, many of which now include herbs.

Now, to keep the record straight, I am all for herbs! But, please, keep in mind that herbs are *MEDICINES!* And medicines should be used only in the treatment of specific conditions of ill health. Healthy people should not take medicines — any kind of medicines, including herbal medicines. Medicinal herbs are divinely created medicines for man's ills. In fact, they are often far superior to synthetic and chemical medicines that orthodox doctors use today. In my book, *How To Get Well*, I recommend medicinal herbs for the treatment of all of our most common diseases. I list specific herbs for specific diseases on virtually every page of the book — but only as *medicines!* You wouldn't think of taking aspirin and penicillin every day in order to prevent headaches and infections; neither should you take strong herbal medicines to prevent illness. Those who take medicinal herbs on a daily basis as a healthful substitute for harmful caffein-containing beverages may find that when the need presents itself to use herbs for the treatment of some acute illness, the herbs will not "work." The body has developed a tolerance to the herbs and will not respond as it should to the medicinal effects.

We must also recognize the fact that many healing herbs contain toxic substances and may have harmful side effects. Those who are "into" herbs often use large quantities of them indiscriminately, not realizing their possible toxicity, and, actually, endangering their lives. Even those herbs that are safe in small quantities may have cumulative effects and cause toxicity when taken over a long period of time. For example, goldenseal, if taken continuously, may affect blood pressure unfavorably; horsetail may damage the kidneys (horsetail contains nicotine and an enzyme that destroys vitamin B_1); and kava kava may irritate the liver and cause skin eruptions. Such herbs should not be used for more than six days at a time. Other herbs that can cause toxic reactions if taken in large quantities are: black cohosh, blue cohosh, poke root, lobelia, mandrake, pennyroyal, lily of the valley, and calamus. Some herbs and common spices contain weak carcinogens: sassafras, mace, nutmeg, cloves, basil, and tarragon. Obviously, they should be used with strict moderation and in small quantities, if at all. Some herbs contain xanthines, which are closely related to caffeine and can produce adverse symptoms; they are: mâté, Mormon tea, guarana, and gota kola. Licorice should not be taken by those who suffer from high blood pressure or have predisposition to it, as it can cause salt and fluid retention and aggravate the condition.

One of the greatest dangers connected with the indiscriminate use of herbs is their tannic acid content. Studies show that there is a correlation between extensive drinking of tannin-rich teas, and the occurrence of cancer of the stomach and of the throat. Regular black tea is, of course, extremely rich in tannic acid. Herbs that are particularly high in tannins are: sarsaparilla, comfrey root, cascara sagrada, rosemary, bayberry bark, uva ursi, peppermint, yellow dock, and cleavers.

In summary, herbal medicines are superior alternatives to chemical drugs for the treatment of many of man's ills. But, they must be looked upon as medicines, not foods or food supplements. In the hands of an experienced herbal practitioner, medicinal herbs can be used effectively in the treatment of virtually every disease. But, since some herbs are toxic in large quantities or when used for extended periods of time, it would be wise not to use them on a regular basis, but only for the duration of the treatment of disease.

Aren't there some mild herbs that could be used as a tasty beverage to replace coffee and regular tea? Yes, some herbs can be used for this purpose:

- if herb teas are made very weak;
- if herb teas are not consumed in excessive quantities;
- if the same herb is not used for too long; and

- if herb teas are drunk with milk. The calcium and the proteins in milk help neutralize tannic acid and other toxic substances in herbs.

The mild herbs most suitable for general, non-medicinal beverage purposes are: rosehips, catnip, lemon balm, lemon grass, alfalfa, camomile, eucalyptus leaves, raspberry leaves, spearmint, dandelion, and nettle leaves.

To achieve desirable flavor, you may combine several herbs.

To make herb tea: Boil the water, remove the pot from heat, add ½ teaspoon dried herbs per cup of water, and let steep 1-3 minutes. Strain, add milk, sweeten with honey, if desired, and enjoy. (For instructions on how to make *medicinal* herb teas, see page 235 in *How To Get Well.*)

Developing Health-Promoting Eating Habits

Not only *what* you eat, but *how* you eat can affect your health. Here are some helpful rules to follow:

- ***Eat only when really hungry.*** Your requirements for food are unique and vary from day to day. If you are not hungry at dinner time, don't eat. Skip the meal. Food eaten without appetite will do you no good. In fact, it will harm you by overburdening the digestive system, causing indigestion, gas, and other discomforts.
- ***Eat slowly and chew well.*** The digestion of food begins in the mouth with the help of enzymes in your saliva. Good chewing increases the assimilation of nutrients and makes you feel satisfied with smaller amounts of food. Always keep in mind that you are not what you eat, but what you assimilate.
- ***Enjoy your food.*** Only food eaten with genuine pleasure will do you any good.
- ***Relax while eating.*** Don't bring your problems to the dining table. A peaceful, unhurried, and happy atmosphere around the table will pay good dividends in improved digestion and assimilation of food — and, hence, in better health.

- ***Eat several small meals in preference to two larger meals.*** This is especially advisable for those with a weight problem. If you put on weight with 1,500 calories a day eaten at two meals, you may find that the same 1,500 calories divided between five or six small meals with 2-3 hour intervals may actually help you to reduce.
- ***Keep it simple.*** Your digestion and assimilation will be enhanced if you do not mix too many foods at the same meal. A mono diet of a single dish or food may be the ideal.
- ***Do not mix raw fruits and raw vegetables at the same meal.*** They are incompatible as far as your digestive enzymes are concerned, and will only result in poor digestion and gas.
- ***Practice systematic undereating.*** This is the *number one* health and longevity secret. As Sylvester Graham used to say, "A drunkard may reach old age; a glutton, never." Overeating, *even of health foods,* is one of the main causes of degenerative diseases and premature aging. The unbelievable truth is: *The less you eat —the better you feel!* This is because the food will be more effectively digested and better utilized if your digestive system is not overloaded.
- ***Do not drink too much of any kind of liquids while eating.*** Liquids only dilute the digestive juices and slow down the process of digestion.
- ***Drink lots of liquids between meals, or an hour before meals.*** Pure spring or well water is the best and healthiest thirst quencher.
- ***Finally, give thanks for the food you eat.*** Think of those who may work harder than you, yet have nothing or little to eat. Be grateful and appreciative for the abundance and the blessings that are yours.

Health Destroyers to Avoid

Here is a short list of health destroyers that you *must* avoid if you wish to achieve Optimum Health. All these factors are scientifically proven to be potential health destroyers.

- ***Excessive proteins*** in the diet, even vegetable proteins. If you follow the Airola Optimum Diet as described in my books, you won't need any protein supplements — you will obtain adequate amounts of high quality protein from your diet.
- ***Excessive fat,*** even vegetable fat. Never use margarine; small amounts of natural butter is preferable. The ideal proportions of the three major dietary factors in the Airola Diet should be (calorie-wise): 15-20 percent fat, 10 percent protein, and 70-75 percent complex natural carbohydrates. The corresponding percentages in the average American diet are 45 percent fat, 25 percent protein, and 30 percent refined carbohydrates. Excessive proteins and fats in the American diet are both linked to cancer development.
- ***Excessive use of salt.*** The average American diet supplies 10 to 15 grams of salt a day. Excessive salt can cause high blood pressure, heart disease, and cancer of the stomach and bowels. Salt consumption must not exceed 5 grams a day, including all dietary sources. Actually, in the Airola Diet, you will obtain all of the salt (sodium) you need from natural unprocessed, unsalted foods. Kelp can be used as a salt substitute. Whole sea salt (sold in health food stores) is better than regular salt, and can be used in moderation.
- ***Refined white sugar and white flour,*** and everything made with them; also, all artificial sweeteners and fructose. Use honey in strict moderation.
- ***Excessive consumption of alcohol.***
- ***Smoking,*** including cigarettes, cigars, and pipes. Avoid also marijuana and chewing tobacco.
- ***Coffee, tea, chocolate, and other caffein-containing beverages*** (colas, etc.).
- ***Harmful spices*** and condiments such as mustard, black and white pepper, white vinegar, etc. (See next chapter.)

- ***Rancid foods.*** Avoid even such popular health foods as wheat germ, seeds, nuts, and vegetable oils, unless they are guaranteed to be absolutely fresh. Rancid foods and rancid fats are major causes of breast cancer and many other cancers.
- ***All processed, refined, canned, and factory-made foods.***
- ***All fried, especially deep-fried, foods.***
- ***All household chemicals,*** such as cleansers, detergents, garden sprays, bug and fly killers, air fresheners, hair sprays, dry cleaning fluids, and other toxic household and environmental chemicals.

2

Culinary Herbs, Spices, And Seasonings In The Airola Diet

The Airola Diet is not only the most nutritious diet, but also the most savory and delicious. Fresh, natural, unprocessed foods have unique, subtle, and distinct flavors. The taste buds in some of us have become dulled by harsh artificial flavorings and additives and excessive salt and pepper that are present in modern factory-made foods, as well as in restaurant and home cooking. Our taste buds have been further damaged by MSG (monosodium glutamate), a chemical "flavor enhancer" which is now used in almost all restaurant cooking. Therefore, some recent converts to natural Optimum Nutrition may not be able to detect and enjoy all the fine nuances of abundant natural flavorings present in all unprocessed whole grains, vegetables, and fruits. Your taste buds can be rejuvenated if you continue with pure natural foods and avoid sugar, salt, and artificial flavorings. Then, you will be able to eat most natural foods *as they are*, in their natural state, without any additional flavorings or seasonings, and savor their fine, exquisite natural flavors.

Although I, personally, use very little seasoning and spices in my own diet, I realize that for some people the palatability of most cooked and even raw foods can be improved and enhanced with the use of various natural spices, seasonings, and culinary herbs. Some herbs and spices, however, are so strong and pungent that they can completely change or mask the inherent natural flavor in the food. These must be avoided. The purpose of seasonings and culinary spices and herbs is not to eliminate or change the natural flavors, but to enhance and accentuate them. It is important for trouble-free digestion of food and effective assimilation of nutrients that foods retain their original, natural, inherent flavors.

The following is a list of culinary herbs, spices, seasonings, and condiments, along with some suggested uses, which can be included in the Airola Diet. Most of them are available in better natural food stores. Always keep in mind the secret of true gourmet cooking: Use seasonings sparingly! This is especially true with natural, unprocessed, whole foods which are naturally filled with subtly delectable and delicious flavors.

(At the end of this section, you will find herbs and spices that are *not* recommended in the Airola Diet.)

AGAR-AGAR: A sea plant gelatin. Can be used as gelatin substitute in salads, salad molds, desserts, or as a neutral-tasting thickener.

ALLSPICE: Cakes, cookies, breads, pies, desserts, fruit punches, soups, eggplant.

ANISE SEED: Cottage cheese, beets, carrots, parsnips, stewed fruits, breads, salads, soups.

APPLE CIDER VINEGAR: Salad dressings, beverages, sauces.

ARROWROOT POWDER: Natural flavorless thickening agent for sauces and soups. Can be used as a substitute for cornstarch or flour as a thickening agent.

BAKING POWDER (Aluminum-Free): Cakes, cookies. To make your own baking powder, take ½ cup potassium bicarbonate to 1/3 cup cream of tartar, and 2/3 cup arrowroot powder. Mix and store in airtight container.

CARAWAY SEED: Cookies, cakes, rye breads, cottage cheese, soups (borsch), red cabbage, potatoes, sauerkraut.

CARDAMOM: Cookies, cakes, baked apples, fruit salads, sweet potatoes, pumpkin, pickles.

CAROB POWDER: Natural healthful substitute for chocolate, with similar taste. Cookies, cakes, beverages, shakes.

CAYENNE (Red Pepper): Salad dressings, beans, chili, guacamole, soups, eggs. Cayenne can help correct the tendency of some vegetables to cause flatulence. Use sparingly.

CELERY LEAVES: Stews, soups.

CELERY SEED: Stews, soups, salad dressings, tomatoes, potatoes, vegetables, eggs.

CHERVIL: Salads, broccoli, soups, stews, eggs. Use as parsley.

CHILI POWDER: Mexican food, beans, soups, salad dressings. Use sparingly.

CHIVES: Salads, salad dressings, potato salad, baked squash, cauliflower, mushrooms, sandwiches, cottage cheese, eggs, soups, sauces. Mild onion-like flavor.

CINNAMON POWDER: Cakes, cookies, puddings, apple pie, applesauce, stewed fruits, hot punch, squash, tomatoes, sweet potatoes. For herb tea, use cinnamon sticks.

CORIANDER: Curries, sauces, apple pie, lentil dishes, soups, pickled vegetables, chili.

CUMIN: Beans, stews, eggs, rice, sauerkraut. Use sparingly.

DILL WEED or DILL SEED: Salads, tomatoes, avocado, green beans, potatoes, eggs, cottage cheese, soups, sauerkraut, pickled vegetables, dill pickles.

FENNEL: Fruit pies, beets, parsnips, turnips, potatoes, soups, stews, sauces, pickled vegetables.

FENUGREEK: Use in East Indian dishes. Also used for herb teas.

GARLIC: Salad dressings, salads, soups, stews, casseroles, eggs, cheese, beans, spinach, tomatoes.

GARLIC POWDER: Use as fresh garlic substitute for all garlic uses.

GINGER: Cakes, cookies, sauces, pumpkin; Chinese, Japanese, and Indian dishes; pickles, applesauce.

HONEY: For all culinary purposes where a sweetener is required. Raw, unfiltered, preferably locally-produced honey is best.

HORSERADISH: Appetizer dips, sauces, pickles, relishes, salad dressings.

JUNIPER BERRIES: Sauerkraut, sour pickles, stews. Use sparingly; remove berries before serving.

KELP: Salad dressings, potatoes, soups, salads. Good natural salt substitute.

LICORICE ROOT: Cakes, cookies, herb teas. Use sparingly. Excessive use may cause fluid retention and aggravate high blood pressure.

MARJORAM: Asparagus, eggplant, zucchini, mushrooms, green peas, spinach, tomatoes, cucumbers, carrots, soups, omelets.

MINT: Fruit salads, fruit punch, peas, carrots, potatoes, pea soup. Fresh mint leaves can be used as a garnish.

MISO: Soups, sauces; in Japanese cooking. Should not be boiled. Add to food just before it is served. Can be used as salt substitute.

NETTLE (Stinging or Common): Fresh or dried; in soups, salads, stews, herb teas.

OLIVE OIL: This is the best and the only oil that I recommend using in Airola Diet cooking, although occasionally sesame seed oil will appear in recipes for those who object to the flavor of olive oil. Make sure olive oil is cold-pressed, virgin, and sold in dark glass bottles or tin cans. You can find good brands in health food stores or Italian delicatessens.

ONIONS (all types): Use abundantly, raw and/or cooked, in salads, and vegetable dishes, sauces, soups, etc.

ONION POWDER or FLAKES: Soups, eggs, salads, stews.

OREGANO: Tomatoes, soups, stews, beans, sauces, eggplant.

PAPRIKA: Salad dressings, stews, potatoes, soups, pickled vegetables, as a garnish.

PARSLEY: Salads, soups, stews, mushrooms, omelets, potatoes, salsify, sweet potatoes, as a garnish.

ROSEMARY: Artichokes, spinach, green beans, eggplant, pea soup, cabbage, tomatoes, soups, eggs, breads, beans. Use sparingly.

SAGE: Soups, sauces, stews, beans. Use sparingly.

SAVORY: French dressings, tomatoes, lima beans, green beans, peas, lentils, soups, eggs, cabbage.

SEA SALT: Soups, stews, pickles, eggs, salad dressings. Use sparingly.

SPEARMINT: Beverages, fruit and vegetable salads, beans, potatoes, cooked vegetables.

TAMARI SOY SAUCE: Soups, stews, beans, vegetables. A fermented soybean product with sea salt. Use sparingly.

THYME: Salads, tomatoes, potatoes, asparagus, spinach, carrots, beets, zucchini, soups, pea soup, mushrooms, beans.

VANILLA: Ice cream, cakes, breads, cookies. Use only natural vanilla extract, never imitation vanilla flavorings.

A NO-NO LIST

The following herbs and seasonings are *not* recommended in the Airola Diet for reasons listed.

BASIL: Toxic in large quantities or when used frequently.

BAYLEAF: Although one of the most popular culinary herbs, bayleaf is quite toxic, and may cause severe symptoms of poisoning, if used in large amounts. If you must use it in cooking, use only the whole leaf (never crushed) and *remove it* before serving the dish.

CHICKORY: Although often used as a coffee substitute, chickory is toxic and can be harmful if used in excess.

CLOVES: Toxic in large quantities or when used frequently.

CURRY POWDER: Commercially sold curry powder usually contains black pepper and tarragon, which are both toxic irritants and possibly carcinogenic. Mix your own curry powder without these ingredients.

MACE: Toxic in large quantities or when used frequently.

MAYONNAISE: Avoid all commercial brands of mayonnaise. They contain sugar, preservatives, or undesirable additives, as well as highly processed oils which are often rancid; some also contain mustard and white pepper. Directions on how to make homemade mayonnaise can be found in Section II (See Index).

MUSTARD: Toxic if used in excess; irritates stomach linings.

MUSTARD SEED: Strong irritant for digestive organs.

NUTMEG: Toxic in large quantities or when used frequently.

PEPPER: Black and white peppers are toxic irritants for stomach, kidney, and bowels.

POPPY SEEDS: Toxic in large quantities or when used frequently.

SALT: Avoid regular refined supermarket brands of salt. Use whole sea salt sparingly. Excessive salt is toxic and can contribute to high blood pressure, cancer of the stomach, and heart disease.

SUGAR: Refined sugar is one of the main contributors to many of our most common diseases such as diabetes, hypoglycemia, tooth decay, obesity, atherosclerosis, and heart disease. Use natural honey as a sweetener.

TARRAGON: Toxic, possibly carcinogenic, in large quantities.

3

Useful Equipment In Your Airola Diet Kitchen

The following kitchen utensils, appliances, and gadgets can be useful in the Airola Diet Kitchen.

Pots and Pans

Use only stainless steel, glass, stoneware, or cast iron cookware. Such cookware is not cheap, but a compromise in this important area is not advisable. Aluminum cookware should never be used. Aluminum utensils can leave residues of highly toxic aluminum in foods they come in contact with. All non-stick type pans are dangerous. They may release harmful gasses when overheated. They can also leave particles of toxic plastic materials in food when scraped. Since high quality stainless steel, glass, or cast iron cookware is very durable and can last a lifetime, it is an one-time investment.

You should have at least three different sizes of pots, skillets, and sauce pans. Two sizes of un-treated black cast iron skillets, six-inch and ten-inch, can be very useful. Food cooked in cast iron pans is actually enriched with natural iron which comes from the gradual oxidation and dissolution of the metal.

Steamer

A stainless steel steamer is used in preparation of steamed vegetables. Steamed vegetables retain more nutrients and flavors than vegetables boiled in water. Steaming is an excellent way of preparing such vegetables as cauliflower, Brussels sprouts, green beans, zucchini, squash, and every kind of cabbage, including Chinese cabbage. Here is how you use the steamer: Place about ½ inch of water in a large pot. Place the steamer in the pot and put vegetables to be steamed on the steamer. Cover the pot and bring water to a rolling boil. Cooking time is determined by how well-done you like the vegetables. The crispier they are, the more nutritious they are. Steamers are inexpensive and will last for years.

Wooden Spoons

In the Airola Diet Kitchen, natural wooden spoons are used for all stirring and mixing during food preparation. They are inexpensive, come in all shapes and sizes, and are long-lasting. Never use painted, stained or varnished wooden utensils.

Cutting Boards

A wooden cutting board, made from a natural and *untreated* hardwood is a must in the Airola Diet Kitchen. Cutting foods on the table or countertops or plates not only ruins the edges of your knife blades and damages the surface of the plates and countertops but it also adds traces of undesirable material from those surfaces to your foods. Cutting boards come in many different sizes. Small ones can be used as a cheese or bread board. Larger boards can be kept on the countertop as a permanent cutting table for all kitchen needs. *Caution:* Do not wash cutting boards in the dishwasher or by immersing in hot water. This can warp them and ruin them. Clean them by wiping first with a wet then with a dry cloth.

Graters

Stainless steel graters are very useful for grating and slicing vegetables, fruits, cheeses, or even dry breads into very fine, medium, or coarse sizes. They come in different shapes and sizes. If you can afford only one, buy a very versatile four-sided grater in which each side is useful for different purposes.

Seed Grinder

This little electric appliance is an absolute must in the Airola Diet Kitchen. It is inexpensive, compact, easy to use, and easy to clean. It resembles a miniature blender with a similar type of cutting blade, but is much smaller and shorter. You can make fine or coarse powder or flour from nuts, seeds, and grains in just a few seconds. Seed grinders are sold in health food stores. Department stores sell a very similar appliance as a coffee grinder.

Since in the Airola Diet it is very important that you never buy seeds, nuts, or grains in milled, crushed, or powdered form, but always whole (to prevent rancidity), a seed grinder becomes a very important gadget to *assure* highest quality optimum nutrition. It is one of the most used appliances in my kitchen. Once you have one, you will never want to be without it.

Food Blender

If you are going to make shakes and mixed drinks of various kinds — and they can be very useful in the Airola Diet, especially if you have children — you need an electric blender. There are many kinds on the market. Make sure the blender container is of transparent glass, not plastic.

Grain Mill

If you go "into" the Airola Optimum Diet all the way, you will want to bake your own whole-grain bread. An electric stone mill is not cheap; nevertheless, it is an excellent investment. If your natural food store does not have a mill so that you can grind your own flour there at the time of purchase, then you had better buy your grains whole and grind them on your own mill at home. To buy whole-grain flour from the store is to take the risk that it may be many weeks old and badly rancid. Such flour will not only be nutritionally inferior, but can also be harmful. Breads and grain cereals are staples in my diet, *but only if the grains are ground just before they are baked or cooked.*

If you don't feel that you can afford an electric stone mill, you can buy a hand-operated mill which is very inexpensive, simple to use, and can be clamped onto a table or countertop. Ask for one in your natural health food store.

Dough Kneader

An electric dough kneader may seem to be an expensive luxury, but if you intend to bake bread regularly it is well worth the investment. It will make bread-baking much easier and also will help to produce better-quality bread with less effort.

Baby-Food Grinder

If you have babies and young children to feed, there is no need to buy nutritionally-inferior canned baby foods — you can make the most nutritious and delicious baby foods in seconds if you have a baby-food grinder. It is a simple, hand-operated, inexpensive, and durable gadget. It will transform fruits, vegetables, cereals, or whatever into fancy finely-mashed baby food. You may find, occasionally, that a baby-food grinder can be useful, too, for making dips, gravies, sauces, dressings, etc.

Juicers

Although juices do not have an overly-important place in the Airola Diet (my basic philosophy being that you should chew and eat your foods, not drink them) a juicer can be very useful, especially if you like to go on an occasional reducing or cleansing juice fast. Also, from time to time, a half glass of freshly-made fruit or vegetable juice can be added to the regular diet or consumed between meals. And, if you have any health disorders at all, fresh fruit or vegetable juices can become a very important natural healing therapy (see *How To Get Well, How to Keep Slim, Healthy, and Young With Juice Fasting,* and *Everywoman's Book).*

There are many types of juicers on the market. The three major types are: hydraulic press, triturator, and centrifugal. Hydraulic juicers are superior, but they are expensive. Other types of juicers are more reasonably priced, and are also useful and durable if they are made from stainless steel. When you buy a juicer, make sure that at least all the parts that can come in contact with the juice are manufactured from stainless steel.

Tableware

Stainless steel tableware (knives, forks, and spoons) is best. However, do not use the kind with plastic handles since toxic plastic material does dissolve gradually and may end up in your food and/or in your stomach in microscopic, yet still toxic, amounts.

Cutting Knives

It is useful to have a large collection of cutting knives of different sizes. Again, make sure the handles are made from wood rather than plastic material, and blades are from stainless steel.

Tea Strainers

Since mild herb tea is a regular fare of many who adhere to the Airola Optimum Diet (especially on winter mornings or as an afternoon refreshment), a couple of simple stainless steel fine-meshed tea strainers can be very handy. There is no need to go for fancy ceramic or bamboo type, which are not only more expensive, but also less efficient.

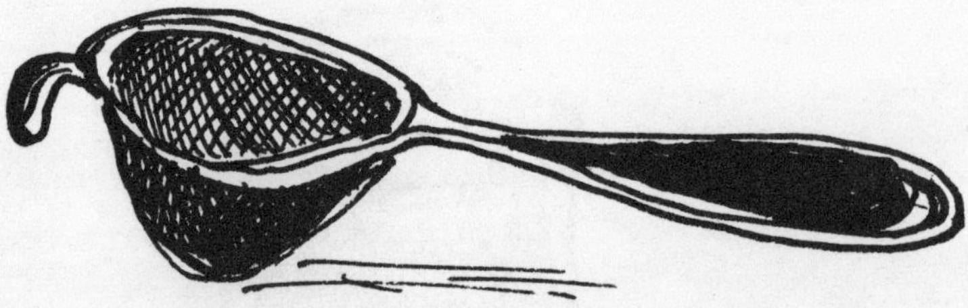

No-No's in the Optimum Diet Kitchen

- Microwave ovens
- Pressure cookers
- Aluminum utensils or kitchenware

- Aluminum foil wrap
- Plastic-coated, non-stick type cookware
- Plastic containers, bottles, or wrap

I can hear millions of distressed voices asking in unison: Why? It would take a book to give you detailed answers, quoting studies upon studies of reliable research on why none of the above can be recommended. Here are just a few reasons, in a nutshell:

- Microwave cooking, by creating a rapid and excessive heat, damages the molecular structure of proteins and fats in the food, more than regular cooking does. There is also always a danger of radiation leakage.
- Pressure cookers develop extremely high temperatures. Remember the lower the cooking temperature, the more nutritious the food.
- Aluminum utensils and wrap dissolve and release harmful amounts of toxic aluminum when they come in contact with foods, especially with acid-containing foods, such as fruits.
- Plastic-coated, non-stick pans can release extremely toxic fumes if accidently left on the burner and they become overheated. Also, the toxic plastic material used in coatings gradually disintegrates, releasing harmful amounts of it into your food.
- Plastic containers, especially plastic bags and wrapping materials, dissolve upon contact with oils, fats, and fatty foods such as cheese, for example. Although plastic bags can be acceptable as storage material for dry foods such as grains, nuts, breads, and even fresh fruits and vegetables, they should never be used for storage or wrapping of butter, cheese, margarine, or any other fat-containing foods. Plastic bottles should never be used for oils or milk, as the fat in the milk or oil may cause a certain amount of disintegration and dissolution of plastic materials, which will end up as a harmful residue in foods.

4

Prescription For A Happy And Healthy Day

The approximate daily menu and health program in a typical day of a faithful follower of the Airola Optimum Diet and Health-Building Lifestyle, should look something like this:

UPON ARISING

Choice 1: One glass of water (warm in winter), plain or flavored with freshly-squeezed juice of ½ lime, or ½ lemon, or 1 orange, or ½ grapefruit. If fresh juice is not available, use a small quantity of pure, unsweetened bottled fruit juice sold in health food stores. Bottled or canned *citrus* juices should never be used, however. Commercially sold citrus juices are usually pressed from unpeeled fruit and such juices may contain harmful amounts of etheric oils from the skins of the citrus fruit. Since most tap water is badly polluted and unsafe to drink, use bottled spring or well water. Distilled water should not be used on a regular basis for prolonged periods of time, as it may cause mineral deficiencies in your body.

Choice 2: One large cup of weak herb tea, sweetened with honey. Choice of rosehips, camomile, spearmint, or any other mild beverage herbs mentioned in the Section on Herbs in Chapter 1.

Choice 3: One glass of freshly-made fruit juice from any locally-grown fruits or berries, in season: apples, pineapple, cherries, pears, citrus, etc. Sweet juices should be diluted with water, ½ and ½. Do not use canned or frozen juices, unless it is totally impossible to obtain freshly-made juices.

MORNING WALK

You should schedule your day in such a manner that you will have at least one hour each morning for a walk combined with deep breathing exercises and mild calisthenics.

Walking is, by far, the best form of exercise. It is also a perfect time for reflection, relaxation, and meditation. Thus, it is not only an excellent way to keep physically fit, but also to keep mentally fit; especially if you can get out of the city and go to the countryside, into the woods, or to the beach. You may walk and jog intermittently. I do not recommend excessive jogging and especially running for women, however. This may cause prolapsed female organs with permanent damage to abdominal structures, as well as sagging breasts. Also, excessive strenuous exercises, such as long distance running, weight lifting, or strenuous competitive sports, may lead to changes in the hormonal balance in the female body — increase in the levels of male sex hormones and decrease in female sex hormones — which can cause not only a pronounced masculine appearance, but also serious disturbances in physiological, mental, and reproductive functions, as several current studies indicate. The best exercises for women are walking, mild calisthenics, hatha yoga, volleyball, swimming, aerobic dancing, etc. Adjust the speed of your walk and exercises to your level of energy and comfort. If you feel tired, stop and rest, then continue. If you have the time, stop in the middle of the walk and do your favorite bending, stretching, and rotating exercises. Do some deep breathing exercises, as you walk.

Caution: Do not walk or jog in smog! Also, do not walk or jog on trafficked streets! It breaks my heart to see joggers on busy streets downtown between the bumper-to-bumper traffic, breathing in tons of lead and carbon monoxide, seemingly totally unaware of the great danger they are exposing themselves to. If you live in a large smoggy city, and the only choice is to walk on the streets, you will be better off without walking. If you are really serious about moving towards a more healthful way of living, you must —before making any other drastic changes in your lifestyle —get into a place to live where you can breathe pure air. Why waste money on vitamins and health foods while killing yourself with polluted air?

If you have a garden, or if you live on a farm, you can skip the walking and jogging, and get in an hour or two of hard physical labor.

SHOWER AND DRY BRUSH MASSAGE

After your walk, take a shower to wash away perspiration. If you are brave, have an intermittent cold and hot shower: ten seconds ice cold — 30 seconds hot; repeat several times. Exquisitely stimulating! Finish with cold water in the summer, and with hot water in the winter.

After showering, dry yourself thoroughly with a coarse towel and then give yourself a 5-10 minute Million Dollar Health and Beauty Treatment — *DRY BRUSH MASSAGE.* Use a special natural-bristle brush with a long handle (sold in health food stores) and brush every part of the body, beginning with the feet and working up towards the heart, using circular motions. If time and circumstances permit, a couple can give the massage to each other — what a pleasant and stimulating way to start the day!! (You will find more details on dry brush massage in any of my major books.)

BREAKFAST

Choice 1: Fresh fruit, in season: apples, bananas, grapes, grapefruit, or any other available fruit or berries — one or several fruits at the same time. It is preferable to use fresh, locally-grown fruit.

½ cup cottage cheese, preferably homemade quark, or one cup of any of the lactic acid milks: yogurt, piima, kefir, or homemade clabbered milk, preferably made from goat's milk or raw cow's milk (see Index).

A small handful (10-20) raw nuts such as almonds or filberts; or a couple of tablespoons of sunflower seeds, pumpkin seeds, or hulled sesame seeds. Nuts and seeds can be ground in your own seed grinder and sprinkled over yogurt. Sesame butter (Tahini) or almond butter can be used occasionally instead of whole nuts and seeds.

1 tbsp. fresh wheat germ, sprinkled over milk or cottage cheese. Use only if fresh, dated, non-rancid wheat germ can be obtained.

Choice 2: A large bowl of fresh Fruit Salad a la Airola (see Index).

Choice 3: A bowl of cooked cereal, such as millet, buckwheat, or oats.

½ cup soaked or cooked unsweetened and unsulfured dried fruits: raisins, prunes, apples, peaches, apricots, etc.; or 2-3 tbsp. of Homemade Applesauce (see Index).
1 glass fresh, raw, unpasteurized milk, preferably goat's milk.

½ tsp. honey, or 1 pat of butter, or 1 tsp. olive or sesame oil (optional).

Choice 4: A bowl of sprouted wheat or other sprouted seeds with a glass of yogurt or milk (see instructions on making sprouts in Section II, "Whole Grains, Cereals, Legumes").

Choice 5: 2-3 Buckwheat Pancakes (see Index).

Choice 6: 1 or 2 eggs, soft-boiled. The best (from a nutritional standpoint) way to prepare eggs: separate the egg yolks from the whites; poach the whites; then scramble the eggs at the table by mixing egg yolks with cooked whites.

1 slice whole-grain bread made without sweeteners or fats (see Index).

1 glass fresh, raw milk, or 1 cup of your favorite herb tea.

1 pat fresh butter (optional).

MID-MORNING SNACK (optional)

1 apple, 1 banana, or an equivalent amount of other fresh fruit or berries in season.

LUNCH

Choice 1: A bowl of cooked, whole-grain cereal, such as millet, buckwheat (kasha), or kruska, if not eaten for breakfast. Any other available whole-grain cereals such as oats, barley, corn or rice can be used. Dry milk powder (non-instant type) can be added to the water in which cereals are cooked. This will raise the protein quantity as well as improve its quality. Molino cereal (see Index) is recommended to those who are bothered by constipation, or extra bran can be added to any cooked cereal.

1 large glass fresh, raw milk, preferably goat's milk.

½ tbsp. olive or sesame seed oil, or 1 pat of butter.

1 tsp. honey, 2 tbsp. homemade applesauce, or dry fruit compote can be used on cereal instead of oil or butter.

Choice 2: A bowl of freshly-prepared vegetable, pea, or bean soup, or any other cooked or steamed vegetable course, such as potatoes, squash, yams, zucchini, green beans, fresh corn on the cob, etc.

1-2 slices whole-grain bread.
1-2 slices natural cheese.
1 pat butter.

Choice 3: Buckwheat Pancakes (see Index), if not eaten for breakfast.

Choice 4: For Mexican food lovers: beans and corn tortillas with fresh salsa made from tomatoes, avocado, onion, garlic, and chili (see Index).

Choice 5: Vegetable salad meal (see DINNER menu).

Choice 6: A large bowl of Fruit Salad a la Airola (if not eaten for breakfast) — or any of the breakfast choices not eaten that morning.

Choice 7: Any of the grain, cereal, bean, pea, or lentil courses traditionally eaten in the ethnic culture of your ancestors. Make sure, however, that in terms of quality of ingredients and the mode of preparation, the basic principles of the Airola Diet are not compromised.

SIESTA

If at all possible, take a ½ to 1 hour rest in bed after lunch. After resting, have a glass of water, a cup of weak herb tea, or fresh fruit juice diluted with water, ½ and ½. Then, take a leisurely walk, and, if possible, do a few stretching, bending and deep-breathing exercises. But, if all this is totally impossible (since many people have jobs that allow only a short time for lunch), at least try to squeeze in 10-15 minutes during which you can sit or lie down, close your eyes and your mind, relax and let the blood flow to your digestive system to help begin the digestive and assimilative processes undisturbed.

MID-AFTERNOON SNACK (optional)

Same as mid-morning snack.

DINNER

Choice 1: A large bowl of fresh, green vegetable salad. Use any and all available vegetables, preferably those *in season*, including tomatoes, avocados, celery, etc. Carrots, shredded red beets, and onions should be staples in every salad; add garlic, if your social life permits. Salads should be attractively prepared and served with homemade dressing (see Index) or lemon juice (or apple cider vinegar) and cold-pressed olive or sesame seed oil, seasoned with herbs, garlic powder, a little sea salt, cayenne pepper, etc. Or, all vegetables, whole or cut, can be placed attractively on the plate without mixing them into a salad, and eaten one at a time — this is by far, the superior way of eating vegetables.

1 or 2 middle-sized boiled or baked potatoes in jackets. Cooked or steamed vegetable course, if desired: eggplant, artichoke, sweet potatoes, yams, squash, zucchini or other vegetables (see Index). Use kelp powder or sea salt sparingly for seasoning; also any or all of the usual garden herbs (see Chapter 2, "Culinary Herbs and Spices").

½ cup homemade cottage cheese (quark), or 1-2 slices of natural cheese.

1-2 slices whole-grain bread, preferably sourdough rye bread (see Index).

1 pat fresh butter.

1 glass yogurt or other soured milk.

Choice 2: Any of the recommended LUNCH choices if not eaten for lunch.

Choice 3: A bowl of soup (see Soup Section for recipes).

2 slices whole-grain bread.

1 slice natural cheese.

1 pat butter.

Choice 4: A large bowl of green vegetable salad, as in Choice 1, or any of the other fresh vegetable salads (see Section on Vegetable Salads), plus a cooked vegetable-based course from your own "nutritional roots." Again, make sure that the quality of the ingredients and the mode of preparation are in harmony with the basic principles of the Airola Diet.

EVENING (BED-TIME) SNACK

Choice 1: 1 glass fresh milk or milk-shake (see Index).

Choice 2: 1 cup yogurt or kefir with 1 tbsp. brewer's yeast powder.

Choice 3: 1 apple, eaten slowly and chewed well.

Choice 4: 1 cup of your favorite herb tea, sweetened with honey, and a slice of whole-grain bread or 1 bran/corn muffin.

Vital Points To Remember

1. The above Menu is an outline, a skeleton, around which an individual diet of optimum nutrition can be built. Or, it can be followed as it is. I know of thousands of people who live on the basic Airola Optimum Diet and enjoy extraordinary health. But my diet is very broad, and,

therefore, so flexible that it can be changed and adapted to your specific requirements and health conditions, your country's own ethnic customs and climate, the availability of foods, your personal preferences, etc.

2. Whatever changes you make, keep in mind, however, that the bulk of your diet should consist of grains, seeds, legumes, and nuts (natural, complex carbohydrates), and fresh vegetables and fruits, preferably organically grown, up to 75-80 percent of them eaten raw. Do not avoid potatoes because you think they are fattening — they are not. Potatoes are a supernutritious food, containing almost as much vitamin C as oranges, and high quality proteins comparable in biological value to those in eggs and meat.

3. The Airola Diet contains all the nutrients you will need, *including adequate amounts of protein.* In addition to grains, nuts, and seeds — especially buckwheat, millet, rice, oats, and almonds — milk, fresh or cultured, and homemade cottage cheese (quark) are good protein sources. A small quantity of eggs, fish, or meat may be added to this diet, if you so desire, *but their inclusion is not necessary.* An adequate amount of protein can be obtained without eggs, meat, or fish on a pure lacto-vegetarian diet.

4. The menus for lunch and dinner are interchangeable. Ideally, a fruit meal should be eaten for breakfast, a cereal meal for lunch, and a vegetable meal for dinner, but if your schedule and lifestyle require differently, do not hesitate to make your own menu plans that will be more suitable for you and your family.

5. It is best to divide all vitamins and supplements into three equal parts and take them with breakfast, lunch, and dinner. If it is more convenient, however, vitamins can be taken with two meals only — breakfast and dinner. If you must take the daily dose of all vitamins with one meal, lunch is the best choice.

6. Do not forget to eat slowly, chew well, and savor your food in a relaxed, pleasant atmosphere; do not overeat; and, most importantly, enjoy your food in a spirit of love and thanksgiving for the great blessings and abundance of health that are yours. Give thanks where thanks are due.

7. Finally, remember that "you do not live by bread alone." As important as good nutrition is, it must not become an obsession or the goal in itself. Also, please remember that although good nutrition is a very important factor in building and maintaining optimal health and prevention of disease, it is not the only factor. Neither is it *the* most important factor. Exercise — sufficient amounts of vigorous physical activity — is just as important, if not more so. The most important nutrient for optimum health and prevention of disease is not a vitamin, mineral, or protein, but *oxygen!* And, you cannot get adequate amounts of oxygen to all parts of your body without vigorous exercise.

Both exercise and nutrition, however, will fail if, in your goal of attaining the highest level of wellness and joy, you overlook other very important factors in building and maintaining good health, preventing disease, and living a long and happy life — relaxation; peace of mind; a positive health-oriented outlook on life; a contented spirit; absence of worries, fears, and jealousies; a cheerful disposition; unselfishness; a caring and loving attitude towards your "neighbors" and all mankind; and faith in God. These are all powerful health-promoting factors without which optimum health cannot be achieved.

Furthermore, the pursuit of better health must not become an obsessive compulsion and the sole purpose and goal in life. As worthwhile and as enjoyable as good health can be, it won't guarantee your happiness and fulfillment. Improving one's health and building a strong, disease-free body can be a rewarding and joyous experience, but only if it is kept in the right perspective. Let's not forget that the true purpose of life is not just building magnificent biceps, slim bodies, and lovely complexions, but perfecting and refining our divine spirits and becoming more God-like. The body is a temple in which the spirit dwells and develops. It should, therefore, be respected and kept healthy. But, the ultimate purpose of life is the development and perfection of the spirit that dwells therein.

True and lasting happiness comes from the realization of the divine origin and purpose of all life and from the directing of our energies towards the expression and the exemplification of the Divine Plan in our daily lives. Supreme happiness can only be achieved by those who give happiness to others and express unconditional love for their fellow men and God in their lives. Only when our pursuits of better health are motivated by such an unselfish and spiritual orientation will they fit into the framework of the purposeful, divinely-designed plan for our lives.

5

Dr. Airola's Weight Loss Program

There are over 40 million "significantly" overweight adults in this country. A total of 75 million Americans are considered to be overweight to some extent. The causes of obesity are many: emotional, glandular, metabolic, psychological, and nutritional. Doctors agree that the ultimate cause of overweight is overeating. They disagree, however, as to what causes overeating. In addition to emotional and psychological factors, such as boredom, unhappiness, frustration, anxieties, low self-esteem, and such health-related factors as hypoglycemia, and glandular disorders, nutritional deficiencies are a major factor in overeating — a factor often overlooked by doctors. Overweight persons are often *over-fed, but undernourished.*

Here is how that works. When you eat a diet of denatured, overprocessed, refined, frozen, overcooked, sugar-laden, pre-packaged, man-made so-called "foods" (the kinds of "junk" foods most Americans eat today), although you are getting a lot of calories, you are not getting adequate amounts of vital nutrients that your body needs because most of these nutrients have been refined out or destroyed in processing and manufacturing. Consequently, even though your stomach is full after a meal of such nutritionless foods, your body, nutritionally speaking, is still hungry. This hunger is expressed in a constant craving for something to eat. So you snack — you take a coke, or potato chips, or sweets. Again, you are loading yourself with *empty* calories while your body is craving real nutrients: vitamins, minerals, trace elements. Such malnutrition by overeating of nutritionless foods sets up a pattern of constant craving for food and chronic overeating — and consequent obesity.

Your appetite is controlled by a mechanism in the brain called the appestat. Normally the appestat creates the sensation of hunger only when there is the actual need for fuel for energy production. Many factors, however, can disrupt the work of the appestat. As mentioned before, negative emotions, insecurity, unhappiness, boredom, etc., can put the appestat out of order. Nutritional deficiencies can do the same.

This is the main reason why reducing diets, the kind you read about each week in the popular tabloids, don't work. They are only concerned with calories. Admittedly, any reducing diet that supplies 800 calories or less a day will help to reduce. But, if the 800 calories are made up of the usual refined, devitalized, and denatured foods that you buy at your supermarket, the end result will be severe nutritional deficiencies, which will lead to excessive hunger and overeating as soon as you go off the diet.

But, this is just one of the minor faults of the average reducing diet. Some of the diets are so dangerously unbalanced and deficient that they can result in severe illness or even death. Liquid protein diets, or any high protein diet, are examples of how improper diets can cause serious health problems or even death by leading to severe auto-toxemia, acidosis, and metabolic and biochemical imbalances in the system. Low- or no-carbohydrate diets are equally harmful. Severe restriction of carbohydrates with no restriction of fats and protein may take weight off effectively, but can have a disastrous effect on health, causing irreparable damage to the brain, nervous system, and heart. The medical racket of "fat doctors" treating obesity with amphetamines, HCG injections, and other anti-obesity drugs (AOD's) may lead not only to drug addiction, but also to serious health damage, such as high blood pressure, liver damage, paranoid psychosis, and changes in libido. Incredibly, many such drugs are now sold without prescription in drugstores.

The only safe and effective way to lose weight and keep weight at normal levels is to

a) eat less;
b) make sure that the foods you do eat are nutritious and health-building; and
c) exercise more.

This common-sense approach to losing weight is slow, not easy, and requires a commitment, *but it is effective.* The program recommended in this chapter will not only take off extra pounds, but it will also improve your health while doing so.

The following diets — one for 800 calories a day, one for 1200 calories, and a 1000-calorie non-dairy diet — are based on the Airola Optimum Diet and should be made up of the high-quality, preferably organically-grown foods recommended in Chapter 1. Select the diet most suitable for your needs and your lifestyle. An 800-calorie diet will help you to lose 3 to 4 pounds a week; a 1000-calorie diet, 2 to 3 pounds a week; and a 1200-calorie diet, 1 to 2 pounds a week, depending upon the amount of exercise.

In addition to diet, please do not overlook many other important factors and reducing aids, such as the following:

Exercise

Since the difference between maintaining weight and putting on weight is the proper balancing between calorie intake and calorie expenditure, and since it is admittedly very difficult to *eat less,* the logical course of action is to increase calorie expenditure. That is, get as much exercise as possible. The more you exercise, the less restrictive you need to be with your diet.

What kind of exercise is best for reducing? *Vigorous* exercise! Any physical activity that burns lots of calories — jogging, tennis, basketball or other vigorous games, swimming, walking briskly, heavy physical labor — are the best forms of exercise for reducing. A combination of intermittent jogging and walking is best for most people, especially those who are not very young. If you haven't jogged or run before, start slowly and increase the time and distance gradually. (See Chapter 4 for more information on exercise.)

New Eating Patterns

Keep all food well out of sight. There is quite a bit of research evidence suggesting that you are more likely to overeat when food is physically visible and within easy reach. Don't store tempting foods in the front of the refrigerator so that if you open the door they are staring you right in the face. You are less likely to snack on them if they are well-hidden; or better yet, not even in the house. "Out of sight, out of mind," is a good rule to remember.

Serve small portions at a meal and keep the rest of the food in the kitchen, not on the table. You are more likely to take second or third helpings if food is left on the table.

Eat slowly and chew well. Eating too fast causes the body to miss the important nerve signals of fullness and satisfaction from the stomach to the appestat. If you eat fast, you may overshoot your biological needs. By chewing well, you also improve the digestibility and assimilability of the foods so that less food will be needed to satisfy the body's needs for nutrients.

Stop eating at the very *first* sign of fullness or satisfaction — even if there is some food left on the plate. "The clean plate syndrome" is one of the worst eating habits, and one of the prime contributing factors to overweight. It is better that the food go to waste than to waist!

Avoid Salt

Train your taste buds to enjoy the natural flavor of unsalted foods. An excess of salt in the diet will interfere with effective reducing by holding excessive amounts of water in the body tissues.

Drink Lots of Liquids

It is important to drink lots of liquids when you are on a reducing diet: herb teas, diluted fruit and vegetable juices, or plain water. The best herbs for reducing are: chickweed, Irish moss, sassafrass, and chaparral. The best fruit juices: lemon, grapefruit, pineapple, papaya. Dilute sweet juices with water, 50-50; the sweeter the juice, the more water. The specific vegetable juices that can help you to reduce are: cabbage, celery, and P & L Juice (see Index).

Take Vitamins and Supplements Daily

The following vitamins and supplements are specifically effective if taken together with a reducing diet:

C — 1,000-3,000 mg.

Cod liver oil — 1 teaspoon

B-Complex, with B_{12} — 100% natural, from concentrated yeast — 1-3 tablets

B_6 — 50-100 mg.

Brewer's yeast powder — 2-3 tablespoons, or equivalent in tablets

E — 400-600 I.U.
Inositol — 500 mg.
Choline — 500 mg.
Lecithin — 2 teaspoons of granules
Kelp — 3-5 tablets, or 1 teaspoon of granules or powder (can be used as a salt substitute on foods)
Calcium — 500 mg.
Magnesium — 250 mg.
"Nature's Minerals" — 6 tablets (multiple mineral and trace element formula without bone meal)

All vitamins should be divided and taken with the major meals. The above dosages are for persons over twenty. Adolescents should take a half dose. Take your vitamins and food supplements *after meals* to minimize the appetite-stimulating effect of some vitamins, notably vitamins from the B-complex. Brewer's yeast should be taken one hour before meals, on an empty stomach, mixed with some acid fruit juice, such as citrus, or pineapple juice. The above mentioned supplements are sold in health food stores. "Nature's Minerals", if your store does not carry them, can be ordered directly from: Sweet Earth Products, P.O. Box 31888, Phoenix, Arizona 85046.

Visualization and Positive Affirmation

Finally, you can program your subconscious mind to work towards a new and slimmer you by visualizing the figure and body you want to have and a daily positive confirmation that you are actually acquiring it.

Here is a very effective method I've devised (called Subconscious Programming Method — SPM) that has helped many people. Cut out the head of one of your own photographs and attach it to a picture of a body that you want yours to look like. Try to find a scantily-clad or nearly nude picture, so you can see the whole body. Each evening before you go to bed, stand in front of a full-length mirror in the nude and take a good, long, and honest look at yourself.

Look at the composite picture for a while, then look again at your own body. Visualize how your whole life may change when your body will look like the one in the composite picture. Every night, as you go through this routine, make a determined decision and commitment: "that's the way I am going to look!"

Then, when you get into bed, relax and feel good about the fact that you are on the way to acquiring a new and beautiful figure. As you are slowly falling asleep, keep repeating, silently, the following words (which are a paraphrase of Dr. Emile Coué's famous words):

"Every day, in every way, I'm getting slimmer, and slimmer, and slimmer!"

Then, throughout the day, as you go about your work, or while driving the car, or on your daily walks, say *loudly* to yourself the same words: "Every day, in every way, I'm getting slimmer, and slimmer, and slimmer!" Say that at least five times a day, and I assure you that wonderful things will begin to happen. Your mental visualization of your ideal body, and conscious positive affirmation of the fact that you are on the way to achieving that body, will register as a work order and a goal in your subconscious mind, which will then "instruct" all the glands, organs, and vital processes of the body to initiate and eventually help to accomplish that goal. Your eating habits, workings of your appestat and all the glands, the digestive, and assimilative mechanisms, effectiveness of fat metabolism, your degree of will power, and desire to work toward the desired goal will all be positively influenced and affected on a subconscious level by such programming of your mind. The power of the mind is limitless. It can accomplish wonders. I have seen miraculous results accomplished by a positive attitude and mind-programming in hundreds of cases. The power of the mind is so great that the above-mentioned method *alone* can help you to lose weight. Imagine how successful you can be if you use it as an adjunct to all the other approaches to reducing recommended in this chapter, including the following reducing diets!

Dr. Airola's Weig

1,200-Calor

	1st DAY	2nd DAY	3rd DAY
BREAKFAST	Mixed fresh fruit salad, 1 cup (100) Yogurt, low fat, plain, 1 cup (120) Raw almonds, 12 to 15 (90)	* Airola Shake, 6 oz. glass (268) Raw pineapple, ¾ cup (52)	Fresh berries, i season, 1 cup (56 * Quark or Cottage Cheese, 1 cup (160) Raw sunflower seeds, 2 tablespoons (9
LUNCH	* Millet Cereal, 1 cup (187) * Unsweetened Applesauce, ½ cup (40) Whole milk, ½ cup (80)	* Cooked Oatmeal, 1 cup (148) Soaked prunes, 5 (125) Whole milk, ½ cup (80)	* Vegetable Juic Cocktail, 1 cup (70) * Cooked Brow Rice, 1 cup (178 * Italian Style Celery, ½ of reci (50)
DINNER	*Vegetable Relish Plate, using 1 medium carrot, ½ tomato, ½ green pepper, ½ cup alfalfa sprouts (70) *Lentil Soup, ¼ of recipe (242) *Whole Grain Bread, 2 slices (140) Natural cheese, 1 oz. (105)	* Basic Tossed Salad, with 1 shredded beet and 1 shredded carrot (80) * Low-Cal Dressing, 1 tablespoon (5) * Swedish Cabbage Rolls, 2 (276) * Cooked Green Peas, ½ cup (50) * Corn Bread, one 2-inch square (93)	* Alfalfa Sprou Salad, ¼ of recip (21) * French Dressing, 1 tablespoon (60 * Mushroom Quiche, ¼ of reci (300) * Cooked Green Beans, 1 cup (31 * Whole Grain Bread, 2 slices (140)

Notes: 1. Recipes marked with asterisk (*) can be found in this book.

Loss Program
Diet

4th DAY	5th DAY	6th DAY	7th DAY
Cantaloupe, ½ (60) Yogurt, low fat, plain, 1 cup (120) Raw pumpkin seeds, 2 tablespoons (94) Fresh wheat germ, 1 tablespoon (18)	* Banana-Berry Shake, 12 oz. glass (250) Mixed raw nuts, 1 tablespoon (85)	Papaya, ½ (or ½ cantaloupe) (60) * Quark or cottage cheese, 1 cup (160) Raw sunflower seeds, 2 tablespoons (92)	* Banana-Date Whip, ¼ of recipe (125) * Quark or cottage cheese, 1 cup (160) Raw almonds, 12 to 15 (90)
* Buckwheat Pancakes, two 4 inch pancakes (180) Stewed fruit, ¼ cup (60) Whole milk, ½ cup (80)	* Cooked Oatmeal, 1 cup (148) Soaked prunes, 4 (100) Fresh wheat germ, 1 tablespoon (18) Whole milk, ½ cup (80)	* Kasha (Buckwheat Cereal), 1 cup (187) * Unsweetened Applesauce, ½ cup (40) Whole milk, ½ cup (80)	* Fresh Carrot Juice, ½ cup (35) * Tabouli Salad, 1/3 of recipe (300)
* Basic Tossed Salad, 2 cups (30) * Low-Cal Dressing, 1 tablespoon (5) Natural cheese, 1 oz. (105) *Baked Sweet Potato, 1 large (254) Cooked Summer Squash, 1 cup (28) * Whole Grain Bread, 2 slices (140)	* Gazpacho, 1 cup (50) * Baked Potato, 1 medium (100) * Cooked Green Peas, 1 cup (100) * Mushroom patty, 1 (109) * Whole Grain Bread, 1 slice (70)	* Airola Salad, 1 cup (60) * Bean Burritos, 2 (400) Cooked zucchini, 1 cup (28) Cooked carrots, ½ cup (35)	* Basic Tossed Salad, 2 cups (30) * Low-Cal Dressing, 1 tablespoon (5) * Vegetable Stew, ¼ of recipe (328) * Whole Grain Bread, 2 slices (140)

Numbers in parenthesis (120) indicate the calorie count.

Dr. Airola's Weigh
1,000-Calori

	1st DAY	2nd DAY	3rd DAY
BREAKFAST	Mixed fresh fruit salad, 2 cups (200) Raw almonds, 12 to 15 (90) Fresh wheat germ, 1 tablespoon (18)	* Pineapple-Banana Shake, 12 oz. glass (257) Raw sunflower seeds, ½ tablespoon, freshly ground and sprinkled over Shake (23)	Fresh berries, in season, 1 cup (56) Scrambled egg, 1 (80) * Rye Bread, lightly toasted, 2 slices (140)
LUNCH	* Millet Cereal, 1 cup (187) * Unsweetened Applesauce, ½ cup (40)	* Garbanzo Bean Spread, ¼ cup (110) * Whole Grain Bread, 2 slices, with lettuce and 2-3 tomato slices (150)	* Vegetable Juice Cocktail, 1 cup (70) * Brown Rice, cooked, 1 cup (178 * Italian Style Celery, ½ of recipe (50)
DINNER	* Vegetable Relish Plate, using 1 medium carrot, ½ tomato, ½ green pepper, ½ cup alfalfa sprouts (70) * Lentil Soup, ¼ of recipe (242) * Whole Grain Bread, 2 slices (140)	* Basic Tossed Salad, 2 cups with 1 shredded beet and 1 shredded carrot (80) * Low-Cal Dressing, 1 tablespoon (5) * Swedish Cabbage Rolls, 2 (276) * Cooked Green Peas, ½ cup (50) Corn Meal Biscuit, 1 (55)	* Alfalfa Sprout Salad, ¼ of recipe (21) * French Dressing, 1 tablespoon (60) * Vegetable Stew (no cheese), ¼ of recipe (153) * Whole Grain Bread, 2 slices (140)

Notes: 1. Recipes marked with asterisk (*) can be found in this book.

ʟoss Program
ɴon-Dairy Diet

4th DAY	5th DAY	6th DAY	7th DAY
Mixed fresh fruit salad, 2 cups (200) Raw almonds, 12 to 15 (90) Fresh wheat ·erm, 1 tablespoon (18)	* Pineapple-Banana Shake, 12 oz. glass (257) Raw sunflower seeds, ½ tablespoon, freshly ground and sprinkled over Shake (23)	Mixed fresh fruit salad, 1 cup (100) Soft boiled egg, 1 (80) * Whole Grain Bread, lightly toasted, 1 slice (70)	* Banana-Date Whip, ¼ of recipe (125) Raw almonds, 10 to 15 (90)
* Buckwheat Pancakes (made without milk), three 4-inch pancakes (216) Iaple syrup, 100% natural, tablespoons (100)	* Cooked Oatmeal, 1 cup (148) * Unsweetened Applesauce, 2 tablespoons (10) Fresh wheat germ, 1 tablespoon (18) Soy milk, ½ cup (70)	* Kasha (Buckwheat Cereal), 1 cup (187) Soy milk, ½ cup (70)	* Fresh Carrot Juice, ½ cup (35) * Tabouli Salad, 1/3 of recipe (302)
* Basic Tossed Salad, 2 cups (30) * Low-Cal Dressing, 1 tablespoon (5) * Baked Sweet Potato, 1 large (254) Summer Squash, ooked, 1 cup (28) * Whole Grain Bread, 1 slice (70)	* Gazpacho, 1 cup (50) * Mushroom Patties, 2 (218) * Baked Potato, 1 medium (100) * Broccoli, cooked, 1 cup (35) * Rye Bread, 1 slice (70)	* Airola Salad, 1 cup (60) * Chili Beans, 1/6 of recipe (304) * Zucchini, cooked, 1 cup (28) * Corn Tortilla, 1 (63)	* Onion Soup, ¼ of recipe (25) * Tofu, Spanish Style (leave out cheese), ¼ of recipe (256) * Whole Wheat Noodles, 1 cup (200)

Numbers in parenthesis (120) indicate the calorie count.

Dr. Airola's Weigh

800-Calor

	1st DAY	2nd DAY	3rd DAY
BREAKFAST	Mixed fresh fruit salad, 1 cup (100) Yogurt, low fat, plain, ½ cup (60) Raw almonds, 10 (70)	* Airola Shake, 6 oz. glass (268)	Fresh berries, in season, 1 cup (56 * Quark or cottag cheese, ¾ cup (12(Raw sunflower seeds, 1 tablespoo (46)
LUNCH	* Millet Cereal, 1 cup (187) * Unsweetened Applesauce, ½ cup (40) Whole milk, 1/3 cup (53)	* Cooked Oatmeal, 2/3 cup (100) Soaked prunes, 2 (50) Whole milk, ½ cup (80)	* Vegetable Juic Cocktail, ½ cup (35) * Cooked Brown Rice, 1 cup (178) * Italian Style Celery, ¼ of recip (26)
DINNER	* Vegetable Relish Plate, using 1 medium carrot, ½ tomato, ½ green pepper, ½ cup alfalfa sprouts (70) * Lentil Soup, 1/6 of recipe (165) * Whole Grain Bread, 1 slice (70)	* Basic Tossed Salad, 2 cups, with ½ shredded beet and ½ shredded carrot (55) * Swedish Cabbage Roll, 1 (138) * Corn Bread, one 2-inch square (93)	* Alfalfa Sprou Salad, ¼ of recip (21) * Low-Cal Dressing, 1 tablespoon (5) * Mushroom Quiche, ¼ of reci (300) * Cooked Green Beans, ½ cup (1

Notes: 1. Recipes marked with asterisk (*) can be found in this book.

oss Program
iet

4th DAY	5th DAY	6th DAY	7th DAY
antaloupe, ½ (60) Yogurt, low fat, olain, 1 cup (122) Raw pumpkin eeds, 1 tablespoon (47)	* Banana-Berry Shake, 12 oz. glass (250)	Fresh papaya, ½ (or ½ cantaloupe) (60) * Quark or Cottage Cheese, ¾ cup (120) Raw sunflower seeds, 1 tablespoon (46)	* Banana-Date Whip, ¼ of recipe (125) Yogurt, low fat, plain, ½ cup (60) Raw almonds, 10 (70)
* Buckwheat Pancakes, two 4-inch pancakes (180) Stewed fruit, ¼ cup (60)	* Cooked Oatmeal, 1 cup (148) * Unsweetened Applesauce, ½ cup (40) Whole milk, 1/3 cup (53)	* Kasha (Buckwheat Cereal), 1 cup (187) * Unsweetened Applesauce, ½ cup (40) Whole milk, 1/3 cup (53)	* Fresh Carrot Juice, ½ cup (35) * Tabouli Salad, 1/6 of recipe (150)
* Basic Tossed Salad, 2 cups (30) * Low-Cal Dressing, 1 tablespoon (5) * Baked sweet potato, 1 small (140) Natural cheese, 1 oz. (105) * Cooked Summer Squash, 1 cup (28)	* Gazpacho, 1 cup (50) * Mushroom Patty, 1 (109) * Baked Potato, 1 medium (100) * Cooked Broccoli, 1 cup (35)	* Airola Salad, 1 cup (60) * Bean Burrito, 1 (200) Cooked zucchini, 1 cup (28)	* Basic Tossed Salad, 2 cups (30) * Low-Cal Dressing, 1 tablespoon (5) * Vegetable Stew, 1/6 of recipe (217) * Whole Grain Bread, 1 slice (70)

2. Numbers in parenthesis (120) indicate the calorie count.

Additional Tips on Weight Loss Program:

1. Those who do not use milk or milk products can replace all milk and yogurt entrees in the 800 and 1,200 Calorie Diets with fresh vegetable and fruit juices, or vegetable broth (see Index). Natural cheese can be replaced with tofu. Or, go on the 1,000-Calorie Non-Dairy Diet.

2. The daily menus are interchangeable.

3. See Index for recipes listed in the Reducing Diet menus.

4. Substitutions are allowed as long as (1) you follow the basic principles of the Airola Diet (see Chapter 1); (2) the substitute has the same amount of calories (see Food Composition Table in Section III for calorie content of various foods); and (3) the substitute belongs to the same basic food group.

5. The menus and the recipes in my reducing diets are simple and rather repetitive. Simplicity and repetitiveness are marks of a healthful diet. Thus, you can eat the same cooked cereal or soup or salad every day, if you prefer: for example, millet every day of the week, rather than oatmeal one day, rice the next day, buckwheat the following day, etc.

6. Do not drink liquids with meals, but drink plenty of liquids the first thing in the morning and between meals: plain water, lemonade (the juice of ½ lime or ¼ lemon in a glass of water), herb teas, etc.

7. The reducing diets in my Weight Loss Program are so nutritious and well-balanced that you can safely diet as long as necessary, or until you reach your desired weight. Once the desired weight is reached, you should follow the basic Airola Optimum Diet as described in Chapter 1 of this book.

8. It is always wise to consult with your doctor before you go on any reducing diet. There are certain health conditions in which dieting is contraindicated.

9. You should never go on any reducing program when pregnant or nursing.

10. Finally, do not forget that, ultimately, the loss of weight is dependent on the balance between the calories you consume and the calories you expend. *Eating less and exercising more* is the supreme secret of successful reducing. When you follow my Weight Loss Program, you'll enjoy an additional bonus: being based on my Optimum Diet it contains all the nutrients needed for the maintenance of Optimum health — consequently, it results in safe and successful weight loss while improving your health.

NOTES AND ADDITIONAL RECIPES: ______________

Section II

Recipes

Vegetable Salads

PREPARING THE VEGETABLE SALAD

1. Choose from the many varieties of lettuce and greens available from your own garden or organic markets in your area: iceberg and crisphead, romaine, Boston or butterhead, leaf, bibb, endive, escarole, watercress, mustard greens, and dandelion leaves.
2. Use only fresh crisp greens. (See Chapter 1 for information on the importance of eating vegetables as fresh as possible.)
3. Store vegetables in refrigerator in plastic bags or tight containers, and prepare just before serving to preserve nutritive value.
4. Remove outer blemished leaves and any tough stems.
5. Wash the leaves thoroughly in cold water and drain.
6. To make the salad more attractive, tear the greens into bite size pieces rather than cutting them.
7. Use a variety of greens for contrast in flavor, color, and texture.
8. Place ingredients in a salad bowl that has been rubbed with a clove of garlic.
9. Add salad dressing *just before serving,* and toss.
10. *Additions to the salad* — tomatoes, cucumbers, celery, onions, garlic, chives, onion and garlic greens, radishes, radish tops, green peppers,

chopped or grated beets, carrots, turnips, kolhrabi, Jerusalem artichokes, zucchini, avocado slices, parsley, early spring nettles, dill, anise, and sprouts.

Caution: Avoid using large amounts of raw spinach, rhubarb, asparagus, chard, white or red cabbage, savoy cabbage, kale, Brussels sprouts, cauliflower, collards, and comfrey leaves in your salad. These plants, if used in considerable quantities, should be cooked before consumption. Although occasional use of these plants in raw form may not do much harm, if consumed in large quantities for protracted periods of time, they can be quite harmful. (See Section I for reasoning behind this caution.)

HOW TO MAKE SPROUTS

First, make sure that the seeds or grains you buy for sprouting are packaged for food. Under no circumstances use seeds that are sold for planting; they more likely than not contain mercury compounds or other toxic chemicals. Play it safe and buy your seeds and sprouting grains at your health food store.

The seeds most commonly used for sprouting are: alfalfa, mung beans, soybeans, and wheat.

There are many different methods for sprouting seeds. Slow germinating seeds, such as wheat or soybeans, can be soaked in water for two days (changing water twice a day) then spread thinly on a plate or paper towel for 2 or 3 days, rinsing them under running water three times a day to prevent molding. If you prefer, you may use one of the very convenient sprouting kits sold in health food stores, with enclosed directions.

Here's my own way of sprouting seeds: Place 1 tablespoon of alfalfa seeds in a quart jar and fill with water. Let soak overnight. Rinse seeds well the following morning and replace them in the glass jar without water, covering the jar with a cheesecloth held on by a rubber band. Keep rinsing the seeds 3 or 4 times a day. In 2 or 3 days, alfalfa sprouts are ready for eating. When seeds are fully sprouted, that is, the sprouts are 1 to 2 inches long, place the top on the jar and keep them in the refrigerator if they are not to be eaten right away. Always rinse sprouts before eating. Alfalfa sprouts can be eaten as they are or mixed with salads or other foods. They can also be ground up in a drink, preferably with vegetable juices.

Important Note: My studies indicate that it is not advisable to eat excessive amounts of raw sprouts, especially mung and soybean sprouts. Occasional consumption won't cause any problems, but if you eat such sprouts often and in large quantities, it would be advisable to cook them slightly (by steaming or gently sautéing them in a wok the way sprout-eating Orientals do) before eating them. This applies also to sprouted wheat or other grains when sprouts are very short. Sprouted grains are best eaten in the form of bread or cooked cereal. This caution does not apply to wheat grass or alfalfa sprouts.

Basic Tossed Salad

assortment of greens
cucumber, sliced
tomato, cut in wedges
parsley, finely chopped
green onions, sliced or chopped

Break the greens into bite size pieces and place in a salad bowl that has been rubbed with garlic. Add the sliced cucumbers, tomatoes, parsley and green onions. Toss with a little oil and vinegar or lemon or lime juice. For reducing diet, use Low-Cal Dressing.

Vegetable Relish Plate

lettuce leaves
carrot sticks
celery sticks
cauliflower florets
marinated mushrooms
pickled cucumbers
turnip slices
deviled eggs
radishes, with tops (which are edible)
green pepper slices
cherry tomatoes
pickled beets
green onions
jicama slices
cheese cubes

Place the lettuce leaves on a large serving dish. Use *some* or *all* of the above suggestions, and arrange them attractively on the lettuce leaves. Serve with a dip, or alone.

Airola Salad

Here is a completely new variety of vegetable salad. It differs from the conventional vegetable salad in two distinctive ways:

1. It is "chunky": it has no soft, leafy vegetables, such as lettuce, parsley, cabbage, spinach, or mustard greens.
2. It is "hot": it has a distinct Mexican flavor, being spiced with chili (cayenne pepper), and lime or lemon.

Use the following fresh vegetables: avocados, carrots, tomatoes, green peppers, cucumbers, red onions, garlic, celery stalks, radishes and Jerusalem artichokes. If any of the above are not available, use what you can get. Tomatoes, cucumbers, avocados, green peppers, celery, onions, and garlic are the basic ingredients.

Chop all vegetables into about 1-inch pieces. Carrots can be sliced into ¼-inch thick slices. Do not peel cucumbers or Jerusalem artichokes.

Place all chopped vegetables in a bowl and add the following ingredients to taste: sea water or sea salt (available in health food stores), chopped onions, garlic, cayenne pepper or chili, paprika, lime or lemon juice. Add some water, stir briskly, and serve.

It is important to have lots of lime or lemon juice — at least the juice of ½ lime or ¼ lemon for each serving. That means if you make a salad for four persons, use 1 lemon or 2 limes. It is best to eat the Airola Salad with a spoon, being sure to consume all the dressing. This salad should be eaten as a main dish, preferably with tortillas. Eat slowly and chew well. It is very filling and satisfying — and fantabulously delicious!

Watercress Salad

1 bunch fresh watercress
¼ pound fresh mushrooms, washed and sliced
1 cup mung bean sprouts
1 tablespoon chopped fresh parsley
1 green onion, chopped
3 tablespoons cold-pressed olive oil
1 tablespoon red wine vinegar
⅛ teaspoon sea salt
dash of cayenne pepper

Wash the watercress and tear into bite-size pieces. Combine the watercress with the sliced mushrooms, bean sprouts, parsley and green onion. Make a dressing with the olive oil, red wine vinegar, sea salt and cayenne and pour over the salad. Makes 4 servings.

Alfalfa Sprout Salad

1½ cups alfalfa sprouts
1 medium tomato, cubed
½ cup diced cucumber
¼ cup diced celery
1 green onion, chopped
2-3 radishes, sliced

Combine all ingredients and serve with Thousand Island Dressing, or Avocado Dressing (see Index). Makes 4 to 6 servings.

Celery and Carrot Slaw

1½ cups thinly sliced celery
1 cup grated carrots
¼ cup yogurt
1 tablespoon apple cider vinegar
1 tablespoon honey
¼ teaspoon sea salt
dash of cayenne pepper

Combine the sliced celery and grated carrots. Make a dressing with the yogurt, apple cider vinegar, sea salt, and cayenne pepper. Pour over the celery and carrots and serve immediately. Makes 6 servings.

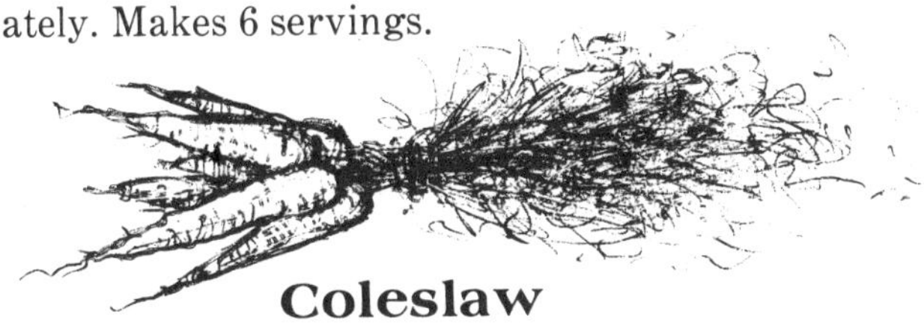

Coleslaw

2 cups shredded cabbage
¼ cup diced green pepper
2 tablespoons Homemade Mayonnaise (see Index)
2 tablespoons yogurt
paprika

Combine the shredded cabbage and green pepper. Stir in the mayonnaise and yogurt. Sprinkle a little paprika on top. Makes 4 to 6 servings.

Black Radish in Sour Cream

1 small black radish
sour cream or yogurt
sea salt

Wash the radish well, but do not peel or scrub the black part off. Slice very, very thinly. Add enough sour cream or yogurt to cover all the slices, and add salt to taste. Serve immediately.

Marinated Sliced Tomatoes

4 medium tomatoes, sliced
2 tablespoons olive oil
1 tablespoon apple cider vinegar
½ teaspoon sea salt
1 small clove garlic, crushed
2 tablespoons chopped parsley
dash of cayenne pepper

Arrange the sliced tomatoes in a serving dish. Combine the other ingredients for the marinade and pour over the tomatoes one hour before serving. Makes 6 servings.

Cucumber Salad

1 medium cucumber, thinly sliced
1 teaspoon dried dill
¼ cup apple cider vinegar
¼ cup water
1 tablespoon honey
¼ teaspoon sea salt
1 tablespoon olive or sesame seed oil

Place the cucumber slices in a small bowl. Combine the dill, apple cider vinegar, water, honey, sea salt and oil to make a dressing and pour over the cucumber slices. Allow to marinate several hours before serving. Makes 4 servings.

Zucchini Tomato Salad

2 cups cubed raw zucchini
2 medium tomatoes, cut in wedges
1/3 cup olive oil
¼ cup lemon juice
1 teaspoon honey
½ teaspoon Homemade Prepared Horseradish (see Index)
½ teaspoon sea salt
dash of cayenne pepper

Place the vegetables in a large bowl. Combine the other ingredients to make a dressing and pour over the vegetables. Marinate several hours before serving. Makes 6 servings.

Stuffed Tomato Salad

4 medium tomatoes
choice of fillings

Wash and core the tomatoes. Cut each tomato into 6 wedges about ¾ through the tomato. Fill the center with the stuffing. Garnish with parsley.

Fillings

1. Green Pepper:

1 cup cottage cheese
2 tablespoons finely chopped green pepper
1 tablespoon finely chopped onion
¼ teaspoon parsley flakes
sea salt to taste
dash of garlic powder
dash of cayenne pepper

Combine all ingredients and spoon into tomatoes.

2. Guacamole Dip (see Index)
3. Egg Salad (see Index)
4. Potato Salad (see Index)
5. Avocado Egg Salad (see Index)

Avocado Egg Salad

1 medium avocado
4 hard-boiled eggs
3 tablespoons Homemade Mayonnaise (see Index)
dash of cayenne pepper

Peel the avocado and the hard-boiled eggs and place in a mixing bowl. Mash with a potato masher until well mixed. Add the mayonnaise and cayenne and stir well. Use as a stuffing for tomatoes, celery or as a sandwich spread. Keep refrigerated.

Marinated Tofu Salad

2 cups cubed tofu, drained
¼ cup apple cider vinegar or lemon juice
2 tablespoons sesame seed oil
¼ teaspoon sea salt
¼ teaspoon parsley flakes
1 tablepsoon chopped onion
1 tablespoon chopped green pepper
1 head of lettuce
1 ripe tomato, chopped
2 medium carrots, shredded
1 green pepper, sliced
1 cup sugar (snow) peas, raw

Make a dressing with the apple cider vinegar, sesame seed oil, sea salt, parsley, chopped onion and green pepper. Pour the dressing over the tofu and marinate several hours in the refrigerator before serving.

Cut or tear the lettuce into bite size pieces and place in a salad bowl. Drain the marinated tofu and place over the lettuce. Garnish with the chopped tomato, shredded carrots, green pepper slices and sugar peas. Serve with your favorite salad dressing. Makes 4 servings.

Cucumber Cottage Cheese Salad

1 cucumber, diced
¼ cup diced green pepper
1 tablespoon chopped fresh chives
1 tablespoon chopped fresh parsley
¼ cup plain yogurt or sour cream
sea salt to taste
2 cups cottage cheese
lettuce
4 radish roses

Combine the cucumbers, green peppers, chives and parsley. Stir in the yogurt and sea salt.

Place ½ cup cottage cheese on each of 4 lettuce leaves to make 4 individual servings. Surround the cottage cheese with the cucumber mixture and top with a radish rose.

Three Bean Salad

2 cups cooked green beans, cut
2 cups cooked kidney beans
1½ cups cooked garbanzo beans
1 tablespoon chopped onion
1 tablespoon chopped green pepper
1/3 cup sesame seed oil
¼ cup apple cider vinegar
½ teaspoon sea salt
½ teaspoon dried herbs
dash of cayenne pepper

Mix together the well-cooked, but not mashed, beans, onion and green pepper. Make a dressing with the sesame seed oil, apple cider vinegar, sea salt and herbs, and pour over the salad. Refrigerate and allow to marinate several hours or overnight before serving. Makes 6 servings.

Egg Salad

6 hard-boiled eggs
2 tablespoons Homemade Mayonnaise (see Index)
2 tablespoons chopped celery
1 tablespoon chopped onion
sea salt to taste

Chop the hard-boiled eggs. Stir in the mayonnaise, celery, onion and sea salt. Use as a sandwich spread or filling for stuffed tomatoes or green peppers.

Chive Stuffed Eggs

6 hard-boiled eggs
2 tablespoons cottage cheese
2 tablespoons yogurt
2 teaspoons finely chopped chives
⅛ teaspoon sea salt

Slice the hard-boiled eggs in half. Scoop out the yolks. Combine the yolks with the remaining ingredients. Spoon back into the eggs and refrigerate.

Tabouli

½ cup bulgar wheat
1 cup water
2 medium tomatoes, chopped
½ cup chopped cucumber
¼ cup chopped celery
1 green onion, sliced
1 tablespoon chopped fresh parsley
¼ cup olive oil
2 teaspoons lemon juice
¼ teaspoon sea salt
dash of cayenne pepper
1 cup alfalfa sprouts

Place the bulgar wheat in 1 cup boiling water and simmer 15 minutes. Cool.

Add the chopped tomatoes, cucumber, celery, onion, parsley, oil, lemon juice, sea salt, and cayenne to the bulgar. Stir well to mix all the ingredients. Chill. Top with the alfalfa sprouts before serving. Makes 6 servings.

Potato Salad

6 medium potatoes, cooked and cubed
6 hard cooked eggs, chopped
2 stalks of celery, diced
¼ cup diced onions
¼ cup diced green pepper
¼ cup diced Home-made Dill Pickles (see Index)
½ cup Homemade Mayonnaise (see Index)
2 tablespoons lemon juice
¾ teaspoon sea salt
⅛ teaspoon garlic powder

Combine the potatoes, eggs, celery, onions, green pepper and pickles in a large bowl. Add the lemon juice, sea salt and garlic powder to the mayonnaise and stir into the salad. Keep refrigerated until served. Makes 6 servings.

Tomato and Potato Salad

2 ripe tomatoes, chopped
2 cups cubed, cooked potatoes
¼ cup chopped onions
¼ cup Homemade Mayonnaise (see Index)
¼ cup plain yogurt
1 tablespoon finely chopped fresh dill or ½ teaspoon dried dill
sea salt to taste

Combine the tomatoes, potatoes and onions. Make a dressing with the remaining ingredients and stir into the salad. Chill. Makes 4 servings.

Beet and Potato Salad

2 cups cubed, cooked potatoes
2 cups cubed, cooked beets
1/3 cup chopped celery
2 tablespoons chopped onion
½ cup Homemade Mayonnaise (see Index)
½ cup yogurt
1 teaspoon Homemade Prepared Horseradish (see (Index)
½ teaspoon sea salt
⅛ teaspoon granular kelp

Combine the potatoes, beets, celery, and onion in a large bowl. Make a dressing with the remaining ingredients. Pour over the salad and stir in, just until blended. Serves 6.

Beet Salad

2 cups cooked, diced beets
1 tablespoon olive oil
1½ teaspoons lemon juice
1/3 cup yogurt
1 tablespoon finely chopped parsley

Place the beets in a serving bowl. Combine the olive oil, lemon juice and yogurt to make a dressing. Pour over the beets and stir to cover all the beets. Sprinkle parsley over the top. Serves 4.

Deviled Eggs

6 hard-boiled eggs
2 tablespoons Homemade Mayonnaise (see Index)
1 teaspoon Homemade Prepared Horseradish (see Index)
sea salt to taste
dash of cayenne pepper
dash of garlic powder

Peel the eggs, cut in half lengthwise and remove the yolks. Mix the yolks with the mayonnaise, horseradish, sea salt, cayenne and garlic powder. Spoon back into the egg whites. Keep refrigerated until served.

Marinated Mushrooms

½ pound fresh small mushrooms
½ cup olive oil
¼ cup apple cider vinegar
1 teaspoon finely chopped parsley
½ teaspoon sea salt
¼ teaspoon oregano

Wash mushrooms well and cook whole in water 5 minutes. Drain. Combine the remaining ingredients, pour over the mushrooms, and stir. Cover and refrigerate overnight.

Salad Dressings, Relishes, and Dips

French Dressing

6 tablespoons sesame seed oil or olive oil
2 tablespoons red wine vinegar
¼ teaspoon sea salt
¼ teaspoon dried herbs
dash of cayenne pepper

Combine all ingredients in a salad dressing bottle. Cover and shake until thoroughly blended. Chill and shake well before using. Store in refrigerator.

Sesame Dressing

½ cup hulled sesame seeds
½ cup sesame seed oil
2 tablespoons apple cider vinegar or lemon juice
2 cloves of garlic, crushed
1 tablespoon soy sauce
2 tablespoons water

Grind sesame seeds in a seed grinder. Place all ingredients in blender and process until well blended. Keep refrigerated.

Homemade Mayonnaise

1 raw egg, preferably fertile
1 teaspoon honey
1 teaspoon sea salt
½ teaspoon Homemade Prepared Horse-radish (see Index)
dash of cayenne pepper
1¼ cups olive oil or sesame seed oil
2 tablespoons apple cider vinegar or lemon juice

In a blender, combine the egg, honey, sea salt, horseradish, cayenne pepper and ¼ cup oil and blend until thoroughly mixed. Continue blending on high speed and slowly add ½ cup oil, one drop at a time, until the mixture is thick. Add 2 tablespoons apple cider vinegar or lemon juice and blend. Gradually add the remaining ½ cup oil and continue blending until thick. Keep refrigerated. Makes 2 cups.

Green Mayonnaise

1 cup Homemade Mayonnaise (see Index)
2 tablespoons minced fresh parsley

Combine the parsley and mayonnaise, mix well. Or place the mayonnaise in a blender and feed in a few sprigs of parsley until the desired color is reached. Chives or dill may be used in place of the parsley. Store in the refrigerator.

Roquefort Dressing

½ cup sour cream
1 ounce Roquefort cheese, crumbled
1 teaspoon Homemade Prepared Horse-radish (see Index)

Combine all the ingredients in a bowl and serve over your favorite vegetable salad.

Pollution Solution

Salad Dressing

1 cup Homemade Mayonnaise (see Index)
1 ripe tomato, chopped
1 small dill pickle, chopped
2 tablespoons chopped onion
2 tablespoons chopped green pepper
3 cloves of garlic, minced
2 teaspoons honey
1 tablespoon plain yogurt
1 tablespoon lemon juice
1 tablespoon algin powder (sodium alginate)
1 tablespoon brewers yeast flakes
2 teaspoons lecithin granules
1 teaspoon kelp
½ teaspoon sea salt
dash of cayenne pepper

Combine all the ingredients and mix well. Store in the refrigerator.

This salad dressing is specially formulated to minimize the damage from environmental pollution. It contains factors that have been scientifically proven* to be effective in protecting the body from the toxic effects of heavy metal poisoning, such as lead, mercury and cadmium, as well as minimizing the damage from x-rays and other sources of harmful environmental radiation.

---

* 1. Airola, Paavo, *How to Get Well,* Health Plus Publishers, 17th Edition, 1981, pp. 165-179.
2. Airola, Paavo, *The Miracle of Garlic,* Health Plus Publishers, 1978, pp. 29-31.
3. Ikezoe, T., and Kitahara, S., *Kiso-to-Rinsbo Medical Journal,* Japan, March, 1975.

Avocado Dressing I

1 cup Homemade Mayonnaise (see Index)
1 medium avocado, peeled and cut up
2 tablespoons lemon juice
2 teaspoons honey
1 clove of garlic, minced
¼ teaspoon sea salt
dash of cayenne pepper

Combine all ingredients in a blender. Chill at least one hour before serving. Makes 1½-2 cups.

Avocado Dressing II

1 ripe avocado
2 tablespoons olive oil
1 teaspoon honey
2 teaspoons apple cider vinegar or lemon juice

Cut avocado in half and remove the pit. Scoop out the pulp with a spoon and place in a blender. Add the other ingredients and blend for a few seconds. If the mixture is too thick, or doesn't cover the blades, add more oil.

Low-Cal Dressing

¼ cup lemon or lime juice
¼ cup water
1 teaspoon honey
⅛ teaspoon sea salt
⅛ teaspoon soy sauce (optional)
⅛ teaspoon of the following herbs of your choice: parsley, oregano, marjoram, chives
dash of garlic powder
dash of cayenne pepper

Place all ingredients in a small glass jar, close tightly and shake vigorously. Store in refrigerator.

This dressing is especially formulated for those who are on reducing diets.

Horseradish Sauce

½ cup sour cream
2 teaspoons Homemade Prepared Horseradish (see Index)
2 teaspoons lemon juice
¼ teaspoon sea salt

Combine all ingredients and chill. Serve over vegetables. Makes ½ cup.

Guacamole Dip

2 large ripe avocados
1 small tomato, diced
2 tablespoons lemon juice
¼ cup minced onions
1 clove of garlic, minced
½ teaspoon sea salt
dash of cayenne pepper

Peel and mash the avocados. Add the other ingredients and stir well. For chunky guacamole add ½ green pepper, diced. Serve as a salad on lettuce leaves; or use for Guacamole Tostada (see Index); or to stuff tomatoes; or as a dip with tostada chips. Makes about 2 cups.

Salsa

4 cups chopped tomatoes
1 small finely diced raw green chili or ¼ cup diced sweet green peppers
2 cloves of garlic, minced
½ cup finely chopped onions
½ teaspoon chili powder
1 tablespoon lime or lemon juice

Combine all ingredients and refrigerate. Use as a dip for corn chips or as a topping for other Mexican foods.

Garlic Mayonnaise

3 large cloves of garlic, minced
2 raw egg yolks
pinch of salt
1 cup olive oil
1 teaspoon apple cider vinegar or lemon or lime juice

Place the garlic, egg yolks, salt and ¼ cup olive oil in the blender and blend until thoroughly mixed. Add the remaining oil slowly while blending at high speed. Finally add vinegar or lemon juice while still blending. Keep refrigerated. Use as a dip or mayonnaise.

Thousand Island Dressing

1 cup Homemade Mayonnaise (see Index)
1 ripe tomato, finely chopped
1 hard-boiled egg, finely chopped
2 tablespoons finely chopped Homemade Dill Pickle (see Index)
2 tablespoons finely chopped onion
2 teaspoons honey
dash of garlic powder
sea salt to taste

Combine all ingredients and refrigerate. Makes 1½ cups.

Homemade Prepared Horseradish

½ cup grated horseradish root
3 tablespoons apple cider vinegar
¼ teaspoon sea salt

Combine all the ingredients. Store in a glass jar. It will keep up to a month if stored in the refrigerator.

Quark Dressing

½ cup quark or cottage cheese
¼ cup water
1 tablespoon olive oil
1 teaspoon grated horseradish
2 teaspoons lemon juice
1 tablespoon chopped chives, parsley, dill or other fresh garden herbs. Onion or garlic tops are excellent, too.
sea salt to taste

Place all the ingredients except the fresh greens in a blender and blend well. Pour into a jar and add the chopped chives or other herbs.

Quark Spread or Dip

Same ingredients as above, but without the water. Mix well in a bowl with a wooden spoon. Excellent as a spread on crackers, bread, or as a dip.

Russian Dressing

½ cup Homemade Mayonnaise (see Index)
½ cup plain yogurt
1 small tomato, chopped
2 tablespoons chopped green pepper
2 tablespoons chopped onion
1 tablespoon chopped celery
1 tablespoon chopped parsley
1 tablespoon chopped chives
1 clove garlic, minced
1 tablespoon lemon juice
1 teaspoon Homemade Prepared Horse-radish (see Index)

Combine all the ingredients and refrigerate.

Buttermilk Salad Dressing

½ cup buttermilk
½ cup Homemade Mayonnaise (see Index)
¼ teaspoon sea salt
½ teaspoon finely chopped parsley
dash of garlic powder

Combine all ingredients. Chill several hours before serving. Makes 1 cup.

Yogurt Dill Dressing

½ cup yogurt
2 teaspoons finely chopped onion
½ teaspoon dried dill or 1 tablespoon fresh dill
¼ teaspoon sea salt

Combine all ingredients and refrigerate several hours before serving. Makes ½ cup.

Vegetables

Preparing Vegetables for Cooking

When preparing and cooking fresh vegetables, use methods that will keep nutrient losses to a minimum and maintain good flavor and color.

To begin with, choose vegetables that are fresh and crisp and have a good color. Just before cooking, wash the vegetables thoroughly. Scrub with a vegetable brush if necessary, but do not allow the vegetables to soak in water as this will leach out water-soluble nutrients. Because most of the nutrients lie near the skin, do not peel vegetables unless the skin is tough, bitter or badly scarred and unattractive and too difficult to clean.

The best way to cook most vegetables is in a covered saucepan with a small amount of water, and cooked as quickly as possible. Many vegetables may also be baked, broiled, water sautéed, or steamed in a vegetable steamer. Cook vegetables only until tender. Do not overcook. They should be served immediately after cooking. Most vegetables are delicious raw and best served in salads and relish plates.

Because of a high oxalic acid content and other unsalubrious qualities, certain vegetables are best cooked and should be eaten raw only in small amounts. These vegetables include spinach, rhubarb, asparagus, cauliflower, cabbage and other vegetables of the cabbage family.

How To Sauté With Water

(without butter or oil)

Fill a cast-iron or other heavy skillet with water, ¼ to ½ inch deep. Heat the water to a boil. Add vegetables (or mushrooms or any other foods you wish to "fry") and sauté as in oil, adding more water if necessary, and stirring until the vegetables are done. A small amount of oil or butter can be added if desired.

This method should be experimented with as some vegetables contain more water, and some take longer to cook than others.

I have developed this Water Sautéing Method to eliminate cooking foods in oils, which become damaged by high heat. Oils heated to temperatures of 350°-400°F, as happens in frying or baking, become not only difficult to digest, but also harmful, even carcinogenic. If a small amount of oil is added during water sautéing, it floats on top of the water, never reaching temperatures higher than that of boiling water, which is 212°F.

Jerusalem Artichokes

Jerusalem artichokes are elongated tubers with beige skins and crisp white flesh resembling potatoes, but are members of the sunflower family. They may be prepared and served any way that you would prepare potatoes.

Choose firm, unblemished artichokes with no soft spots. Wash and scrub well with a vegetable brush. Jerusalem artichokes do not need to be peeled. If you prefer to peel them, sprinkle with lemon juice to keep them from darkening, or peel after cooking.

Place in boiling water and cook just until tender, 15-20 minutes. If overcooked they will become tough. When cooked, drain and serve immediately.

They may also be grated or sliced raw in salads, or juiced.

The carbohydrates in Jerusalem artichokes are well tolerated by diabetics and hypoglycemics.

Globe Artichokes

The globe artichoke is the flower bud from a plant belonging to the thistle family. The heart and ends of the leaves are edible. When buying globe artichokes, choose those with a bright green color. Brown spots on the leaves indicate age or injury. A spreading of the leaves indicates overmaturity and toughness.

The artichokes may be boiled or steamed and served hot as a vegetable or cold in a salad.

To prepare, trim the stem and trim the tough outer leaves from the base. Wash well to remove dirt between the leaves.

To cook, stand the artichokes upright in a saucepan of boiling water and cook over medium heat 20-30 minutes or until tender. Or place on a steamer rack over boiling water, cover, and steam 30-40 minutes or until tender. When tender, the leaves can be pulled out easily.

As you pull off the leaves with your fingers, bite off the soft and tender inner ends, or scrape them off between your teeth. When all the leaves are removed, cut out the thistle-like center part with a knife, and discard. Eat the remaining solid part of the artichoke, dipping it in butter or your favorite dip or sauce.

Asparagus

Asparagus does not store well, so it must be used as soon as possible after picking or buying. Wash the asparagus thoroughly and break the stem above the white part where it snaps easily. Place asparagus in a large pot of boiling water and simmer for 8-12 minutes, or until tender. Drain the asparagus and discard the water — do not use it for soups.

Asparagus — any asparagus, even the young, fresh shoots from your own garden — should never be eaten raw. It contains toxins which can be removed by cooking as suggested above. Steaming or frying will not destroy or remove these toxins.

Avocados

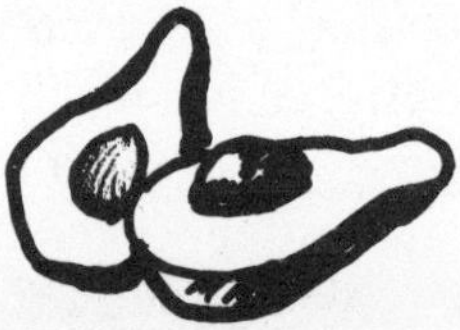

If you live in an area where fresh, locally grown avocados are available, you are fortunate, since avocados are both nutritious and delicious. Although, botanically speaking, avocados are fruits, they are usually eaten with vegetables, in salads, Mexican dishes, Guacamole, etc. Avocados are also a main ingredient in the Airola Salad (see Index for the above-mentioned recipes).

There are many kinds of avocados. Even as a novice, you will clearly distinguish between bright green, smooth-skinned avocados and darker, rough-skinned ones. It is important to eat avocados at the precise time of full ripeness. By pressing gently with your finger, you will soon learn when the avocado is edible. It must be soft, but not too soft. Make sure the whole avocado is ripe, since often one end or side softens before the other. Smooth-skinned avocados can be peeled, but with hard-skinned ones, it is better to cut in half, remove the pit, and scoop out the pulp with a spoon. If the avocado is too ripe, with some discolored or black areas, remove these blemishes before eating.

See Index for various avocado recipes.

Green Beans

Use only young tender beans which snap easily when bent in a 45° angle. They should be picked while young, when they are about 4 inches long and the beans inside the pod are still small. Wash and cut off the stem ends. The beans may be cooked whole, cut in 1-2 inch pieces, or cut in diagonal French-style lengthwise strips. Boil in a small amount of water or steam 15-20 minutes until tender. Serve with sautéed mushrooms, sliced water chestnuts or onions, or cheese sauce.

Note: To preserve the nutritive value of the green beans, they should be cooked whole, uncut; stem ends can be removed after cooking.

Lima Beans

Fresh lima beans may be bought shelled or in the shell. If purchased in the shell, scald the pods to make shelling easier. Rinse, and remove any discolored beans. Cook fresh lima beans in boiling water 12-15 minutes or until tender. They may be seasoned with sautéed onions or mushrooms, tomatoes, and cheese.

Fava, broad, and butter beans are similar to lima beans and may be prepared in the same way.

Important caution: raw lima and fava beans contain a toxic substance which is destroyed by heat, and, therefore, should never be eaten raw.

Beets

Good quality beets are smooth, firm and heavy for their size. Beets that are too large or have deep scars tend to be tough and woody. If you have beets in your garden, the thinnings can be cooked and eaten whole. Harvest the beets when only a few inches in diameter. They will be more tender and sweet than if allowed to get larger.

To prepare, trim off the tops leaving 1 inch of stem. Scrub well with a vegetable brush and cook in boiling water until tender, 30-40 minutes. Drain, plunge into cold water and slip off the skins. Then use whole or slice or dice as desired.

To bake, place whole washed beets in a pan and bake at 350°F for 30-60 minutes until tender. Cool slightly and slip off the skins.

Beet greens are a good source of vitamin A and iron.

Broccoli

Select broccoli that is a dark green or purple green in color with tightly closed buds. Open, yellowing buds indicates overmaturity and toughness. Stalks should be tender and free of bruises.

To prepare, wash well, remove the large leaves, and trim the stalks. If the stalks are thick, slash lengthwise so that they will cook in the same time as the buds. Steam the broccoli in a vegetable steamer or place upright in a saucepan so that only the stalks are in water and steam 10-15 minutes or until tender. The broccoli should still be bright green and crisp.

The leaves can be cooked and served as greens. The stalks can also be sliced diagonally and sautéed in water.

Broccoli is a good source of vitamin A and vitamin C.

Brussels Sprouts

Select sprouts that are hard, compact, and bright green in color with no yellow, wilted leaves or black spots. Small sprouts will be more tender than larger ones.

To prepare, cut off the stem ends and wash well. Remove any loose or discolored leaves. Cook in boiling water 10-12 minutes or until tender. Do not overcook or they will become bitter and lose their bright green color.

Cabbage

Cabbage should be compact and heavy for its size. The leaves should be crisp with a fresh green color.

Remove the outer leaves only if they are damaged or discolored. Wash and cut just before cooking. Cabbage may be cooked whole, or cut into wedges, shredded, or stuffed. To cook, place in boiling water and cook until tender, 10-15 minutes. Drain and serve. Do not overcook. When over-cooked, sulfur compounds break down and produce an unpleasant strong taste and odor.

To cook red cabbage, add a little apple cider vinegar or lemon juice to the water to maintain the red color.

Green cabbage is an excellent source of vitamin C and also provides roughage.

The most beneficial way to incorporate cabbage into your diet is in the form of sauerkraut. See Section of Lactic Acid Foods for instructions on Homemade Sauerkraut.

Carrots

Choose carrots that are firm, clean and bright orange in color. If tops are used for salad they should be fresh and green. If the carrots are grown in your garden, begin harvesting when they are about half an inch in diameter. They are best if used before they get larger than one inch in diameter and 4-5 inches in length.

To prepare, scrub with a vegetable brush and trim the ends. They may be eaten raw — whole, sliced, diced, cut in julienne strips or grated. To cook, steam or cook in boiling water 20-30 minutes or until tender.

Carrots are one of the best sources of vitamin A.

Cauliflower

Select cauliflower with a firm compact head and white, unblemished florets. The outer leaves should be crisp and green.

To prepare, wash, remove the outer leaves, and trim the stem. The leaves, if fresh, can be cooked and served like greens and the stem can be cut up and used in soup. Separate the cauliflower into florets, place in boiling water and cook 10-12 minutes; or cook whole for 15-20 minutes. One to two teaspoons lemon juice added to the cooking water will help keep the cauliflower white.

Cauliflower is a good source of vitamin C and is low in calories.

Celeriac

Celeriac, also known as celery root or turnip rooted celery, has a flavor similar to celery, but more delicate. It may be used in soups and stews, raw in salads, or served mashed or pureed.

To prepare, trim the tops and scrub well. Celeriac is difficult to peel, so cut into wedges first and then peel. Steam it 20 minutes or until tender. Or you may cook it whole in boiling water and then peel it.

Celery

Buy thick, green stalks that snap easily. Trim off the root end and wash well. Celery may be served raw in salads, as an appetizer with a dip, or stuffed. Water sauté it, add to soups or stews, or juice it.

Celery is very low in calories and an excellent source of roughage. It is rich in natural sodium.

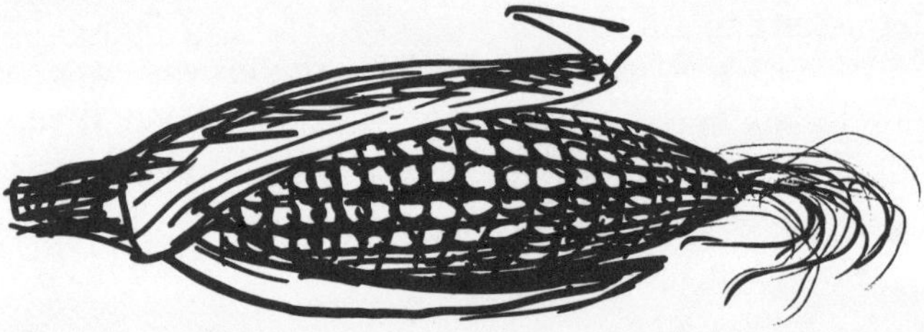

Corn on the Cob

Corn is best if eaten within 2-3 hours of being picked. After a few hours the sugar begins to turn to starch and the corn loses some of its sweetness.

To prepare, strip the husks, remove the silk, and wash. If the corn is tender and fresh it may be eaten raw — and it is most nutritious and delicious that way.

To boil, drop into rapidly boiling water and cook 3-5 minutes. To roast, leave the husks on and bake at 325°F, 20-30 minutes.

Cucumbers

Select firm, bright green cucumbers. Avoid those that have been waxed. Serve raw in salads, relish plates, sandwiches, as a garnish for soup, or pickled. Cucumbers may also be cooked, using the same methods as for summer squash (see Index).

Cucumbers don't have to be peeled, unless you happen to pick a bitter one, or if you are not sure if they have been waxed. The wax can also be removed by washing and scrubbing with hot water and plenty of soap. Rinse well to remove soap.

The most beneficial and delicious way to eat cucumbers is in pickled form, when they develop beneficial lactic acid. See the Section on Lactic Acid Foods for instructions on Homemade Dill Pickles.

Dandelions

Dandelions grow abundantly in lawns and fields. The nutritious young shoots have more vitamin A activity than many cultivated vegetables and are high in minerals such as calcium and iron. The leaves should be picked while they are still small and tender, and before the plant blooms. The leaves become too bitter to eat after the plant has flowered.

Wash the leaves, chop finely, and add to a salad.

Caution: Do not pick dandelion leaves from road sides or someone else's lawn unless you are certain that they haven't been sprayed with weed killers.

Eggplant

Eggplant, also known as *aubergine,* should be firm, smooth and a glossy dark purple in color with no soft spots. Harvest when about 4 inches in diameter and 6 inches long, or less. If allowed to get larger they will be tough and seedy. Handle carefully to avoid bruising.

To prepare, wash and cut off the stem. It is not necessary to peel if the eggplant is young and tender.

Bake it whole in the oven for 20-30 minutes, then cut into cubes and use in salads or cooked dishes. It may be sliced or cubed and steamed or water sautéed, or hollowed out, stuffed and baked. Eggplant is especially good seasoned with garlic, onion, oregano, tomatoes, or cheese.

Fennel or Anise

Fennel, with its bulbous white root and bright green tops, has a flavor similar to licorice. To prepare, simply wash and slice or chop into a salad. The tops can be used to add flavor to soup. The large stalks can also be sliced and water sautéed, alone or with other vegetables.

Greens

Beet tops
Chinese cabbage
collards
comfrey
kale
mustard greens
spinach
Swiss chard
turnip tops
watercress.

If fresh and young, most greens are best chopped and served raw in salads or steamed until just tender.

Prepare the greens by washing thoroughly to remove all the dirt. Cut out the damaged areas and trim the tough stems. Steam 5-10 minutes.

Cautions: 1. Greens that contain substantial amounts of oxalic acid — spinach, chard, and rhubarb are best cooked in a large amount of water. Discard the cooking water. If these greens are eaten raw, use only in small amounts.

2. Comfrey leaves, especially young ones, can be toxic, and, therefore, should not be used in large quantities. Never use comfrey leaves when making juices such as Formula P & L (see Index).

Kohlrabi

Kohlrabi, a relative of the cabbage family, has a bulbous stem that grows above the ground. It is not a root. It has a sweet turnip-like flavor and is crisp and tender if no larger than 2 inches in diameter. Larger bulbs tend to be tough and woody. The tops may be used as greens if fresh, green, and tender.

To serve raw, wash and peel the bulbs. Then slice, cut in julienne strips, or grate for a salad.

To cook, steam 15-20 minutes or until tender and then peel. Kohlrabi may also be sliced and water sautéed.

Okra

Choose young tender pods with soft seeds. If they are too mature, the pods will be tough and fibrous. Okra, when cooked, produces a thick gluey sap that serves to thicken soups and stews. It may also be served alone as a vegetable dish.

To prepare, remove the stem and wash. Cook whole or sliced by boiling or steaming until tender, 5-8 minutes.

Young pods of okra can be eaten raw. They can also be pickled, alone or with other vegetables, such as green peppers, chili peppers, etc. See pickling instructions in the Section, *Lactic Acid Foods.*

Onions

There are many types of dry onions, the most common being mild sweet Bermuda and Spanish onions, and the strong flavored globe onions.

The Bermuda onion is a flat onion 2-5 inches in diameter with a white, yellow, or red skin. The Spanish onion is globular in shape with a white or yellow-brown skin. Both the Bermuda and Spanish onions are good eaten raw in salads and sandwiches.

The globe onions are globular in shape, but smaller than the Spanish onion. They have a white, yellow, or red skin, and are used for cooking.

Green onions are any of the above varieties before maturing. They have small round ends with a white stalk and tubular green leaves. Scallions are green onions pulled before the bulb has formed. They may be eaten raw in salads or with a dip, or can be cooked. They are excellent when water-sautéed with other vegetables. To prepare, wash and trim off the roots and remove the outer skin.

Leeks have a large thick white stem and flat green leaves. When washing, be sure to get all the dirt out from between the leaves. They are milder in flavor than onions and are usually served cooked. They can also be used raw, finely chopped, in salads.

Shallots are small bulbs in a cluster, similar to garlic, but milder in flavor. To peel, cut the root end and stem and then slip off the skin. Rinse and slice or chop as required.

Chives have thin grass-like blades and are used mainly in salads, sandwiches, and omelets.

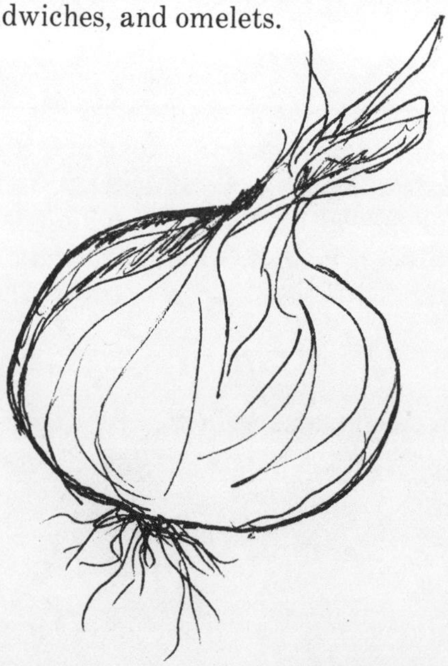

Mushrooms

Fresh mushrooms are firm and white, with no soft spots. The freshest mushrooms have a closed cap, but open mushrooms are sometimes preferred for their more pungent flavor. They are low in calories, but have a blotter-like capacity for fats when cooked. Mushrooms can be eaten raw in salads; used as a main dish, appetizer, or garnish; used in sauces and stuffings; and to give a distinctive flavor to soups. (See Index for mushroom recipes.)

To prepare, wash or wipe with a damp cloth. Do not soak, as the mushrooms will take up water and also lose nutrients and flavor. Trim the stem ends. Since most of the flavor is in the skin, avoid peeling. Mushrooms can be used whole, halved, quartered, sliced, or chopped. To keep them from darkening, sprinkle with lemon juice.

Ten minutes is usually enough time to cook mushrooms. Do not overcook. They may be steamed, water sautéed, broiled, baked, etc.

Parsnips

Select firm, smooth parsnips of small-medium size. Scrub well with a vegetable brush and trim the ends. Steam whole parsnips in a small amount of water for 20-30 minutes. If sliced or cut into strips they will take less time to cook. Parsnips will enhance the flavor of soups and stews and are very good combined with carrots.

Green Peas

Choose green, well filled pods. They are best eaten just after being picked as the sugar turns to starch quickly and they lose their good flavor. Shell and wash just before cooking. If young and tender, they are good raw in salads.

The French method of cooking fresh peas is to line a saucepan with damp lettuce leaves, pour the peas in, and cover with more lettuce. No water is added. The water from the lettuce is sufficient. Cook over medium heat 5 minutes or until tender. Or the peas may be steamed over boiling water 5-7 minutes.

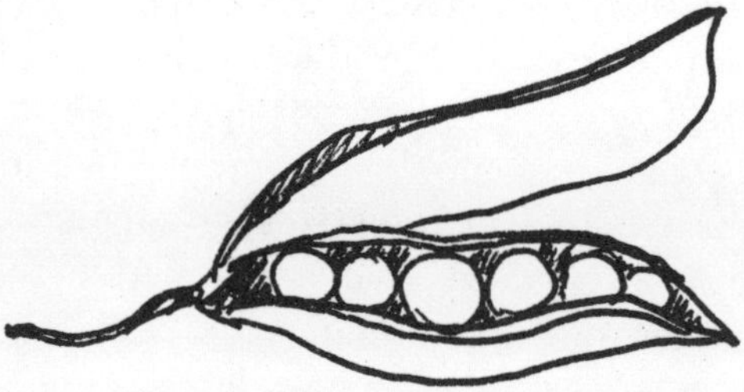

Sugar Peas

Sugar peas, also known as snow peas or Chinese peas, are often used in Oriental cooking. They should be picked before the peas fully develop. The fibrous inner lining found in green peas is absent in sugar peas and the whole pod can be eaten.

To prepare, wash and trim off the ends. Sugar peas may be cooked like green beans, steamed or water sautéed, 3-5 minutes. Do not overcook. They should still be crisp and bright green in color.

Sugar peas are also delicious eaten raw, served whole on a vegetable relish plate, or mixed with salads.

Sweet Bell Peppers

Sweet bell peppers are eaten either green or red. Choose those that are firm, shiny and well shaped and have a thick flesh. Wash and remove the stem and seeds. They may be cut into slices for a salad or left whole and stuffed. If cooked, they may be water-sautéed or stuffed and baked.

Green sweet peppers are high in vitamin C and A, low in calories.

Green or red bell peppers are a basic ingredient in Airola Salad (see Section on Vegetable Salads).

Potatoes

Choose potatoes that are firm and unbruised with no green spots. Potatoes exposed to light turn green and develop a toxic substance called *solanine.* You should never eat such potatoes. Also, avoid sprouted potatoes or frost-bitten ones. Frost-bitten potatoes are apt to be watery and have a dark ring under the skin. Store potatoes in a "light-tight" paper bag in a dark, cool place.

To prepare, scrub well with a vegetable brush. Remove bad spots and sprouts, but don't peel. Many nutrients just under the skin would be lost.

To boil potatoes, place in boiling water and cook over medium heat for 20-30 minutes, just until tender. As soon as they are cooked, pour off the water and shake the pan over low heat for a minute or so to dry the potatoes. If kept in the water, they will get watery and lose flavor. The cooking water can be used in bread doughs or added to soups. Serve the potatoes whole, or mash with a little milk and butter.

To bake, select potatoes of uniform size. Scrub well, remove bad spots and sprouts, and bake at 350°F for 1 hour. Prick the skins with a fork when the potatoes are half done to allow the steam to escape, and prevent the potatoes from bursting in the oven.

Potatoes are a good source of vitamins C and A, thiamine, iron, calcium, and high-quality protein. Protein in potatoes is comparable in quality to that in eggs and milk.

Sweet Potatoes or Yams

Choose those that are firm and clean and have no soft spots. Yams have a bright orange, moist flesh while sweet potatoes are drier and light orange-yellow in color. They should be stored at room temperature, but since they spoil easily they can not be kept very long.

To cook, scrub well with a vegetable brush, drop into boiling water, and cook covered 25 minutes or until tender. They may be baked at 350°F for 40-60 minutes. Be sure to prick the skin with a fork half way through baking to let the steam escape and keep the potato from bursting.

Sweet potatoes are especially high in vitamin A.

Radishes

Choose radishes that are firm and smooth. Radishes should be harvested as soon as they are fullly grown. If left in the ground too long they will become bitter, tough, and may split. The many varieties of radishes — red, white, black, and Diakon — are usually eaten raw as appetizers, or in salads, or on sandwiches, but may be cooked using the same methods as for turnips (see Index). To prepare, cut off the tops and wash thoroughly. If radish tops are fresh and healthy looking, they could be eaten as greens together with the radish. Black radish is delicious with yogurt or sour cream (see Index).

Rutabagas

Choose rutabagas that are firm, round, and smooth. They should be heavy for their size, but not too big, or they will be tough and bitter. Rutabagas may be steamed, boiled, or baked; added to casseroles, soups, and stews; or eaten raw, sliced, diced, or grated into a salad.

To prepare, scrub well and remove the tops and root end. Peel and slice.

In case you don't know the difference between rutabagas and turnips, rutabagas are yellow inside, and turnips are white.

Rutabagas are a good source of vitamin C.

Turnips

Choose turnips that are firm and smooth with white roots and purple shading on the top. They are best when 2-3 inches in diameter; if they are bigger than that they tend to be tough and bitter. Turnips may be steamed or baked either whole or sliced, and used in soups and casseroles. They are also good eaten raw.

To prepare, scrub well and remove tops and root ends. Peel, slice, and steam 15-20 minutes, or until tender.

Salsify or Oyster Plant

Salsify is a slender white root similar to parsnips, with a flavor like oysters. The root will discolor and shrivel up when exposed to air so it should be cooked unpeeled. If it is necessary to peel, add a little lemon juice to the cooking water to prevent discoloring. Salsify may be cooked using the same methods as for parsnips (see Index). Steam whole 20-30 minutes.

Summer Squash

The many varieties of summer squash all have in common a thin skin that is easily punctured with the fingernail. They should be firm and heavy for their size. It is not necessary to peel them or to remove the seeds. They are best if picked before they get longer than eight inches.

Zucchini is long and thin with a deep green skin and white flesh.

Cocozelle is similar to zucchini, but the skin is paler green in color with lighter green stripes.

Scallops or cymlings (also known as pattypan squash) are dish shaped with a scalloped edge and are pale green in color.

Straight neck or crooked neck squash is yellow with a lumpy skin.

Chayote is a pale green, pear-shaped summer squash with a smooth or ribbed rind.

To prepare, wash and trim the ends. Steam whole or sliced for 10-20 minutes or until tender. Summer squash can also be baked, broiled, stuffed, used in casserole dishes, and soups, grated and baked in breads, eaten raw in salads, and pickled.

Winter Squash

Winter squash is available from fall to early spring and includes acorn, buttercup, turban, butternut, hubbard, and banana squash. Except for the butternut, they all have a hard shelled skin.

Choose squash with dry hard rinds that do not yield to pressure. They should be heavy for their size. Avoid squash with watery or soft spots, which indicates decay.

To prepare, wash and cut in half. Remove the seeds and the stringy portion. (If the seeds are large and mature, they can be washed, dried, and, when hulled, used like sunflower seeds.) Place in a pan with a small amount of water in the bottom and bake at 350°F for 30-60 minutes, depending on the size. Larger squash may be cut into serving size pieces before baking.

To steam squash, peel and cut into 1-inch cubes and steam 15-20 minutes, or until tender. Serve as is, or puree or mash.

Winter squash can also be stuffed or used in breads or pies.

Pumpkin

Pumpkin is most often used in pies, but it is excellent eaten as a vegetable.

To prepare, wash and cut in half. Scoop out the seeds. The seeds can be washed and dried and, when hulled, eaten like sunflower seeds. Place the pumpkin in a baking dish with a small amount of water in the bottom and bake 30-60 minutes depending on the size. Serve whole or mashed. The pumpkin may also be peeled and cut into 1-inch cubes and then steamed 15-20 minutes or until tender. To use in a pie or custard, puree it after cooking.

Tomatoes

Tomatoes are best eaten raw, but may also be stuffed and baked, broiled, made into juice or tomato sauce, used in soups and stews. Tomatoes should be ripe, uniformly red, and firm when picked. To prepare, wash and core just before serving.

Unfortunately, commercially-sold tomatoes are almost always picked green, then ripened artificially — and consequently, lack both the taste and the nutritive value of real vine-ripe tomatoes.

Tomatoes are high in vitamin C and vitamin A, and low in calories.

Sweet and Sour Beets

2 cups diced cooked beets
¼ cup apple cider vinegar
¼ cup honey
2 whole allspice berries
2 teaspoons arrowroot flour

Combine the apple cider vinegar, honey, allspice, and arrowroot flour in a saucepan. Cook over medium heat until the sauce thickens, but do not allow to boil. When thickened, add the beets and cook over medium heat until the beets are hot, but do not allow to boil. The sauce will thin out at higher temperatures. Remove the allspice and serve. Makes 4-6 servings.

Brussels Sprouts Surprise

1 pound Brussels sprouts
3-4 large tomatoes, sliced
1 tablespoon chopped onions
1 cup shredded cheese

Steam the Brussels sprouts in a little water for 10 minutes, until almost tender. Place in a single layer in a baking dish. Cover with the sliced tomatoes and chopped onion. Sprinkle with the shredded cheese. Pre-heat oven to 350°F and bake until the cheese melts, 10-15 minutes. Serves 6.

Green Beans in Sour Cream

1 pound fresh green beans
¼ pound fresh mushrooms, sliced
¼ cup chopped onions
½ cup sour cream

Cut the green beans into 1-inch pieces and steam until tender, about 15 minutes. Sauté the mushrooms and onions in ¼ cup water until tender. Add more water if necessary. When cooked, add the green beans and sour cream. Makes 6 servings.

Italian Style Celery

2 cups sliced celery
½ cup chopped onion
1 clove garlic, minced
½ cup water
1 fresh tomato, chopped
1 tablespoon chopped parsley
dash of cayenne pepper
sea salt to taste

Sauté the celery, onion, and garlic in the water until almost tender, about 5 minutes. Add the chopped tomato, parsley, cayenne, and sea salt. Cover and cook a few more minutes until heated through. Serves 4.

Mexican Style Corn

2 cups cut corn
1 tablespoon chopped onion
¼ cup chopped green pepper
¼ cup chopped sweet red pepper
½ cup water
dash of cayenne pepper
sea salt to taste

Cook the corn, chopped onion, green and red pepper in the water about 5 minutes or until tender. Add more water if needed. Season with a dash of cayenne pepper and sea salt. Serves 6.

Parslied Carrots

1 pound carrots, sliced
1 small garlic clove, minced
2 tablespoons butter
1 tablespoon lemon juice
1 tablespoon fresh minced parsley

Cook the carrots until tender and drain. Add the garlic, butter, lemon juice, and parsley and heat just until the butter melts. Makes 4-6 servings.

Carrots in Dill

1 pound carrots, cut in julienne strips
2 tablespoons butter
2 teaspoons chopped fresh dill (½ teaspoon dried dill)

Cook the carrots until tender, 15-20 minutes. Drain. Add the butter and dill. Makes 6 servings.

Mashed Rutabagas and Carrots

3 medium carrots, sliced
2 medium rutabagas, peeled and sliced

Steam the rutabagas and carrots until tender. Mash together, or puree in the blender. Serves 4-6.

Oriental Style Vegetables

2 small zucchini, cut in julienne strips
2 stalks celery, sliced
½ pound mushrooms, sliced
1 medium onion, sliced
2 tablespoons butter
4 teaspoons soy sauce
sea salt to taste

Water sauté all the vegetables in a large skillet using ¼ cup water. Add more water if necessary. Cook for about 5 minutes, until the vegetables are tender, but still crisp, stirring constantly to prevent burning. Remove from heat, add the butter and sprinkle with soy sauce and sea salt. Serve immediately. Makes 6 servings.

Ratatouille

3 cups cubed eggplant
2 cups sliced zucchini
1 green pepper, chopped
1 onion, chopped
1 clove garlic, minced
¼ cup olive oil
¼ cup water
½ teaspoon sea salt
2 tablespoons fresh chopped parsley
2 tomatoes, chopped

Combine all ingredients except the parsley, oil and tomatoes in a skillet and cook covered over medium heat 10-15 minutes until the vegetables are tender. Add the parsley and tomatoes. Cook another 5 minutes. Remove from heat, add oil, and stir well. Serve hot or chilled. Makes 6 servings.

Stewed Tomatoes

6 ripe tomatoes, peeled and quartered
¼ cup chopped celery
¼ cup chopped onion
1 clove of garlic

Place all the ingredients in a covered saucepan. Bring to a boil, reduce heat and cook on low heat until the tomatoes are tender, about 20 minutes. Makes 6 servings.

Vegetable Sauté

2 cups sliced zucchini
2 medium sized carrots, sliced
½ cup chopped onion
½ cup chopped celery
¼ cup water
1 green pepper, cut in strips
2 medium tomatoes, cut in wedges
1 clove of garlic, minced
½ teaspoon sea salt

Water sauté the zucchini, carrots, onion and celery for 5 minutes. Stir frequently and add more water as needed. Add the green pepper, tomatoes, garlic, and sea salt. Continue cooking until the vegetables are tender, but still crisp, about 5 minutes. Serve immediately. Makes 6 servings.

Potato Souffle

2 cups mashed potatoes
1 egg yolk
1 tablespoon butter
½ teaspoon dried dill or 1 tablespoon fresh dill
1 egg white

Combine the egg yolk, butter, and dill with the mashed potatoes. Beat the egg white until stiff and fold into the potato mixture. Place in a buttered 1-quart baking dish and bake at 350°F for 25-30 minutes. Serves 4.

Potato Porridge

2 cups water
3 medium potatoes

Bring the water to a boil. Scrub the potatoes well and grate directly into the boiling water to prevent oxidation. Cook for 2 minutes stirring constantly. Lower the heat and simmer 10-15 minutes until the potatoes are tender. Serve with milk and/or butter. Makes 4 servings.

Green Pepper Sauce

2 large sweet green peppers, sliced
1 yellow onion, sliced
2 tablespoons water
2 cups Homemade Stewed Tomatoes (see Index)
½ teaspoon dried marjoram leaves

Sauté the sliced green peppers and onions in the water until tender, but still crisp. Stir frequently and add more water if needed. Add tomatoes and marjoram leaves. Cook over medium heat 3-5 minutes to heat through. Serve over cooked brown rice or whole-grain noodles. Makes 6 servings.

Sautéed Kohlrabi

2 medium kohlrabi, peeled and sliced
½ onion, sliced
1 tablespoon chopped parsley
2 tablespoons olive oil
dash of cayenne pepper
sea salt to taste

Sauté the kohlrabi and onion in ½ cup water 5 minutes, or until tender. Add the fresh parsley and olive oil. Season with a little cayenne pepper and sea salt.

Sautéed Yellow Crookneck Squash

3 small yellow crookneck squash, sliced
2 tablespoons chopped onion
1 clove garlic, crushed
¼ cup water
2 tablespoons olive oil
¼ teaspoon salt
dash of cayenne pepper

Sauté the squash, onion, and garlic in the water 5 minutes or until tender. Stir frequently and add more water as needed. Add the oil, sea salt, and cayenne pepper. Serve immediately. Makes 6 servings.

Sauces

Basic White Sauce

2 tablespoons butter
1 tablespoon cornstarch
1 cup milk
¼ teaspoon sea salt

Melt the butter in a saucepan. Combine the cornstarch and milk and add to the melted butter. Add the sea salt. Cook over medium heat, stirring constantly until the sauce comes to a boil. Continue to boil one minute. Makes 1 cup.

For a thicker sauce use 3 tablespoons butter and 2 tablespoons cornstarch.

Whole Wheat White Sauce

2 tablespoons butter
2 tablespoons whole wheat flour
1 cup milk
¼ teaspoon sea salt

Melt the butter in a saucepan. Stir in the whole wheat flour. Add the milk and sea salt. Cook over medium heat, stirring constantly until the sauce comes to a boil. Continue to boil one minute. Makes one cup.

For a thicker sauce use 3 tablespoons butter and 3 tablespoons whole wheat flour to 1 cup milk.

Cheese Sauce

Basic White Sauce recipe (see Index)
½ cup shredded mild cheese
dash of cayenne pepper

Make the white sauce. Remove from heat and stir in the cheese and pepper. The cheese will melt slowly as you stir it. Makes 1¼ cups.

Mushroom Sauce

Basic White Sauce recipe (see Index)
1 cup sliced raw mushrooms

Make the white sauce. Water sauté the mushrooms for about 5 minutes or until cooked. Add the mushrooms to the sauce. Makes 1½ cups.

Scott's Creamy Corn-Squash Sauce

2/3 cup yellow squash
1/3 cup fresh corn
herb seasonings

Boil squash, crockneck or other type, and fresh corn off cobb in small amount of water until done. Mix well in blender with herb seasonings, if desired. Makes delicious creamy sauce which is non-dairy and fat-free. Terrific on yams, potatoes, or vegetables.

Be careful not to use too much liquid when blending, or sauce will be too watery. To monitor consistency, add cooking water slowly while blending.

Arrowroot White Sauce

2 tablespoons butter
1 tablespoon arrowroot flour
1 cup milk
¼ teaspoon sea salt

Melt the butter in a saucepan. Add the arrowroot flour and blend well. Slowly stir in the milk. Add the sea salt. Cook over medium heat, stirring constantly until the sauce thickens, 3-5 minutes. Do not allow to boil or it will become thin again. Makes one cup.

For a thicker sauce use 3 tablespoons butter and 1½ tablespoons arrowroot flour to 1 cup milk.

Parsley Sauce

Basic White Sauce recipe (see Index)
2 teaspoons finely chopped fresh parsley

Make the white sauce and add 2 teaspoons finely chopped fresh parsley when the sauce has thickened. Makes 1 cup.

Homemade Tomato Sauce

16 ripe tomatoes, quartered
½ cup chopped onions
½ cup chopped celery with tops
¼ cup chopped parsley
2 cloves of garlic
1 teaspoon sea salt

Place the tomatoes in a saucepan with the onions, celery, parsley and garlic. Bring to a boil. Then reduce heat and simmer 30 minutes. Strain, return to saucepan and simmer uncovered 1-1½ hours, until thick. Season with sea salt. Makes approximately 3 cups.

Soups

Airola Souper Soup

Have you ever wished to be an expert soup maker — to be able to make every kind of delicious vegetable soup without failure? Here is my "discovery" which will transform you into an instant gourmet chef, to the delight of your hungry family. You can sit back and enjoy the appreciative superlatives that will be sure to come your way.

Take any or all vegetables you happen to have in your refrigerator or in your own backyard garden. You can make this soup with as few as one vegetable, or as many as several dozen. Place vegetables in a pot and cover with water. Do not use aluminum utensils. Bring to a boil and simmer for 15-25 minutes, until vegetables are done. Do not overcook; vegetables must not be mushy.The length of cooking time depends on the vegetables. Such vegetables as rutabagas and carrots require longer cooking time. If fast-cooking leafy vegetables are mixed with slow-cooking vegetables, add them near the end of the cooking time. Season to taste with sea salt and your favorite herbs such as dried parsley leaves, dill weed, paprika, cayenne, celery seed, garlic and/or onion powder, or other favorites. Note: do not use black or white pepper. You may use vegetized seasonings or other ready-made seasonings, such as soy sauce, miso, etc.

If you prefer, you may mash vegetables with a potato masher, or place soup in the blender, making it into a puree before serving.

Now, obviously, you have known all this before — so where is my "discovery"? Here: As I said earlier, use any vegetables you happen to have on hand. Whatever vegetable happens to be the predominant contributor to the flavor gives the soup its name! If the predominant ingredient is potatoes, you created Potato Soup; if the predominant ingredient is onions, you created Onion Soup; if you used mostly carrots in your soup, it is Carrot Soup; if zucchini predominates, it is Zucchini Soup, etc., etc. Your imagination is the limit! You can now create any vegetable soup you wish — all from one simple Souper Soup recipe! One enthusiastic student of mine told me that when she brings steaming Souper Soup to the table, her children often ask, "Mom, what kind of soup is it?" She replies, "You tell me!" The kids taste the soup and announce the verdict, "It's zucchini soup, right?" "You're absolutely right again, today it's zucchini soup!"

Garlic Soup

1½ quarts water
4 potatoes
1 carrot
2 stalks celery
1 onion
2 large bulbs (heads) of garlic
½ teaspoon thyme
dash of oregano
dash of cayenne
sea salt to taste

Bring the water to a boil. Cut the potatoes, carrots, celery, and onion into ½-inch pieces and place in the boiling water. Break the garlic bulbs and peel the individual cloves. Place them in the soup together with the spices. Cook the soup over medium heat for 20-30 minutes. When the soup is ready, it can be served in either of two ways: 1) strain and serve as a clear broth with 1 raw egg dropped into each serving; 2) eliminate eggs and puree in the blender and serve as a "cream of garlic" soup.

Potato Soup

2 cups diced potatoes
2 medium carrots, diced
1 tablespoon finely chopped onion
1½ cups water
½ teaspoon sea salt
1 cup milk
2 teaspoons finely chopped parsley

Combine all ingredients except milk and parsley in a saucepan. Bring to a boil. Reduce heat and simmer 20-30 minutes until the vegetables are tender. Remove from heat. Stir in the milk and parsley and serve. Makes 4 servings.

Lentil Soup

1 cup lentils
1 stalk celery, chopped
1 medium carrot, chopped
1/3 cup chopped onion
1 clove of garlic, minced
3 cups water
¼ cup lemon juice
¼ teaspoon sea salt
¼ teaspoon granular kelp

Simmer the lentils, celery, carrots, onion, and garlic in water 1½ hours, until tender. Add the lemon juice, sea salt, and kelp and cook another 5 minutes. Serves 4-6.

Bean Soup

2 cups dry pinto beans
6 cups water
2 medium carrots, diced
1 onion, chopped
1 stalk celery with tops, chopped
1 teaspoon chili powder
sea salt to taste

Soak the beans overnight in the water and then cook until tender, 3-4 hours. Add the diced carrots, chopped onions, and celery. Simmer until the vegetables are tender, about one hour. Add the chili powder and sea salt about ½ hour before the beans are finished. Makes 4-6 servings.

Borsch

1 quart water
4 medium fresh raw beets
1 small carrot
1 stalk celery
½ small onion, chopped
½ cup chopped beet tops
1 dill pickle, chopped, or ½ cup sauerkraut
2 tablespoons lemon juice or red wine vinegar
1 tablespoon honey
1 teaspoon salt
½ teaspoon dried dill
1 cup sour cream or yogurt

Bring the water to a boil. Shred the beets, carrots and celery and place in the boiling water. Add the chopped onion. Cook 15-20 minutes over medium heat until the vegetables are tender. Add the chopped dill pickle or sauerkraut, lemon juice, honey, salt, and dill. Simmer a few more minutes. Serve hot with a spoonful of sour cream or yogurt on top. Makes 6 servings.

Summer Borsch

Prepared as above, the Borsch can be chilled in the refrigerator and served cold on hot summer days as a most refreshing and cooling dish.

Okra Soup

1 medium carrot, chopped
1 cup diced potatoes
¼ cup chopped onion
2 cups chopped okra
2 cups chopped tomatoes
1 teaspoon chopped parsley
sea salt to taste

Place the carrots, potatoes and onions in a saucepan and cover with water. Bring to a boil, lower heat and cook covered for 15 minutes. Add the okra, tomatoes, parsley and sea salt and cook another 15-20 minutes. Makes 4 servings.

Tomato Zucchini Soup

2 cups chopped peeled tomatoes
2 cups diced zucchini
½ cup chopped celery with tops
¼ cup chopped onion
1 small clove garlic
½ teaspoon chopped parsley
½ teaspoon sea salt
water

Place all ingredients in a saucepan. Cover with water. Bring to a boil. Reduce heat and simmer 20-30 minutes or until the vegetables are tender. Serves 4-6.

Gazpacho

2 cups tomato juice
½ cup carrot juice
½ cup finely chopped cucumber
¼ cup finely chopped green pepper
¼ cup finely chopped celery
1 small green onion, chopped fine
1 tablespoon finely chopped parsley
1 clove of garlic, minced
1 tablespoon lemon juice
dash of cayenne pepper

Combine all the ingredients in a large bowl and chill. Serve cold. Makes 6 servings.

Cold Cucumber Soup

1 medium cucumber, cubed
1 tablespoon chopped green onion
1 tablespoon finely chopped parsley
dash of cayenne pepper
2 cups buttermilk

Put all the ingredients in a blender and blend at high speed for several minutes. Serve cold with a sprig of parsley. Makes 4 servings.

Cream of Mushroom Soup

2 cups fresh clean mushrooms
½ cup chopped onions
1 cup water
1 cup milk
1 tablespoon chopped parsley
½ teaspoon miso or sea salt
dash of cayenne pepper

Slice the mushrooms and place in a saucepan with the chopped onions and water. Bring to a boil and cook over medium heat about 10 minutes, until the mushrooms and onions are tender. Add the milk, parsley, miso or sea salt and cayenne pepper. Serve at once. Makes 4 servings.

Becky's Vegetable Soup

1½ quarts water
¼ cup barley
½ cup dried soup vegetables
2 carrots, sliced
1 onion, chopped
2 potatoes, chopped
¼ cup cooked lima beans
1 cup tomato juice
sea salt to taste

Combine all ingredients in a large saucepan. Bring to a boil and simmer 1 hour.

Vichyssoise

1½ quarts water
3 cups diced potatoes
2½ cups sliced leeks, white part only
1 teaspoon sea salt
½ cup cream
2 tablespoons finely chopped chives

Bring the water to a boil. Add the potatoes and leeks and simmer 20-30 minutes, or until tender. Pour into a blender jar, add the salt and blend until smooth. Stir in the cream and chill. Serve cold with chopped chives sprinkled on top. If you don't have chives, you may use the green parts of the leek. Makes 6 servings.

Mushroom Potato Soup

2 cups diced potatoes
1 tablespoon chopped onion
1½ cups water
½ teaspoon sea salt
1½ cups sliced mushrooms
½ cup milk
1 tablespoon finely chopped parsley

Combine the potatoes, onions, water, and sea salt in a saucepan. Bring to a boil. Reduce heat and simmer 20 minutes, until the potatoes are tender. Mash the potatoes in the cooking water. Add the mushrooms and cook another 5-8 minutes, until the mushrooms are cooked. Remove from heat. Stir in the milk and parsley and serve. Makes 4 servings.

Vegetable Barley Soup

3 medium carrots, cut in julienne strips
1 cup sliced celery
1 small onion, chopped
1 clove of garlic, minced
1 teaspoon sea salt
½ teaspoon dried parsley
½ teaspoon oregano
dash of cayenne pepper
½ cup barley
6 cups water
4 medium tomatoes, chopped
2 cups cut-up broccoli

Combine the carrots, celery, onion, garlic, sea salt, parsley, oregano, cayenne, barley and water in a large saucepan. Bring to a boil. Reduce heat and simmer 35 minutes. Add the tomatoes and broccoli and simmer another 20 minutes. Makes 3 quarts.

Spanish Bean Soup

1 cup dry garbanzo beans
3 cups water
2 cups Homemade Tomato Sauce (see Index)
1 small onion, chopped
1 large green pepper, chopped
½ cup sliced raw mushrooms
¼ cup minced chives

Soak the garbanzo beans overnight. Discard the water and cook in 3 cups fresh water until tender, 2-3 hours. When the garbanzo beans are tender add the tomato sauce and onion and cook 15 minutes. Add the green peppers and cook another 5 minutes. Season with sea salt if desired. Serve with sliced mushrooms and chives sprinkled on top. Makes 4-6 servings.

Vegetable Noodle Soup

1 small beet, diced
1 medium carrot, diced
1 cup chopped yellow squash
1 cup chopped zucchini
1 medium tomato chopped
1 cup chopped cabbage
½ cup chopped okra
½ cup cut-up green beans
2 tablespoons chopped onion
fresh dill weed
fresh celery leaves
sea salt
2 cups uncooked Whole Wheat Noodles (see Index)

Combine all the vegetables with a sprig of fresh dill and a few celery leaves in a saucepan. Cover with water. Bring to a boil, reduce heat, and cook over medium heat until the vegetables are almost tender, about 20 minutes. Add the noodles and more water if necessary and cook 8-10 minutes, until the noodles are cooked. Season with sea salt if desired. Makes 6 servings.

Cream of Tomato Soup

2 cups cut-up tomatoes
2 tablespoons chopped celery
1 tablespoon chopped onion
2 tablespoons butter
2 tablespoons whole wheat flour
1 cup whole milk
¼ teaspoon sea salt
chopped parsley

Simmer the tomatoes, celery and onion 15 minutes. Melt the butter in a small saucepan. Add the flour and stir until well blended. Pour the milk in slowly, stirring constantly. Cook over medium heat stirring constantly until the mixture comes to a boil. Add the sea salt. Pour the sauce into the tomato mixture and mix well. Serve with chopped parsley sprinkled on top. Serves 4.

Split Pea Soup

1 cup dried split peas
3 cups water
½ cup chopped onion
1 small carrot, diced
1 stalk celery, diced
1 teaspoon sea salt

Wash peas, place in a saucepan with the vegetables, and cover with water. Bring to a boil. Reduce heat and simmer for 1½ hours, or until peas are tender. Add sea salt and your favorite herb seasonings. Puree in the blender or serve as is. Makes 4-6 servings.

Potato and Leek Soup

1½ quarts water
3 cups diced potatoes
2½ cups sliced leeks
1 teaspoon sea salt
1/3 cup milk
2 tablespoons finely chopped chives

Bring the water to a boil. Add the potatoes and leeks and simmer 20-30 minutes or until tender. Pour into a blender jar; add the sea salt and milk, and blend until smooth. Serve with chopped chives sprinkled on top. If leeks are not available yellow onions may be used. Serves 6.

Onion Soup

2 medium onions, sliced
1 clove of garlic, minced
¼ cup water
4 cups Vegetable Broth (see Index)
1 teaspoon soy sauce

Sauté the sliced onion and garlic in the ¼ cup water until tender. Add more water if necessary.

Add the vegetable broth when the onions are tender and cook over low heat 20 minutes. Stir in the soy sauce and serve. Makes 4 servings.

Entrees

Vegetable Stew

4 potatoes, cut in ¾-inch thick slices
2 carrots, sliced
1 stalk celery, cut in 1 inch pieces
1 turnip, sliced
1 small parsnip, sliced
1 small onion, sliced
1 beet, sliced
1 medium zucchini, cut in ½-inch slices
½ small head cabbage, cut in wedges
2 cups shredded cheese

Combine the first 7 vegetables in a sauce pan with a small amount of water in the bottom. When the vegetables have been cooking for 10 minutes, add the zucchini and cabbage. Cook over medium heat for 30 minutes or until the vegetables are tender. Add water as needed. Arrange the vegetables on a serving platter and sprinkle with the shredded cheese. Place under the broiler until the cheese is melted. Serves 6.

Mushroom Quiche

¼ pound mushrooms, sliced
¼ cup chopped onion
1½ cups milk
3 eggs
¼ teaspoon sea salt
one 9-inch pie crust (see Index)

Water sauté the mushrooms and onions for 3-5 minutes. Place in a 9-inch pie plate lined with the pie crust. Combine the milk, eggs, and sea salt and pour over the mushrooms and onions. Bake at 375°F for 30-35 minutes, or until a knife inserted in the center comes out clean. Serves 4-6.

Zucchini Quiche

3 cups raw sliced zucchini
¼ cup chopped onion
1 cup shredded Swiss cheese
3 eggs, slightly beaten
1¼ cups milk
¼ teaspoon sea salt
one 9-inch pie crust (see Index)

Water sauté the zucchini and onions for 3 minutes. Line a 9-inch pie pan with the pie crust. Sprinkle half the cheese in the bottom of the pie, and add half the zucchini. Repeat with the remaining cheese and zucchini. Beat the eggs with the milk and sea salt. Pour over the zucchini and cheese. Bake at 350°F for 40 minutes, or until a knife inserted in the center comes out clean. Serves 6.

Whole Wheat Macaroni Casserole

2 cups uncooked whole wheat macaroni
3 tablespoons butter
3 tablespoons whole wheat flour
2 cups milk
½ teaspoon sea salt
2 cups shredded cheddar cheese
¼ pound raw mushrooms, sliced
1 carrot, shredded
½ cup chopped onion
¼ cup chopped celery
1 tablespoon minced parsley
½ teaspoon marjoram

Cook the macaroni in 3 quarts boiling water 8-10 minutes until tender. Drain and set aside.

Melt the butter in a saucepan. Stir in the flour and mix well. Pour in the milk and bring to a boil, stirring constantly. Remove from heat. Add the sea salt and shredded cheese. Stir until the cheese is melted.

Pour the sauce over the cooked macaroni. Add the remaining ingredients and mix well. Bake covered in a casserole dish at 350°F for 30 minutes. Top with a little more shredded cheese if desired and bake a few more minutes to melt the cheese. Makes 6 servings.

Tofu, Spanish Style

1 large green bell pepper, sliced
1 medium onion, sliced
1 stalk celery, chopped
1 clove of garlic, minced
2 cups Homemade Tomato Sauce (see Index)
dash of cayenne pepper
one 16-ounce package tofu, drained and cubed
¼ cup freshly grated Romano or Parmesan cheese
4 cups cooked Homemade Whole Wheat or Buckwheat Noodles (see Index)

Water sauté the green pepper, onions, celery, and garlic in ¼ cup of water until tender, about 5 minutes. Add the Tomato Sauce, cayenne, and cubed tofu. Cook a few minutes to heat the tofu.

Pour the vegetables and tofu mixture over the cooked noodles and sprinkle with grated Romano or Parmesan cheese. Serve immediately. Serves 4-6.

Stuffed Green Pepper

4 green bell peppers
1 cup chopped fresh mushrooms
½ cup chopped onions
¼ cup chopped celery
1 clove of garlic, minced
2 tablespoons olive oil
½ cup Homemade Tomato Sauce (see Index)
1 tablespoon chopped parsley
2 cups cooked brown rice

Wash the green peppers. Remove the seeds and membranes. Water sauté the chopped mushrooms, onion, celery and garlic in ¼ cup water until tender, about 5 minutes. Add more water if necessary. Stir in the olive oil, Tomato Sauce, parsley and cooked brown rice. Stuff the green peppers with the mixture. Place in a baking dish. Bake at 350°F, 20-30 minutes or until the green peppers are tender. Serves 4.

Stuffed Zucchini

2 medium zucchini
¾ cup bread crumbs
½ cup shredded cheese
⅛ teaspoon dried parsley
dash of ground oregano

Wash the zucchini and steam them whole for 10-15 minutes, until almost tender. Drain and cool. Cut in half and scoop out the pulp. Chop the pulp and drain off the excess liquid. Mix the pulp with the bread crumbs, cheese, parsley, and oregano. Fill the squash halves with the mixture and sprinkle with a little more shredded cheese. Place in a baking dish and bake at 350°F for 10 minutes just until hot and the cheese has melted. Serves 4 as a side dish or 2 as a main course.

Onion Cheese Pie

3 cups creamed cottage cheese
2 large eggs
1 medium onion, chopped
1 Rye Pie Crust (see Index)

Water sauté the onion until tender, about 5 minutes. Beat the eggs slightly and add to the cottage cheese. Stir in the onions. Pour into the Rye Pie Crust. Bake at 400°F for 5 minutes. Reduce the heat to 350°F and bake 15-20 minutes.

Green Chili and Cheese Squares

4 eggs, beaten
2¾ cups shredded Monterey Jack cheese
1 small green chili, finely diced
1 teaspoon chopped onion
2 tablespoons milk

Combine all the ingredients and pour into a buttered 8-inch square baking pan. Bake at 325°F, 20-25 minutes until firm. Cut into squares and serve. Makes 4 servings.

Swedish Cabbage Rolls

1 large head cabbage
3 cups cooked brown rice
2 eggs, slightly beaten
¼ cup chopped onions
¼ cup chopped celery
¼ cup chopped green pepper
2 cups Homemade Tomato Sauce (see Index)
1 clove of garlic, minced
½ teaspoon ground allspice
½ teaspoon sea salt
dash of cayenne pepper

Cut the core out of the cabbage and place the cabbage in a large pot of boiling water. Pull off the outer leaves as soon as they become tender. You will need 8-10 leaves. Let them cool.

Mix together the cooked brown rice, eggs, onions, celery, green pepper, 1 cup of the Tomato Sauce, garlic, allspice, sea salt and cayenne.

Place a large spoonful of filling on each cabbage leaf. Then, fold the right and left sides of the leaf over the filling. Roll up, starting at the bottom of the leaf. The cabbage roll may be held together with a wooden toothpick, tied with thread or placed seam side down in the baking dish. Pour the remaining 1 cup of Tomato Sauce over the cabbage rolls. Bake in a covered casserole dish at 350°F for 30-40 minutes. Makes 4-5 servings.

Fresh Corn Pudding

6-8 medium ears of corn
4 eggs, slightly beaten
1 cup milk
½ teaspoon sea salt

Shred the corn (using vegetable grater) to remove all the kernels from the cob. There should be 2 cups shredded corn. Add the eggs, milk and sea salt to the corn. Pour into a 1½-quart casserole dish. Place the casserole dish in a larger pan filled ½-inch deep with hot water. Bake in the oven at 350°F for 30-40 minutes. Serves 4-6.

Black Beans and Rice

1½ cups dried black beans
1 cup chopped onions
1 clove of garlic, minced
1 teaspoon sea salt
cooked Brown Rice (see Index)

Cover the beans with water in a large sauce pan and soak overnight. Add the onions and garlic and simmer 2½ hours or until tender. Add more water if needed. When cooked, add the sea salt. Serve over brown rice. Makes 6 servings.

Grains and Vegetables

3 parts water
1 part grains (millet, buckwheat, or brown rice)
fresh vegetables (carrots, broccoli, onions, cabbage, zucchini, pea pods, green peppers, and/or other available vegetables)
sea salt to taste

Heat water to boiling. Add sea salt to taste. Add grains. Cook millet ten minutes, buckwheat or brown rice twenty minutes, stirring occasionally to prevent burning.

Add the vegetables and cook another 15 minutes on low heat. Carrots or other vegetables which require longer cooking time could be added 5 minutes earlier than remaining vegetables, while the grains are boiling.

Enjoy as is, or top with raw butter, cheese, and/or tamari soy sauce. Optional extra toppings: cayenne, kelp.

Those who are "into" Oriental foods can add approximately 1 tablespoon rinsed hijiki seaweed to boiling water before adding grains. Hijiki is rich in trace minerals from the sea and will give the dish a delightful flavor of the ocean.

Garbanzos

Garbanzos, or chick peas, are traditional food in the Middle East. They are often combined, half and half, with bulgar, or crushed wheat. Such combinations result in improved protein quality.

Garbanzos are difficult to cook to a soft texture, but it can be done. Try this method: soak 1 pound of well-washed garbanzos in 7 cups of water overnight. Drain, add fresh water and desired spices, and cook briskly for several hours until soft.

Cooked garbanzos can be added to vegetable salads, soups, and stews. Mashed, they make an excellent filling for Pita or Bible bread. Here is the recipe:

Garbanzo Filling (Hummus)

2 cups cooked garbanzos (follow cooking instructions above)
½ cup water
1 onion, chopped
1 clove of garlic, chopped
2 tablespoons minced parsley
1 teaspoon soy sauce
2 tablespoons fresh wheat germ
½ cup homemade Salsa (see Index)
½ teaspoon sea salt
1 tablespoon lemon juice

Grind all ingredients in a food grinder or baby food grinder, or chop in the blender if you can do it without adding too much water. Mix thoroughly. Place in a glass baking dish with cover. Bake at 350°F for 30 minutes. Serve hot as a filling for Pita or Bible bread.

When cold, the Garbanzo Filling can be mixed with some olive oil and served as a dip or relish with vegetables.

Zucchini Cheese Casserole

2 medium zucchini, cut in 1/8 inch slices
3 medium carrots, cut in julienne strips
3 medium tomatoes, sliced
3 tablespoons cornstarch
1¾ cups milk
1 cup shredded mild cheese
dash of cayenne pepper
½ cup fresh bread crumbs

Cook the carrots in boiling water 5 minutes. Place all vegetables in a baking dish in layers. Combine the cornstarch and milk in a saucepan and heat until thick. Remove from heat. Add ½ cup of the shredded cheese and a dash of cayenne pepper and stir until the cheese melts. Pour the sauce over the vegetables. Sprinkle the bread crumbs and remaining cheese over the sauce. Bake at 350°F, 30-40 minutes or until the vegetables are tender. Makes 6 servings.

Lentil Casserole

1 cup lentils
2 cups water
1 cup chopped tomatoes
1 green onion, chopped
1 clove of garlic, minced
1/8 teaspoon chili powder
dash of cayenne pepper
1 cup shredded cheese

In a saucepan, bring the lentils and water to a boil. Reduce the heat and simmer 1-1½ hours, until tender. Add the tomatoes, onion, garlic, chili powder, and cayenne. Place in a baking dish. Bake, covered, 20 minutes. Sprinkle the cheese on top and bake, uncovered, 5 minutes longer, or until the cheese melts. Makes 4-6 servings.

Enchiladas

3 cups Homemade Tomato Sauce (see Index)
1 cup water
1 teaspoon chili powder
¼ teaspoon garlic powder
dash of cayenne pepper
12 corn tortillas
3 cups shredded mild cheddar cheese
1 medium onion, chopped

Combine the Tomato Sauce, water, chili powder, garlic powder and cayenne in a saucepan and heat until the mixture boils. Remove from heat. One at a time, dip the tortillas in the sauce. Place the tortilla in a baking dish, sprinkle with cheese and onions, roll up and place seam side down. Repeat with all the tortillas. Pour the remaining sauce over the enchiladas. Sprinkle more shredded cheese on top. Bake at 350°F for 15-20 minutes. Makes 4 to 6 servings.

Refried Beans

2 cups dry pinto beans or yellow Mexican beans
6 cups water
1 cup shredded cheese
1 clove of garlic, minced
1 teaspoon sea salt
1 teaspoon chili powder
dash of cayenne pepper

Soak the beans in the water overnight and then cook until tender, about 3-4 hours. Mash the cooked beans. Add ½ cup of the shredded cheese, the minced garlic, salt, chili powder, and cayenne pepper, and mix well. Place in a baking dish and sprinkle the remaining cheese on top. Bake at 350°F for 15-20 minutes. Makes 6 servings.

Bean Tostadas

6 corn tortillas
2 cups Refried Beans (see Index)
1½ cups shredded Monterey Jack cheese
1 tomato, diced
2 cups alfalfa sprouts

Heat the tortillas uncovered in a 350°F oven until crisp, 3-5 minutes. Spread mashed beans over the tortillas and top with shredded cheese. Place under the broiler until the cheese melts. Remove from the oven and top with the diced tomatoes and alfalfa sprouts. Makes 6 servings.

Vegetable Tostadas

6 Corn Tortillas (see Index)
½ cup chopped zucchini
1 medium onion, chopped
½ pound fresh mushrooms, chopped
¼ cup chopped celery
½ cup chopped green pepper
1 clove of garlic, minced
2 medium tomatoes, chopped
1 tablespoon chopped fresh parsley
sea salt to taste
2 cups shredded Monterey Jack or cheddar cheese
homemade Salsa (see Index)

Heat the tortillas, uncovered, in a 350°F oven until crisp, 3-5 minutes.

Water sauté the zucchini, onion, mushrooms, celery, green pepper, and garlic in ¼ cup water until tender, but still crisp, about 5 minutes. Add the chopped tomatoes and parsley and cook another 2 minutes. Season with sea salt if desired.

Sprinkle shredded cheese on each tortilla and melt under the broiler. Cover with a spoonful of the vegetable mixture and top with a spoonful of homemade Salsa (see Index). Makes 6 servings.

Guacamole Tostadas

6 corn tortillas
1½ cups shredded mild cheddar cheese
2 cups homemade Guacamole Dip (see Index)

Sprinkle shredded cheese on each tortilla and melt under the broiler. Cover with 2-3 tablespoons of Guacamole and serve. Makes 6 servings.

Bean Burritos

6 corn tortillas
2 cups Refried Beans (see Index)

Soften the tortillas in a covered baking dish in a 350°F oven for 5-10 minutes. Heat the Refried Beans. Place a heaping spoonful of mashed beans in the center of the tortilla. Fold the right and left sides of the tortilla over the beans. Then fold over the top and bottom. Makes 6 servings.

Chili Beans

2 cups dry pinto beans
6 cups water
2 cups Homemade Stewed Tomatoes (see Index)
1 cup Homemade Tomato Sauce (see Index)
1 medium onion, chopped
1 clove of garlic, minced
1 tablespoon chili powder
2 teaspoons ground cumin
1 teaspoon sea salt
dash of cayenne pepper

Soak the beans in the water overnight and then cook until tender, at least 3-4 hours. Add the Stewed Tomatoes, Tomato Sauce, onions, garlic, chili powder, cumin, sea salt and cayenne. Simmer until the flavors have blended, 30-40 minutes. Serve with shredded cheese. Makes 6 servings.

Bean Burgers

2 cups cooked pinto beans
1 cup fresh bread crumbs
2 tablespoons chopped onion
½ cup shredded mild cheese

Mash the beans and combine with the remaining ingredients. Make 8 patties. Place in a well-buttered baking pan and bake 10 minutes at 400°F. Turn over and bake an additional 10 minutes.

Brown Rice and Carrot Casserole

3 cups cooked brown rice
½ cup chopped onion
2 medium carrots, chopped
¼ cup chopped celery
2 tablespoons olive oil
1 tablespoon finely chopped parsley
½ teaspoon sea salt
1 cup shredded cheese

Water sauté the onions, carrots, and celery in ¼ cup water until almost tender, about 5 minutes. Add more water if necessary. Stir in the olive oil, parsley and sea salt. Add the cooked rice. Bake in a covered casserole dish 20 minutes. Sprinkle the shredded cheese on top and bake uncovered a few minutes, or until the cheese melts. Makes 4-6 servings.

Mushroom Patties

1 pound fresh mushrooms, finely chopped
½ cup chopped onion
1 cup rolled oats
2 large eggs
1 teaspoon soy sauce
½ teaspoon sea salt

Water sauté the mushrooms and onions until tender, about 5 minutes. Stir in the rolled oats, eggs, soy sauce, and sea salt. Shape into patties and place in a well-buttered baking dish. Bake 10 minutes at 400°F, turn the patties over and bake another 10 minutes. Make a Whole Wheat White Sauce (see Index) or onion sauce, and pour over the patties before serving. Makes 6 patties.

Mushroom Stroganoff

1 pound fresh mushrooms, sliced
2 green onions, chopped
2 cups vegetable broth
2 tablespoons cornstarch
sea salt to taste
1 cup sour cream
Whole Wheat Noodles (see Index)

Water sauté the sliced mushrooms and onions in ¼ cup water until tender, about 5 minutes. Add more water if needed. Dissolve the cornstarch in the vegetable broth and add to the mushrooms and onions. Bring to a boil. Reduce heat and simmer 5 minutes. Season with sea salt if desired. Stir in the sour cream and serve over cooked Whole Wheat Noodles. Makes 4 to 6 servings.

Whole Grains, Cereals and Legumes

Cooking Grains

Before cooking, rinse the grain in cold water. Bring the required amount of water to a boil and slowly add the grain. Stir so that each grain is quickly surrounded by hot water. Reduce heat. Cover and cook over low heat until tender. Do not stir or uncover until the grain is cooked. Cereal that is cooked slowly over low heat has a more sweet and nutty flavor than if cooked quickly.

For finely ground cereals (corn meal, wheat flour, rice flour, etc.) use 4 cups water to 1 cup cereal. Cook 20-30 minutes.

Coarsely ground cereals (cracked or flaked grains, steel-cut oats, bulgar, etc.) will require 2 to 2½ cups water to 1 cup cereal. Cook 20-30 minutes.

Whole grain cereals, (wheat, rye, brown rice, oats, barley, millet, buckwheat etc.) also need 2 to 3 cups water to 1 cup cereal. Cook 40-60 minutes.

To cook cereals in a crock pot, place the cereal and required amount of water in the crock pot and cook over low heat 4-6 hours.

Millet Cereal

1 cup hulled millet
3 cups water
½ cup powdered skim milk (optional)

Method 1: Rinse millet in warm water and drain. Heat mixture of water, powdered skim milk, and millet to boiling. Simmer for 10 minutes, stirring occasionally to prevent sticking and burning. Remove from heat, cover, and let stand for a half an hour or more. Serve with milk, honey, oil, or butter — or Homemade Applesauce — and treat yourself to the most nutritious cereal in the world! Makes 4 servings.

Method 2: Here's another, even better, way to make millet cereal (or any other cereal, for that matter). Place all ingredients in a pan with a tight cover. Use ovenproof utensils: glass, earthenware, or stainless steel, if possible. Place in the oven turned to 175° to 200°F and leave for 3-4 hours. The cereal can be left in the oven longer if necessary, but it should be ready to eat after about 3-4 hours. To speed the process, the cereal can be heated to the boiling point before putting into the oven.

This cooking method is superior because of the low temperature, which makes the nutrients — especially the proteins — of millet or other grains more easily assimilable.

Method 3: First bring millet, water, and powdered skim milk to a boil on the stove. Pour mixture into a crockpot, and cook on low for 3-4 hours.

Millet is a truly wonderful, complete food. It can rightfully be called the king of all cereals, possibly sharing this distinction with buckwheat. It is very easily digested and never causes gas and fermentation in the stomach as some other starchy cereals often do. Famed nutritionist Dr. Harvey Kellogg said that millet is the only cereal that can sustain or support human life when used as the sole item in the diet. Besides complete proteins, millet is rich in vitamins, minerals, and important trace elements, such as molybdenum and lecithin.

Kasha
(Buckwheat cereal)

1 cup hulled raw buckwheat grains (not toasted)
2 to 2½ cups water

Bring water to a boil. Stir the buckwheat into the boiling water and let boil for 2-3 minutes. Turn heat to low and simmer for 15 to 20 minutes, stirring occasionally. If seasoning is desired, use a very little sea salt. When all the water is absorbed, remove cereal from the stove and let stand, covered, for another 15 minutes. Kasha must never be mushy. Serve hot with olive oil, sesame seed oil, butter, Homemade Applesauce (see Index), or milk. Serves 4.

Kasha is a favorite cereal in Russia and many other Eastern European countries. It has an unique, mellow flavor, and is extremely nutritious. It contains complete proteins of high biological value, equal in quality to animal proteins, as shown in recent studies.

This is a quick way to prepare Kasha if you do not have much time. For those who do have the time, the oven or crockpot methods, as described in the recipe for millet cereal, are preferable.

Molino Cereal

1 cup water
1 tablespoon coarse whole wheat flour
2 tablespoons wheat bran
2 tablespoons whole flaxseed
2-3 chopped figs or soaked prunes
1 tablespoon unsulfured raisins

Place all ingredients in a pan and boil for 5 minutes, stirring occasionally to prevent burning. Serve immediately with sweet milk, a little honey, or Homemade Applesauce (see Index). Makes 2 servings.

This cereal is beneficial for people with a tendency toward constipation.

Potato Cereal

2 large raw potatoes
2 tablespoons whole wheat flour
1 tablespoon wheat bran
4 cups water

Heat water to boiling. Add flour and bran and simmer for 2 to 3 minutes. Place a fine shredder over pan and quickly shred potatoes directly into simmering mixture. Stir vigorously. Remove from the stove and let stand for a few minutes. Serve hot with milk, butter, or cream; sprinkle fresh wheat germ on top, if desired. Makes 3-4 servings.

Airola "Granola"

2 cups rolled oats
½ cup raw bran
½ cup puffed millet
½ cup puffed rice
1 cup nuts and seeds mixture (almonds, sunflower seeds, sesame seeds, etc.), ground coarsely in the seed grinder
1 cup unsulfured raisins
½ cup chopped dried apples
½ cup fresh wheat germ

Mix all ingredients and store in a glass jar in the refrigerator. Serve with milk and/or Homemade Applesauce (see Index) for breakfast or lunch.

This "granola" may not taste as sweet, nor as crunchy as the usual coated, toasted, roasted, sweetened, and otherwise denatured varieties, but it is far superior to all of them in wholesomeness, nutritional value, and digestibility. However, it should be only eaten occasionally and not used as a substitute for such basic cooked cereals as buckwheat, millet, rice, oats, etc., which are indispensable "must" foods in the Airola Diet. Also, to prevent rancidity, do not prepare and store more than a two to three day supply at a time.

Finnish Rye Porridge

1 cup whole rye flour
2 cups water
dash of sea salt (optional)

Bring water to a boil. Stir in the flour with a wire whip. Cook 10 minutes over medium heat, stirring constantly. Remove from heat, cover, and let stand for 5 minutes. Spoon porridge into large soup plates, press pat of butter in the center, and serve with milk. Makes 4 servings.

Millet with Onions

2 cups cooked millet (see Index)
1 onion, sliced
1 clove of garlic, minced
2 tablespoons sesame seed oil
1 tablespoon chopped parsley
½ teaspoon sea salt

Water sauté the sliced onions and garlic in 2 tablespoons water just until tender, about 5 minutes. Add more water if needed. Stir in the cooked millet, oil, parsley and sea salt. Cook over medium heat a few minutes to heat through. Serves 4.

Millet and Tomatoes

2 cups cooked millet
½ cup chopped celery
1/3 cup chopped onion
1 clove of garlic, minced
1 cup chopped fresh tomatoes
2 tablespoons olive oil
½ teaspoon sea salt
sour cream or yogurt

Water sauté the celery, onion and garlic in 2 tablespoons water 5 minutes. Add more water if necessary. Stir in the chopped tomatoes, olive oil, sea salt and cooked millet. Cook 5 minutes to heat through. Serve with a spoonful of yogurt or sour cream on top. Makes 4 servings.

Millet Spoon Bread

1¾ cups cooked millet
1/3 cup corn meal
2 cups milk
2 eggs, beaten

Combine all the ingredients. Pour into a 1½-quart casserole dish. Bake at 325°F, 40-50 minutes. Serves 6.

Waerland Five-Grain Kruska

1 tablespoon whole wheat
1 tablespoon whole rye
1 tablespoon whole barley
1 tablespoon whole millet
1 tablespoon whole oats
1 tablespoon wheat bran
2 tablespoons unsulfured raisins
1-1½ cups water

Grind the 5 grains coarsely in your grinder. Place all ingredients in a pot and boil for 5-10 minutes, then wrap the pot in a blanket or newspapers and let it stand for a few hours. Experiment with the amount of water used —Kruska must not be mushy, but should have the consistency of a very thick porridge. Serve hot with sweet milk and Homemade Applesauce (see Index) or stewed fruits. Makes 4 servings.

This is another cereal that can be used by those who have a tendency towards constipation.

Oatmeal

1 cup old fashioned rolled oats
2 cups water

Bring the water to a boil. Stir in the oats. Cook 5-10 minutes over medium heat, stirring frequently. Reduce heat, cover, and cook another 5 minutes. Makes 3-4 servings.

Buckwheat Noodles I

1/3 cup buckwheat flour
1/3 cup whole wheat flour
1 egg
1 tablespoon water
1 teaspoon sesame seed oil

Measure the flour into a small mixing bowl. Combine the egg, water and oil and add to the flour. Mix well until the dough can be rolled into a ball. Knead the dough for 5 minutes. Cover and let stand 1 hour. Using a rolling pin, roll and stretch the dough as thinly as possible. Hang it over a chair or towel rack over a clean towel and let it dry 20-30 minutes. Before it becomes brittle, roll it up and cut into strips ½ inch wide. Cook the noodles 8-10 minutes in rapidly boiling water. Makes 4 cups of cooked noodles.

Buckwheat Noodles II

1/3 cup buckwheat flour
1/3 cup whole wheat flour
3-4 tablespoons water

Measure the flour into a small mixing bowl. Stir in enough water to make a stiff dough. Knead the dough for 5 minutes. Cover and let stand 1 hour. Using a rolling pin, roll out the dough as thinly as possible. This dough will not be as thin as Buckwheat Noodles I and will not hold together as well. Let it dry 20-30 minutes, on a flat surface. Cut into strips ¼ inch wide. Cook the noodles 8-10 minutes in rapidly boiling water.

Brown Rice

2 to 2½ cups water
1 cup brown rice, washed

Bring the water to a boil. Add the brown rice and cover. Reduce heat and simmer 30-40 minutes until all the water is absorbed. Makes 3 cups cooked brown rice.

Brown Rice Pudding

1 cup raw brown rice
3 cups milk
2 tablespoons butter

Wash the rice and put in a crock pot with the milk. Cook on low heat 5-6 hours until the rice is cooked. Add the butter after 4 hours of cooking. This rice pudding may be served with a little honey and cinnamon sprinkled on top. Makes 6 servings.

Spanish Rice

2 cups cooked brown rice
2 cups cut-up fresh tomatoes
2 green onions, chopped
¼ cup chopped celery
1 clove of garlic, minced
½ teaspoon chili powder
⅛ teaspoon ground cumin
1 green pepper, sliced

Simmer the tomatoes, green onions, celery, garlic, chili powder and cumin 10-15 minutes, until tender. Add the green pepper and cook 2-3 minutes. Stir in the rice, heat and serve. Makes 4 servings.

Bulgar Pilaf

2 cups Vegetable Broth (see Index)
¼ cup chopped celery with tops
1 green onion, chopped
1 cup bulgar

Place the vegetable broth, chopped celery, and onion in a saucepan. Bring to a boil. Stir in the bulgar. Reduce heat and simmer 15 minutes. Makes 4 servings.

Parslied Rice

3 cups cooked brown rice
2 tablespoons olive oil
1 clove of garlic, minced
¼ cup chopped fresh parsley

Combine all ingredients and serve while still hot.

Whole Wheat Noodles

¾ cup whole wheat flour, freshly ground
1 egg
1 tablespoon water
1 teaspoon sesame seed oil

Measure the flour into a small mixing bowl. Combine the egg, water, and oil and add to the flour. Stir well until the dough can be rolled into a ball. Knead the dough for 5 minutes. Cover and let stand 1 hour. Using a rolling pin, roll and stretch the dough as thinly as possible. Hang it on a chair or towel rack over a clean towel and let it dry 20-30 minutes. Before it becomes brittle, roll it up and cut into strips ½ inch wide. Cook the noodles 8-10 minutes in rapidly boiling water. Makes 4 cups of cooked noodles.

Whole Wheat Crepes

¾ cup whole wheat flour
3 eggs
2 tablespoons non-instant nonfat dry milk
⅛ teaspoon sea salt
1 cup water

Place all the ingredients in a blender and blend until smooth. Chill in the refrigerator one hour before cooking. STir batter frequently while using, to keep the whole wheat flour from settling to the bottom. Cook in a crepe pan, or lightly buttered griddle or skillet over medium heat, making pancakes as thin as possible. Makes approximately 12-15 crepes.

Serve the crepes with a variety of fillings. Here are just a few choices.

1. Cooked vegetables: broccoli, carrots, summer squash, green beans, etc., topped with Mushroom Sauce, Cheese Sauce, or Cream of Tomato Soup used as a sauce (see Index for sauce recipes)
2. Ratatouille (see Index)
3. Green Pepper Sauce (see Index)
4. Mushroom Stroganoff (see Index)
5. Fresh fruit or berries topped with yogurt or sour cream
6. Blueberry Filling:

2 cups fresh blueberries	1 tablespoon cornstarch
2 tablespoons honey	2 tablespoons water

Place the blueberries and honey in a saucepan. Dissolve the cornstarch in the water. Add to the blueberries. Cook over medium heat, stirring constantly until the mixture thickens. Fill the crepes while hot or cooled. Top with yogurt or sour cream.

7. Apricot Filling:

1 cup dried apricots	1 tablespoon cornstarch
2 cups water	2 tablespoons water
2 tablespoons honey	dash of cinnamon

Soak the dried apricots in the 2 cups of water overnight. The next day, add the honey, bring to a boil, and simmer 5 minutes. Dissolve the cornstarch in the 2 tablespoons water and stir into the apricot mixture. Continue cooking until the mixture thickens. Season with a dash of cinnamon. Use hot or cold to fill the crepes. Top with yogurt or sour cream.

Sprouted Wheat Pancakes

2 cups sprouted wheat (1/8"-1/4" sprouts)	*1 cup milk*
2 large eggs	*3/4 cup whole wheat flour*

Grind the sprouted wheat in a blender. Add the eggs, milk and whole wheat flour. Blend on high speed until smooth. Cook the pancakes in a lightly buttered skillet over medium heat. Makes 12-18 small pancakes.

Zucchini Pancakes

1 cup whole wheat flour
½ teaspoon sea salt
2 large eggs
2 cups shredded zucchini

Combine all the ingredients and mix well. Drop by spoonfuls onto a well buttered skillet, spread with the back of a spoon to make a round pancake, and cook over medium heat 2 to 3 minutes on each side. Makes 2 dozen two-inch pancakes.

Fresh Corn Pancakes

6-8 medium ears of corn
2 cups whole wheat flour
2 large eggs
1½ cups milk

Shred the corn (using vegetable grater) to remove all the kernels from the cob. There should be about 2 cups of shredded corn. Stir the whole wheat flour, eggs and milk into the corn. Cook the pancakes in a buttered skillet over medium heat. Makes about 1½ dozen 6-inch pancakes.

Corn Meal Pancakes

¾ cup whole wheat flour
½ teaspoon baking soda
¾ cup yellow corn meal
¾ cup cooked brown rice
2 eggs, slightly beaten
1½ cups buttermilk

Sift together the whole wheat flour and baking soda. Stir in the corn meal, brown rice, eggs and buttermilk. Cook the pancakes in a lightly buttered skillet over medium heat. Makes 8-12 pancakes.

Buckwheat Pancakes

1 cup whole raw buckwheat, or buckwheat flour
½ cup rolled oats or fresh wheat germ
2 eggs
2 cups buttermilk, yogurt, or kefir
pinch of sea salt

Place buckwheat and oats or fresh wheat germ in blender or seed grinder and grind well until a fine flour is obtained. Mix flour in a medium-sized bowl with remaining ingredients and blend well. If batter is too thick, add fresh milk to desired consistency. Fry on a lightly-buttered griddle on low heat.

Serve with butter, olive oil, or Homemade Applesauce (see Index). Makes 6 delicious medium-sized pancakes.

Potato Pancakes

3 large eggs
1 cup milk
1½ cups whole wheat flour
2 tablespoons grated onion
1 teaspoon parsley flakes
½ teaspoon sea salt
4 large potatoes

Beat the eggs and milk together. Add the flour, onion, parsley, and sea salt and mix well. Shred the potatoes (there should be about 4 cups of shredded potatoes) and add to the batter, mixing well. Drop the batter onto a lightly buttered skillet and spread with the back of the spoon to make a round pancake. Cook over medium heat 2-3 minutes on each side. Makes 12-15 four-inch pancakes.

Dried Legumes

There are over 25 types of dried beans and peas available. They include pinto and kidney beans, garbanzos, navy beans, black beans, dried limas, lentils, black-eyed peas, split peas, and soy beans.

One cup of beans, peas or lentils will expand to 2-2½ cups when cooked.

Wash beans thoroughly and remove discolored beans. Soak overnight using 3 cups of water for each cup of beans. Bring the beans to a boil using the soaking water*, reduce the heat, and simmer until tender. For most pre-soaked beans this will take 1-1½ hours. Lentils and split peas will be tender in 20-30 minutes.

A quick method for soaking beans — if you have forgotten to soak them overnight — is to cover the washed beans with water, bring to a boil and simmer 2 minutes. Remove from heat, cover and soak 1 hour. Then cook as for soaked beans.

Various spices and herbs can be used to enhance the flavor of beans including onions, tomatoes, sea salt, chili powder, cumin, garlic, and cayenne pepper. The seasonings should be added during the last hour of cooking. If added too soon, the flavor will cook out before the beans are finished.

**Note:* When soaking garbanzos and soy beans overnight, discard the soak water and replace it with fresh water before cooking.

Soybeans

Soybeans are one of the most versatile beans. They may be used whole, ground into flour, made into soy milk or soybean curd (tofu), or sprouted. Green soybeans may be cooked much like lima beans. To shell them, immerse the pods in boiling water and boil 5 minutes. Drain and cool, and squeeze the pods to remove the beans. Cook the *fresh* beans in boiling water for 15 minutes, or until tender.

Dried soybeans contain an enzyme inhibitor that makes them very difficult to digest. To remove the enzyme inhibitor, dried soybeans should be soaked in water for 24 hours, changing water every 8 hours. After that, the soybeans can be cooked for 3-4 hours in fresh water. Because they boil over easily, use a large saucepan and check them frequently during cooking. Their bland flavor can be improved by seasoning with tomatoes, cheese, soy sauce, onions, garlic, oregano, thyme, etc.

Garbanzo Bean Spread
(Hummus)

2 cups cooked garbanzo beans (see Index)
3 tablespoons lemon juice
2 tablespoons sesame seed oil
1 clove of garlic, minced
2 tablespoons chopped parsley
2 tablespoons fresh wheat germ
1 teaspoon soy sauce
½ teaspoon sea salt
¼ teaspoon ground cumin
dash of cayenne pepper

Grind the cooked garbanzo beans in a food mill or food processor. Add the remaining ingredients to the garbanzo beans and mix well. Use as a filling for Pita bread or as a dip for vegetables. (See also Garbanzo Filling recipe in Entreé section).

Lentil Barley Stew

1 cup lentils
1/3 cup barley
3 cups water
2 cups Homemade Stewed Tomatoes (see Index)
¼ cup chopped onion
¼ cup chopped celery
¼ cup chopped carrots
1 clove of garlic, minced
sea salt to taste
dash of cayenne pepper

Cook the lentils and barley together in the 3 cups of water until tender, about 1½ hours. Add the stewed tomatoes, onion, celery, carrots, garlic, sea salt and cayenne and mix together. Pour into a casserole dish and bake at 350°F for 35-40 minutes.

Lima-Mung Beans

2 cups dry lima beans
6 cups water
3 cups mung bean sprouts
½ cup chopped green pepper
1 tablespoon olive oil
1 teaspoon sea salt
½ teaspoon turmeric

Soak the lima beans overnight, then cook until tender in the 6 cups water. Drain

Water sauté the mung bean sprouts and green pepper in ¼ cup water until tender, about 5 minutes, stirring constantly. Add the cooked lima beans, olive oil, sea salt and turmeric. Simmer 10-15 minutes. Makes 6 servings.

NOTES:

Breads

Sourdough Rye Bread

8 cups freshly-ground whole rye flour
3 cups warm water
½ cup sourdough culture

Mix 7 cups of flour with the water and sourdough culture. Cover and let stand in a warm place for 12 to 18 hours. Add remaining flour, mix well, and knead for 5 minutes, using a dough mixer if you have one. Place in buttered and floured pans. Let rise in a warm place for approximately 1-2 hours, or until the loaf has risen noticeably. Always save ½ cup of dough as a culture for the next baking. Keep the culture in your refrigerator. For the initial baking, it will be necessary to obtain a sourdough culture from a friend or from a commercial baker.

Preheat oven to 350°-400°F and bake for 1 hour or more, if needed. This recipe makes one 2-pound loaf.

Sourdough bread baking is a delicate art. If you do not succeed at first, don't give up — keep experimenting until you bake a sublimely delicious loaf that will not only fill your house with Old-Country aroma, but will delight your family and justify the Biblical reference to bread as the "Staff of Life."

How to Make Sourdough Starter

You will get the best results with sourdough bread if you have an old well-used starter. Try to get it from someone you know who bakes sourdough bread regularly, or possibly you can get it from a commercial bakery.

If you do not succeed in obtaining a culture, you can always make your own. It won't be as good as an old culture, but it will get better and better with time.

To make sourdough starter, take 2½ cups of fresh finely ground pure rye flour. Mix with 2½ cups of warm water in a deep glass or stainless steel bowl. Add 1 packet of active dry yeast, and mix with a wooden spoon. Cover with a plate or damp cloth and let stand in a warm place for 4 days. Stir once a day. On the 5th day, add 1 cup warm water and 1 cup flour. Stir well, cover, and return to a warm place. The next day your culture is ready to be used.

You need 1 cup of starter to bake 2 loaves of bread. Save the rest and store in the refrigerator.

The culture will keep for 10 days - 2 weeks. Every time you take a cup of it for baking, add ½ cup warm water and ½ cup flour to the old culture and keep in a warm place for 24 hours before returning it to the refrigerator. Store the culture in a tight container, preferably in something other than glass, as glass may break when the culture expands. If you do not bake for a prolonged period of time, you must add ½ cup flour and ½ cup warm water every 10 days - 2 weeks, keeping the culture at room temperature for a day before returning to the refrigerator.

Sprouted Wheat Bread

2½ cups warm water
2 packages active dry yeast
1/3 cup honey
2-3 teaspoons sea salt (optional)
3 tablespoons non-instant nonfat dry milk
6-8 cups whole wheat flour
2 cups sprouted wheat

Dissolve the yeast in ¼ cup warm water. Add the remaining water and honey to the dissolved yeast and let stand several minutes. Add the sea salt. Measure out two cups of whole wheat flour. Add to it the 3 tablespoons nonfat dry milk and mix well. Stir this mixture into the liquid ingredients and mix until smooth. Cover and let stand 15 minutes.

Grind the sprouted wheat in a blender or food mill, and add to the batter. Stir in the remaining flour as needed to make a soft dough. Let the dough rest for 15 minutes, then turn out onto a well floured surface. Knead for 5 minutes. Place in a buttered bowl and turn the dough so that the buttered side is up. Cover with a damp cloth and let rise until double in size, about 1½ hours. Punch down, turn out onto a floured surface and shape into two loaves. Place in buttered pans, cover and let rise until almost double, about 30 minutes. Bake at 350°F, 30-40 minutes.

Chapatti

2 cups whole wheat flour
10-12 tablespoons water

Mix the flour and water together. Knead until smooth. Cut the dough in half. Divide each half into 6 pieces and roll each into a ball. On a floured surface roll it into a thin 6-inch circle with a rolling pin. Cook on a hot ungreased cast-iron skillet about one minute on each side. Makes 12 chapattis.

Whole Wheat Bread I

2 cups warm water
2 packages active dry yeast
*¼ cup honey**
1-2 teaspoons sea salt (optional)
4-5 cups whole wheat flour

Dissolve the yeast in the warm water, add honey and let stand for several minutes. Add the salt and two cups whole wheat flour. Mix until smooth. Cover and let stand for 15 minutes. Add the remaining flour as needed to make a soft dough. Knead well for 5 minutes. Cover with a damp cloth and let rise in a warm place until double in size, about 1-1½ hours. Punch down, shape into 2 loaves, and put in buttered pans. Let rise until amost double in size, about 30 minutes. Bake at 350°F, 30-40 minutes.

Whole wheat bread can be made without salt, if you prefer. In such a case, the rising time will be reduced.

*The honey in the recipe is used not for the sweetening of the bread, but to facilitate the growth of the yeast culture.

Whole Wheat Bread II

2½ cups warm water
2 packages active dry yeast
1/3 cup honey
2-3 teaspoons sea salt (optional)
3 tablespoons non-instant nonfat dry milk
5-6 cups whole wheat flour

Dissolve the yeast in ½ cup warm water. Add the remaining water and honey to the dissolved yeast and let stand several minutes. Add the salt. Measure out two cups of whole wheat flour. Add to it the 3 tablespoons nonfat dry milk and mix well. Stir this mixture into the liquid ingredients and mix until smooth. Cover and let stand 15 minutes. Add the remaining flour as needed to make a soft dough. Let the dough rest for 15 minutes, then turn out onto a well floured surface. Knead for 5 minutes. Place in a buttered bowl, and turn the dough so that the buttered side is up. Cover with a damp cloth and let rise until double in size, about 1½ hours. Punch down, turn out onto a floured surface and shape into two loaves. Place in buttered pans, cover and let rise until almost double, about 30 minutes. Bake at 350°F, 30-40 minutes.

Five-Grain Bread

2 packages active dry yeast
2 cups warm water
1-2 teaspoons sea salt (optional)
2 tablespoons honey
3 tablespoons unsulfured black strap molasses
¼ cup oat flour
¼ cup barley flour
½ cup rye meal
½ cup millet flour
3-4 cups whole wheat flour

Dissolve the yeast in ¼ cup warm water. Add the dissolved yeast to the remaining water, sea salt, honey and molasses in a large mixing bowl. Gradually mix in the oat flour, barley flour, rye meal, and millet flour. Add enough whole wheat flour to make a soft dough. Cover and let the dough rest for 15 minutes.

Turn the dough out onto a well floured surface and knead for 5 minutes. Place the dough in a buttered bowl and then turn the dough so that the buttered side is up. Cover with a damp cloth and let rise until double in size, about 1½ hours. Punch down, shape into 2 loaves and place in buttered loaf pans. Cover and let rise until almost double, about 30 minutes. Bake at 350°F for 30-40 minutes. Remove from the pans and cool.

Millet Bread

2 cups warm water
2 packages active dry yeast
¼ cup honey
1 teaspoon sea salt (optional)
2 cups millet flour
2-3 cups whole wheat flour

Dissolve the yeast in the warm water, add honey, and let stand for several minutes. Add the sea salt and the millet flour. (To make millet flour, grind millet grain in your seed grinder into a fine powder.) Mix until smooth. Add the whole wheat flour as needed to make a soft dough. Cover and let rest for 15 minutes. Knead well for 5 minutes. Cover with a damp cloth and let rise in a warm place until double in size, 1-1½ hours. Punch down, shape into two loaves and put in buttered pans. Let rise until almost double in size, about 30 minutes. Bake at 350°F, 30-40 minutes.

Pita Bread

1 package active dry yeast
1 cup warm water
2 tablespoons honey
1 teaspoon sea salt (optional)
2½-3 cups whole wheat flour

Dissolve the yeast in the warm water. Stir in the honey, salt and flour to make a soft dough. Knead well for 5 minutes. Cover with a damp cloth and let rise until doubled in size, 1-1½ hours.

Punch down and divide into 6 parts. Shape each part into a ball. Cover and let rise 15 minutes.

Roll each ball into a 6-inch circle, ¼ inch thick. Place on an ungreased baking sheet. Bake on the lowest oven rack in a preheated 475°F oven for 8-10 minutes, until puffed and lightly browned. Wrap the pita breads in a towel to keep from hardening as they cool. Makes 6 pitas.

Buckwheat Bread

2 cups warm water
2 packages active dry yeast
¼ cup honey
1 teaspoon sea salt (optional)
2 cups buckwheat flour
2-3 cups whole wheat flour

Dissolve the yeast in the warm water, add honey, and let stand for several minutes. Add the salt and the buckwheat flour. Mix until smooth. Add the whole wheat flour as needed to make a soft dough. Cover and let stand for 15 minutes. Knead well for 5 minutes. Cover with a damp cloth and let rise in a warm place until double in size, 1-1½ hours. Punch down, shape into two loaves and put in buttered pans. Let rise until almost double in size, about 30 minutes. Bake at 350°F for 30-40 minutes.

The addition of millet or buckwheat to wheat bread improves its protein quality and gives it a unique, pungent flavor.

Corn Meal Muffins

1 tablespoon active dry yeast
1¾ cups lukewarm water
2-3 tablespoons honey
2 eggs, slightly beaten
1 teaspoon sea salt
2 cups yellow corn meal
2 cups whole wheat flour
1/3 cup non-instant non-fat dry milk

Dissolve the yeast in ¼ cup lukewarm water. Add the honey, eggs, salt and the remaining 1½ cups water. Combine the corn meal, whole wheat flour and non-fat dry milk and add to the liquid ingredients. Stir just until blended. Fill buttered muffin tins ½ full and let rise in a warm place 15 minutes. Bake at 400°F 20-25 minutes. Makes 2 dozen muffins.

Corn Tortillas

2 cups masa (corn) flour
1¼ cups water

Combine the flour and water and knead well. Divide the dough in half. Shape each half into 8 balls. Roll each ball between two sheets of waxed paper to make a 6-inch circle. Bake on an ungreased skillet. When the edges begin to curl (after about 30 seconds) turn the tortilla and cook one minute. Turn again and cook another 15-30 seconds. Makes 16 tortillas.

Masa flour is sold in most supermarkets in the Southwest.

Corn Bread

2 cups yellow corn meal
3 teaspoons aluminum-free baking powder (see Index)
½ teaspoon sea salt
1 cup milk
1 egg, slightly beaten
3 tablespoons honey

Combine the corn meal, baking powder and sea salt. Mix the milk, egg, and honey together and stir into the dry ingredients until just blended. Pour into a buttered 8-inch square pan. Bake at 350°F for 20 minutes. Serve hot.

Corn Meal Biscuits

2 teaspoons honey
1 cup boiling water
1 cup yellow corn meal

Melt the honey in the water and pour over the corn meal. Stir until well blended. Drop from a spoon onto a buttered baking sheet. Bake at 400°F, 15-20 minutes. Makes 1 dozen biscuits.

Fruits

Fruits are refreshing and cleansing foods and are best eaten in the morning for breakfast. They can also be eaten as a refreshing snack between meals. Generally, fruits should not be eaten together with raw vegetables. Lemon, papaya, and pineapple are exceptions to this rule. Since in the ideal, ultimate Airola Optimum Diet there are no desserts, fruits or fruit-based courses should preferably form a meal by themselves, rather than be eaten as a concluding course after a large meal.

Keep in mind the following rules regarding fruits:

1. Eat all fresh fruits in season.
2. Choose fruits that are indigenous to your own area and climate.
3. Eat sun-dried fruits out of season.
4. Do not use commercially processed fruits. Frozen fruits or berries, without sugar, can be used sparingly out of season.
5. Do not mix watermelon, cantaloupe, casaba, or other melons with other fruits. Melons mix well with other melons, but not with other fruits. Melons are best eaten separately, between meals.

Fruit Salad a la Airola

1 bowl fresh fruits, organically grown if possible
1 handful raw nuts and/or sunflower seeds
3-4 soaked prunes or handful of unsulfured raisins
3 tablespoons Home-made Cottage Cheese (see Index)
1 tablespoon fresh raw wheat germ
3 tablespoons yogurt
2 tablespoons natural unpasteurized honey
1 teaspoon fresh lemon or lime juice

Wash and dry all fruits carefully. Use any available fruits and berries in season, but try to get at least 3 or 4 different kinds. Peaches, grapes, pears, papaya, bananas, strawberries, and fresh pineapple are particularly good for producing a delightful bouquet of rich, penetrating flavors. A variety of colors will make the salad festive and attractive to the eye.

Chop or slice bigger fruits, but leave grapes and berries whole. Place them in a large bowl and add prunes and half of the nuts or sunflower seeds (nuts and sunflower seeds could be crushed). Make a dressing with 1 teaspoon honey (or more, if most of the fruits used are sour), 1 teaspoon of lemon or lime juice, and 2 tablespoons of water. Pour over the fruit, add wheat germ, and toss well. Mix cottage cheese, yogurt, and 1 teaspoon honey in a separate cup until it is fairly smooth in texture, and pour it on top of the salad. Sprinkle with remaining nuts and sunflower seeds. Serve at once.

This is not only a most delicious dish, but it is one of the most nutritious and perfectly balanced meals I know of. It is a storehouse of high-grade proteins and all the essential vitamins, minerals, trace elements, and fatty acids you need for optimum health.

Ambrosia Salad

4 oranges
1 grapefruit
½ cup freshly grated coconut
¼ cup chopped nuts

Peel and slice the oranges and grapefruit. Arrange attractively on the serving plate. Sprinkle with the grated coconut and chopped nuts. Garnish with mint. Serves 4.

Pineapple-Apricot Salad

3 tablespoons agar-agar flakes
1 cup orange juice
2 cups puréed apricots
1 cup unsweetened crushed pineapple
¼ cup honey
1 cup apricot halves
½ cup chopped nuts

Add the agar-agar flakes to 1 cup orange juice in a saucepan. Bring to a boil, cover, reduce heat, and simmer for 15 minutes to dissolve the agar-agar. Cool slightly. Stir in the puréed apricots, crushed pineapple and honey. Chill in the refrigerator. When slightly thickened, top with apricot halves and chopped nuts. Chill until set. Serves 6.

Agar-agar flakes can be obtained at better health food stores. Readers who do not object to using gelatin (an animal product) may replace the agar-agar flakes with 2 tablespoons of gelatin.

Minted Cottage Cheese Fruit Salad

1½ cups cottage cheese
1 tablespoon finely chopped fresh mint
assortment of fresh fruits

Mix the mint with the cottage cheese. Place the cottage cheese in the center of the plate. Wash and cut up the fruit and arrange attractively around the cottage cheese. Serves 4.

Fresh Fruit Salad with Yogurt Dressing

2 cups pineapple cut into 1 inch cubes
2 cups fresh strawberries
1 cup sliced fresh peaches
2 medium bananas, sliced
1 cup fresh green grapes
1 cup plain yogurt
2 tablespoons honey
2 tablespoons orange juice

Combine the fruits in a large bowl. Mix the yogurt, honey, and orange juice and pour over the fruit salad. Serves 6-8.

Jelled Strawberry-Banana Salad

2½ tablespoons agar-agar flakes
2 cups grape juice
1 cup sliced fresh strawberries
1 medium banana, sliced

Add the agar-agar flakes to the grape juice in a saucepan. Bring to a boil, cover, reduce heat and simmer for 15 minutes to dissolve the agar-agar flakes. Cook slightly. Pour over the sliced strawberries and bananas and chill until set. Makes 6 servings.

One tablespoon gelatin may be substituted for the agar-agar flakes.

Hawaiian Fruit Plate

Papaya, sliced
Pineapple wedges
Bananas, sliced
Kiwi, sliced
Strawberries
Mint leaves

Arrange the sliced fruits attractively on a serving platter. Garnish with fresh mint leaves.

Molded Strawberry Salad

3 tablespoons agar-agar flakes
2 cups apple juice
3 tablespoons honey
2 cups sliced strawberries
2 peaches, sliced
1 tablespoon lemon juice

Add the agar-agar flakes to the apple juice in a saucepan. Bring to a boil, cover, reduce heat and simmer for 15 minutes to dissolve the agar-agar. Cool slightly. Add the honey, strawberries, peaches and lemon juice. Chill until set. Serves 6.

Two tablespoons gelatin may be used in place of the agar-agar flakes.

Banana Logs

Ripe bananas
Plain yogurt
Sesame seeds, freshly grated coconut, or chopped sunflower seeds

Peel the bananas and cut into 1-inch pieces. Dip each piece into the yogurt and then roll in the sesame seeds, grated coconut or chopped sunflower seeds.

Baked Apples

6 large baking apples
¼ cup honey
cinnamon

Wash the apples and core from the top, leaving the bottom intact. Fill the center of each apple with about 2 teaspoons honey and sprinkle with cinnamon. Put in a baking pan with ½ inch water in the bottom of the pan. Bake at 350°F, 50-60 minutes or until tender. Serve hot or cold. Makes 6 servings.

Raw Cranberry Sauce

1 pound raw cranberries
1 cup honey
½ cup orange or apple juice

Mix the cranberries, honey, and juice and process in a blender or food grinder until well blended. Serve at once.

Lemon Sauce

1/3 cup honey
1/3 cup fresh lemon juice
1 tablespoon cornstarch

Combine the lemon juice and cornstarch in a saucepan and cook over low heat until thick, stirring constantly. Stir in the honey. Serve over fresh fruit. Makes 2/3 cup.

Prune Whip

2 cups dried prunes

Cover the prunes with hot water and soak overnight. Pit the soaked prunes and puree in a blender until smooth. Pour into individual serving dishes. Makes 6 servings.

Homemade Applesauce

All kinds of organically grown apples may be used, but Pippins, Roman Beauty, Jonathan, Northern Spy, Granny's etc., are preferable.

Wash apples well and remove stems. Cut into approximately 1-inch pieces. Note: Do not peel or remove core or seeds — use the whole apple. Place in a pan, and add one inch of water (only enough water to cover the bottom and prevent burning).

Cover and bring to a boil. Simmer until apples are soft. Mash with potato masher or place in a blender if finer texture is desired. Do not use sugar or honey, but pectin may be added if desired. When sauce is cooled, place in jars and refrigerate. Keeps for approximately 1 week.

Banana Date Whip

2 medium bananas
½ cup pitted dates
1 tablespoon lemon juice

Place all the ingredients in a blender and puree until smooth. Pour into individual serving dishes. Makes 4 servings.

Cold Berry Soup

2 cups fresh berries (strawberries, blackberries, raspberries, boysenberries, blueberries, black or red currants, gooseberries — any available berries in season)
1/3 cup honey
2 cups buttermilk or yogurt

Combine all ingredients in a blender and blend until smooth. Serve cold. Makes 4-6 servings.

Dried Fruit Compote

1 cup dried prunes
½ cup dried apricots
½ cup dried pears
½ cup dried apples
½ cup raisins
1 cinnamon stick
3 tablespoons cornstarch
water

Make sure all fruits are unsulfured. Buy them at a health food store or dry them yourself. Combine the fruits in a saucepan. Add the cinnamon stick and cover with water. Soak overnight in the refrigerator.

Dissolve the cornstarch in ¼ cup water and add to the soaked fruits. Place over medium heat and bring to a boil, stirring frequently. When the compote thickens, remove from heat and pour into individual serving dishes. Serve hot or chilled. Makes 6 servings.

Lactic Acid Foods

Homemade Dill Pickles

Use only small, fresh, firm cucumbers. Place them in cold water overnight, then remove and dry well.

Place cucumbers in a wooden barrel or a large earthenware or glass container. Put a few leaves of black currants or cherries, caraway or mustard seeds, and several dill branches in with the cucumbers. If fresh dill is not available, use dry dill weed.

Boil a sufficient amount of salt water, using about 4 ounces of sea salt for 5 quarts of water. Let the water cool down, then pour it over the cucumbers. Cover with a cheesecloth, place a wooden board over it, and on the top a clean heavy stone. There should be enough salt water to cover the board. Keep the container in a warm place for about 1 week, then move to a cooler place. Pickles are ready for eating in about 10 days to 2 weeks. It may take a little longer if the temperature is cold. Every 5 days or so, remove the stone and the covers and wash them well, first in warm water, then in cold water, and replace them. Keep the top of the water clear of foam and mildew. When pickles are ready for eating, they can be placed in glass jars and kept in the refrigerator.

Homemade Sauerkraut

Cut white cabbage heads into narrow strips with a large knife or grater, and place in a wooden barrel or an earthenware pot. A large stainless steel pail or a glass container could possibly be used, but under no circumstances use an aluminum utensil.

When the layer of cabbage is about 4 to 6 inches deep, sprinkle with a few juniper berries, cummin seeds, and/or black currant leaves — use your favorite or whatever you have available. A few strips of carrots, green peppers, and onions can also be used. Add a little sea salt — not more than 2 ounces total for each 25 pounds of cabbage. Continue making layers of grated cabbage and spices until the container is filled. Each layer should be pressed and pounded very hard with your fists or a piece of wood so that there will be no air left and the cabbage will be saturated with its own juice.

When the container is full, cover the cabbage with a clean cheesecloth, place a wooden or slate board over it, and on the top place a clean heavy stone. Let stand for 10 days to 2 weeks — longer if the temperature is below 70°F. Now and then remove the foam and possible mildew from the top, from the stone, and from the container's edges. The cheesecloth, board, and stone should occasionally be removed, washed well with warm water and then cold water, and replaced. When the sauerkraut is ready for use, it can be left in the container, which now should be stored in a cold place, or (preferably) put into glass jars and kept in the refrigerator.

Sauerkraut is best eaten raw — both from the point of taste and for its health-giving value. Drink the sauerkraut juice, too. It is an extremely beneficial and wonderfully nutritious drink.

Homemade Pickled Vegetables

Use the same method as described in the recipe for Sauerkraut to make health-giving lactic acid vegetables. Beets, carrots, green and red peppers, beet tops, and celery are particularly adapted for pickling.

After vegetables are washed and chopped to about 1-1½ inch pieces, pack them tightly into a jar or other suitable container, fill the container with water (which must first be boiled, then cooled to room temperature), add salt and spices, place the board or slate on top to keep vegetables under the water, and cover the container with a cloth. Keep in a warm place, not below 70°F. When pickled vegetables are ready, place them, with juice, in glass jars and store in the refrigerator.

Homemade Soy Yogurt

For those who prefer not to eat dairy products, or are unable to digest them well, here is a recipe for a non-dairy yogurt that is both delicious and nutritious.

Begin by making soy milk: Soak 1 cup dry soy beans in water for 2-3 days. Keep in refrigerator, and change water morning and evening. Rinse beans, put in the blender with 1 quart of fresh water and blend well. Strain through two layers of cheesecloth. Bring the soy milk to a boil, and strain again. Sweeten with 1 teaspoon honey.

Take 1 quart of soy milk cooled to 100°-110°F, and stir in 4 tablespoons of yogurt culture. Pour into glass jars and place in automatic yogurt maker or thermos bottle, or keep in a pan of warm water over very low heat on the stove, or in a warm oven. The yogurt should set in 4-8 hours, depending on the temperature. As soon as the yogurt is solidified, store in the refrigerator. Use as regular yogurt. Save 4 spoonfuls of the soy yogurt for the next batch.

Homemade Kefir

To make your own kefir, you will need kefir grains. Perhaps you can get some from your friends. If not, you can order kefir grains from R.A.J. Biological Laboratory, 35 Park Ave., Blue Point, Long Island, New York. The kefir grains will last indefinitely — there is never any need to reorder. Merely follow the instructions which will come with the grains. They multiply rapidly, so please, share them with your friends.

Place 1 tablespoon of kefir grains in a glass of milk, stir, and allow to stand at room temperature overnight. When the milk coagulates, it is ready for use. Strain and save the grains for the next batch. Kefir is a true "elixir of youth," used by centenarians in Bulgaria, Russia, and Caucasus as an essential part of their daily diet.

Freeze-dried kefir culture, sold in health food stores, can also be used in making kefir. It is not re-usable, however.

Homemade Piima

Viili piima is Finnish lactic acid milk which is becoming increasingly popular in the U.S. and Canada. It is made with a special culture — *Streptococcus lactis var. hollandicus.* Starter culture can be bought from some health food suppliers or from biological supply laboratories. Also try Piima, P.O. Box 582, Leeds, Utah, 84746, or perhaps you can get some starter culture from friends who make piima regularly.

Stir ½-1 teaspoon piima culture into a pint of warm (body temperature) milk in a clean porcelain jar or bowl. Cover loosely and set in warm place overnight. When solidified, store in the refrigerator. Always save 1 or 2 spoonfuls for the next batch.

There are many who feel that piima is the most delicious of all cultured milks. Most of them are Finns, of course!

Homemade Cultured Milk

Use only unpasteurized, raw milk. Place a bottle of milk in a pan filled with warm water, and heat it to about body temperature. Fill a cup or a deep plate, stir in a tablespoon of yogurt, cover with a paper towel (to keep dust off) and keep in a warm place — for example, near the stove, radiator, or wherever there is a constant warm temperature. The milk will coagulate in approximately 24 hours.

Use 1 or 2 spoonfuls of soured milk as a culture for your next batch (use yogurt or commercial buttermilk only as a starting culture for the first batch).

Homemade Cottage Cheese
(Quark)

Warm Homemade Cultured Milk (see Index) to about 110°F by placing the container in a pan of warm water. When the milk has curdled, place a clean linen cloth or cheesecloth in a deep strainer and pour the curdled milk over it. Wait until all liquid whey has seeped through the strainer. What remains in the strainer is fresh, wholesome, and delicious Homemade Cottage Cheese. If the cheese is too hard, add a little sweet or sour cream, and stir. The higher the temperature, the harder the cheese, and vice versa. Raw Homemade Cottage Cheese (Quark) can be made by straining cultured milk through a fine cheesecloth, without warming it first.

Whey

Liquid whey, which will be a by-product of cottage cheese or quark, should never be discarded. It is an exceptionally wholesome and beneficial drink, loaded with important minerals.

Chilled, it can be used as a delicious beverage on a hot summer day, possibly with some lemon juice added. Or, it can be used in soups, borsch, and other recipes. In bread baking it can be used in the place of water.

Homemade Yogurt

Heat one quart of skim milk almost to boiling, then cool to room temperature. Add 2-3 tablespoons of plain yogurt. Stir well. Pour into a wide-mouth thermos bottle, cover, and let stand overnight. In lieu of a thermos bottle, you can use an ordinary glass jar, placing it in a pan of warm water over an electric burner switched on "warm" for 4-5 hours, then switch to "off" and let jar remain in warm water until the milk is solid. If you prefer, you can use a convenient automatic yogurt maker, which can be bought in health food stores.

Use 2-3 spoonfuls of your fresh homemade yogurt as a culture for the next batch.

Apple Cider

Apple cider is natural, raw, unprocessed, and unsweetened apple juice which is kept in a warm place until it is slightly fermented. During fermentation, some of the fruit sugar is changed into beneficial lactic acid.

To make your own apple cider, start with fresh, pure, unsweetened apple juice. Let stand in an uncorked bottle for a few days. You must be careful not to let fermentation continue too long, in which case the juice will eventually turn into wine, with gradually-increasing amounts of alcohol. As soon as the juice becomes bubbly, cork and store in the refrigerator.

Desserts

Oatmeal Carob Cookies

2 tablespoons honey
¼ cup butter
1 egg
1½ cup old-fashioned rolled oats, or steel-cut oats
¼ cup Homemade Carob Chips (see Index)

Cream the honey and butter together. Add the egg and mix well. Grind the oats in a blender or nut grinder to make a flour. Add the oat flour and the carob chips to the butter mixture and mix well. Drop by small spoonfuls onto a buttered baking sheet. Bake at 350°F for 10 minutes. Makes 1½ dozen.

Oatmeal Raisin Cookies

½ cup raisins
½ cup hot water
½ cup butter
¾ cup honey
2 eggs slightly beaten
1 teaspoon natural vanilla extract
2 cups whole wheat flour
1 teaspoon baking soda
1 teaspoon ground cinnamon
2 cups rolled oats

Soak the raisins in the hot water 20-30 minutes. Cream the butter and honey together. Add the eggs, vanilla, and the water the raisins were soaking in. Sift the dry ingredients together and add to the liquid ingredients. Add the raisins and rolled oats. Drop by spoonfuls 2 inches apart on a buttered baking sheet. Bake at 400°F, 8-10 minutes.

Oatmeal Currant Cookies

2 tablespoons honey
¼ cup butter
1 egg
¼ cup Homemade Applesauce (see Index)
1½ cups quick rolled oats
¼ cup currants
¼ teaspoon ground cinnamon

Cream the honey and butter together. Add the egg and applesauce and mix well. Grind the rolled oats in a blender or nut grinder to make a flour. Add the oat flour, currants and cinnamon to the batter and mix well. Drop by spoonfuls onto a buttered baking sheet. Bake at 350°F for 10 minutes. Makes 1½ dozen.

Baked Custard

2 cups milk
3 eggs, slightly beaten
3 tablespoons honey
dash of cinnamon (optional)

Mix the milk, eggs and honey together. Pour into a baking pan. Set the pan in a larger pan with ½-inch of water in the bottom. Bake in 350°F oven for 35-45 minutes, or until set. Sprinkle with cinnamon before serving. Makes 4 servings.

Blueberry Rye Pudding

1 cup rye flour
2 cups water
3 cups blueberries, fresh or frozen
¼ cup honey

Combine the rye flour and water in a saucepan; stir until well blended. Add the blueberries and honey. Place over medium heat and cook, stirring frequently, until the mixture comes to a boil. Reduce heat, cover and cook on low heat 30 minutes. Stir frequently. Serve with milk or cream. Makes 6 servings.

Banana Date Bars

½ cup butter
½ cup honey
1 large egg, slightly beaten
2 medium bananas, mashed
¾ cup chopped pitted dates
1 tablespoon lemon juice
1 cup whole wheat flour
½ teaspoon baking soda
½ teaspoon ground cinnamon
¼ teaspoon ground allspice
1 cup quick rolled oats
½ cup freshly shredded coconut

Cream the butter and honey together. Stir in the egg, mashed bananas, dates and lemon juice. Sift together the whole wheat flour, baking soda, cinnamon, and allspice and add to the liquid ingredients. Mix well. Stir in the rolled oats and coconut. Pour into a buttered 8 x 8-inch pan. Bake at 350°F for 20 minutes.

Apple Bars

½ cup rye flour
½ cup noninstant nonfat dry milk
½ teaspoon baking soda
¼ teaspoon ground cinnamon
2 large apples, shredded
2 teaspoons lemon juice
3 tablespoons honey

Sift together the rye flour, nonfat dry milk, baking soda and cinnamon. Combine the shredded apples, lemon juice and honey and add to the dry ingredients. Stir until well blended. Pour into a buttered 8 x 8-inch pan. Bake at 350°F for 15 minutes. Cool and cut into squares.

Date Bars

½ cup honey
½ cup butter
2 eggs, separated
1 teaspoon natural vanilla extract
1 cup water
1½ cups whole wheat flour
½ teaspoon baking soda
2 cups chopped, pitted dates
2 cups quick rolled oats

Cream the honey and butter together. Add the two egg yolks, vanilla and water. Mix thoroughly. Combine the flour and baking soda and add to the liquid ingredients. Add the dates and rolled oats and mix well. Beat the egg whites until stiff but not dry and fold into the batter. Pour into a buttered 9 x 13-inch baking pan. Bake at 350°F for 30-40 minutes. Cool and cut into squares.

Pineapple Carrot Cake

¾ cup butter
¾ cup honey
3 large eggs, separated
1 teaspoon natural vanilla extract
1 cup crushed, unsweetened pineapple
2 cups grated raw carrots
2 cups whole wheat flour
2½ teaspoons aluminum-free baking powder
1 teaspoon ground cinnamon

Cream the butter and honey. Beat in the egg yolks. Add the vanilla, crushed pineapple and carrots. Sift the whole wheat flour, baking powder and cinnamon together. Add to the liquid ingredients and beat until well mixed. Beat the egg whites until stiff, but not dry, and fold into the batter. Pour into a 9 x 13-inch pan. Bake at 350°F for 25-30 minutes. Serve plain or with a frosting.

Oatmeal Spice Cake

1½ cups whole wheat flour
2 teaspoons aluminum-free baking powder
1 teaspoon ground cinnamon
¼ teaspoon ground allspice
1 cup quick rolled oats
½ cup butter
½ cup honey
2 tablespoons unsulfured black strap molasses
2 large eggs
1 cup milk

Sift together the whole wheat flour, baking powder, cinnamon, and allspice. Stir in the rolled oats. Cream the butter and honey together. Beat in the eggs and add the milk. Stir the dry ingredients into the liquid ingredients and beat until well blended. Bake in a buttered and floured 9-inch round cake pan at 350°F for 30-35 minutes.

Carrot Cake

¾ cup butter
¾ cup honey
3 large eggs, separated
1 teaspoon natural vanilla extract
¼ cup hot water
2 cups grated raw carrots
2 cups whole wheat flour
2½ teaspoons aluminum-free baking powder
1 teaspoon ground cinnamon

Cream the butter and honey. Beat in the egg yolks. Add the vanilla, hot water, and grated carrots. Sift the whole wheat flour, baking powder and cinnamon together. Add to the liquid ingredients and beat until well mixed. Beat the egg whites until stiff but not dry, and fold into the cake batter. Pour into a buttered 9 x 13-inch cake pan. Bake at 350°F for 25-30 minutes. Serve plain or with vanilla or cream cheese frosting.

Orange Bread

½ cup honey
¼ cup butter
2 eggs
¾ cup orange juice
2 cups whole wheat flour
2½ teaspoons aluminum-free baking powder

Cream together the honey and butter. Add the eggs and orange juice. Sift together the whole wheat flour and baking powder, and stir into the creamed mixture. Pour into a small loaf pan. Bake at 350°F for 25-30 minutes.

Pumpkin Pie

2 cups pureed cooked pumpkin
2 eggs
½ cup honey
1 teaspoon ground cinnamon
¼ teaspoon ground ginger
¼ teaspoon ground allspice
1½ cups light cream or milk
one 9-inch unbaked pie crust (see Index)

Combine the pumpkin, eggs, honey and spices and mix until smooth. Add the cream or milk. Pour into the pie shell. Bake at 450°F for 15 minutes. Reduce heat to 350°F and bake 30 minutes or until a knife inserted in the center comes out clean. Cool and serve.

Karjalan Rahka Piirakka
(Karelian Cheese Pie)

3 cups creamed cottage cheese
3 tablespoons honey
2 eggs
Rye Pie Crust (see Index)

Combine the cottage cheese, honey and eggs in a blender and blend until smooth. Prepare the rye pie crust and place in a 9-inch pie pan. Pour in the cheese filling. Bake at 400°F for 5 minutes. Reduce the heat to 350°F and bake 25 minutes or until done. Served hot or cold.

Rye Pie Crust

1 cup rye flour
6 tablespoons water
sea salt to flavor (optional)

Stir the water and sea salt into the flour with a fork until it forms a ball. Roll out one pie crust ⅛-inch thick.

Whole Wheat Pie Crust

1¾ cups whole wheat flour
¼ teaspoon sea salt (optional)
½ cup chilled butter
3 tablespoons cold water

Combine the flour and salt. Cut in half of the butter with a pastry blender until mixture resembles corn meal. Cut in the remaining butter until dough particles are the size of peas. Add the water one tablespoon at a time and stir until the dough is moist enough to form into a ball. Divide the dough and roll out two crusts ⅛-inch thick.

Carob Fudge

¾ cup soft unsalted butter
½ cup honey
1 teaspoon natural vanilla extract
2 tablespoons water
1 cup noninstant nonfat dry milk
¼ cup carob powder
2 cups chopped nuts and seeds (pecans, walnuts, sunflower seeds, pumpkin seeds, etc.)

Cream together the butter and honey. Add the vanilla and water. Combine the nonfat dry milk and carob powder and add to the butter and honey mixture. Mix on high speed for several minutes. Stir in the chopped nuts and seeds. Spread in a buttered 8 x 8-inch pan. Chill and cut into squares.

Applesauce Bread

½ cup butter
½ cup honey
2 eggs, slightly beaten
1 cup Homemade Applesauce (see Index)
¼ cup unsulfured raisins
2 cups whole wheat flour
2½ teaspoons aluminum-free baking powder
½ teaspoon ground cinnamon
¼ teaspoon ground allspice

Cream the butter and honey. Add the eggs, applesauce and raisins. Sift together the whole wheat flour, baking powder, cinnamon and allspice and add to the liquid ingredients. Blend well. Pour into two buttered 7½ x 3½ x 2¼-inch loaf pans. Bake at 350°F for 30-35 minutes.

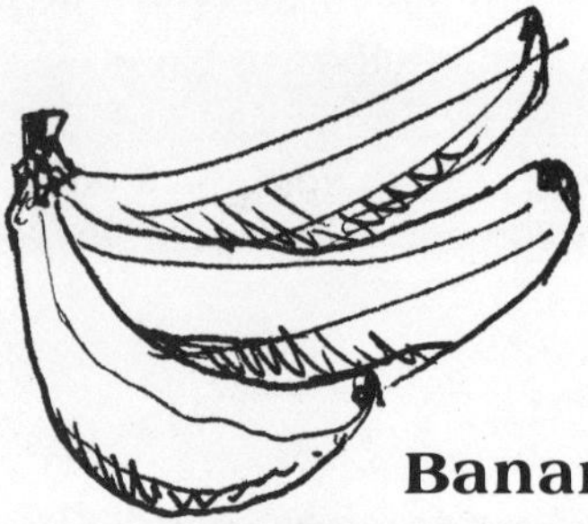

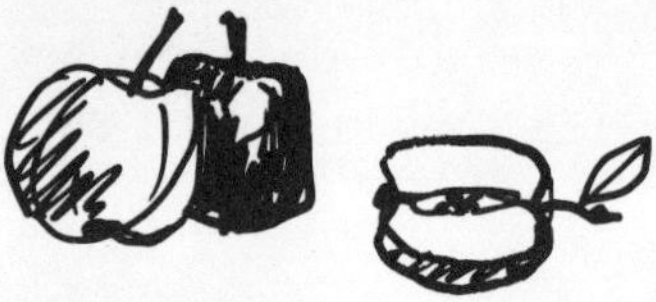

Banana Bread

½ cup honey
½ cup butter
2 eggs
1 teaspoon natural vanilla extract
2 ripe bananas, mashed
2 cups whole wheat flour
½ cup oat flour
2½ teaspoons aluminum-free baking powder

Cream the butter and honey together. Add the eggs, vanilla and mashed bananas. Mix well. Sift the whole wheat flour, oat flour and baking powder together and add to the banana mixture. Blend thoroughly. Pour into a loaf pan. Bake at 350°F for 40-50 minutes.

Zucchini Bread

½ cup butter
½ cup honey
2 large eggs
1 cup grated raw zucchini
1 teaspoon natural vanilla extract
2 cups whole wheat flour
2½ teaspoons aluminum-free baking powder
1 teaspoon ground cinnamon

Cream together the butter and honey. Beat in the eggs. Add the zucchini and vanilla. Sift together the whole wheat flour, baking powder and cinnamon and add to the liquid ingredients. Beat until well mixed. Pour into 2 buttered 7½ x 3½ x 2¼-inch loaf pans. Bake at 350°F for 25-30 minutes.

Zucchini Cookies

¾ cup butter
¾ cup honey
2 eggs
2 cups grated raw zucchini
2 teaspoons lemon juice
2 teaspoons natural vanilla extract
2 cups whole wheat flour
2 teaspoons ground cinnamon
2 teaspoons baking soda
2 cups quick rolled oats

Cream together the butter, honey and eggs. Add the zucchini and vanilla. Sift the whole wheat flour, cinnamon and baking soda together and add to the liquid ingredients. Mix well. Stir in the rolled oats. Drop by spoonfuls onto a buttered baking sheet. Bake at 350°F for 8-10 minutes. Makes 3½ dozen.

Vanilla Frosting

¾ cup soft, unsalted butter
½ cup honey
2 teaspoons natural vanilla extract
2 tablespoons water
1 cup noninstant nonfat dry milk

Cream the honey and butter together. Add the vanilla and water. Stir in the nonfat dry milk and mix on high speed for several minutes. Spread on cooled cake. Makes 2 cups frosting.

Carob Frosting

¾ cup soft, unsalted butter
½ cup honey
1 teaspoon vanilla extract
2 tablespoons water
1 cup noninstant nonfat dry milk
¼ cup carob powder

Cream the honey and butter together. Add the vanilla and water. Combine the nonfat dry milk and carob powder and add to the honey and butter mixture. Mix well on high speed for several minutes. Spread on cooled cake. Makes 2 cups frosting.

Homemade Ice Cream

2½ cups raw sweet cream
2 large eggs, separated
½ cup raw honey
1 teaspoon pure natural vanilla extract

Separate eggs. Beat egg yolks and honey together. Add the cream and vanilla and stir well. Place in ice cube trays and freeze. When solidly frozen, remove from trays and put in a mixing bowl. As it thaws, mix until smooth, adding beaten egg whites as you mix. Replace in trays and refreeze.

"Ice cream" can also be made by substituting yogurt for cream. For flavors other than vanilla, add carob flour, chopped fruits, or berries for desired flavor of ice cream.

Bran Muffins

6 tablespoons butter
¾ cup honey
1 egg (optional)
1 cup buttermilk
1 cup bran
2 cups whole wheat flour
1½ teaspoons baking soda
¼ teaspoon sea salt (optional)
½ teaspoon allspice
¾ cup unsulfured raisins

Cream butter and honey. Add egg, buttermilk, and bran, and mix well. Sift together the whole wheat flour, baking soda, allspice, and sea salt. Add dry ingredients and raisins to liquid ingredients and mix just until blended. Fill buttered muffin tins 2/3 full. Bake at 350°F for 20-25 minutes. Makes 1½ dozen.

No-Bake Carob Cookies

½ cup honey
½ cup butter
½ cup milk
3 tablespoons carob powder
½ cup sesame Tahini
1 teaspoon natural vanilla extract
3 cups quick rolled oats
½ cup chopped nuts

Combine the honey, butter, milk and carob powder in a saucepan. Bring to a boil and boil one minute. Remove from heat. Beat in the Tahini, vanilla, rolled oats and chopped nuts. Drop by spoonfuls onto a baking sheet and chill in the refrigerator. Makes 2 dozen.

Homemade Carob Chips

¼ cup butter
½ cup honey
2 teaspoons liquid lecithin (sold in health food stores)
1 teaspoon natural vanilla extract
2 cups noninstant nonfat dry milk
½ cup carob powder

Cream together the butter and honey. Add the lecithin and vanilla. Sift the carob powder and nonfat dry milk together and stir into the butter and honey. The mixture will be stiff. Knead it with your hands until it forms a smooth ball. Roll out into long thin strips, ¼ inch in diameter. Chill in the refrigerator several hours. Cut the strips into small chips. Store in the refrigerator. Makes 2 cups of chips.

NOTES:

Snacks for Children

Halvah

1 cup hulled sesame seeds

2 teaspoons honey, preferably coagulated solid honey

Grind sesame seeds in a small electric seed grinder. Pour sesame meal into a small bowl and knead honey into the meal with a large spoon until honey is well mixed in and the halvah acquires the consistency of a hard dough. Serve it as is, or make small balls and roll them in whole sesame seeds or sunflower seeds. This is an excellent, nutritious, and delicious candy, loved by children and grown-ups alike.

Tropical Yogurt Delight

½ banana
3 tablespoons fresh papaya
2 tablespoons yogurt
few drops lemon or lime juice

Mash all ingredients together with a fork or potato masher.

Juice Popsicles

Pour fresh juice (apple, orange, grape, watermelon, etc.) into ice cube trays or popsicle holders and freeze.

Frozen Yogurt Treats

Prepare one of the recipes below, spoon into popsicle holders or ice cube trays and freeze. Each recipe makes approximately 6 popsicles.

1. *Applesauce:*

    1 cup plain yogurt
    1 cup applesauce
    1 tablespoon honey

    Combine all ingredients.

2. *Banana:*

    2 medium bananas
    1 teaspoon lemon juice
    1 cup plain yogurt

    Mash the bananas with the lemon juice. Stir in the yogurt.

3. *Carob-Banana:*

    2 medium bananas
    1 teaspoon lemon juice
    1 cup plain yogurt
    2 tablespoons carob powder

    Mash the bananas with the lemon juice. Blend the yogurt and carob powder together and stir into the mashed bananas.

4. *Peach:*

2 large ripe peaches, sliced
1 teaspoon lemon juice
1 cup plain yogurt

Puree the peaches with the lemon juice in a blender. Stir in the yogurt.

5. *Berry:*

2 cups fresh or frozen berries (strawberries, raspberries, blueberries, blackberries, boysenberries, etc.)
1 tablespoon honey
1 cup plain yogurt

Puree the berries with the honey in a blender. Stir in the yogurt.

Nutty Fruit Bars

1/3 cup honey
1/3 cup raisins
¼ cup chopped pitted dates
¼ cup chopped dried apricots
1/3 cup raw sunflower seeds
½ cup raw nuts
1 cup hulled sesame seeds

Melt the honey in a saucepan. Stir in the dried fruits, nuts and seeds. Make sure all fruits are unsulfured. Mix well and pour into a buttered 9-inch pan. Allow to dry at room temperature 3-4 hours. Cut into bars. Makes 2 dozen bars.

No-Bake Date Cookies

½ cup honey
2 beaten eggs
1 cup chopped dates
1 cup quick rolled oats
1 cup puffed rice
1 cup chopped nuts

Mix the honey, eggs, and dates in a saucepan. Cook over medium heat 5 minutes, stirring constantly. Remove from heat. Stir in the rolled oats, puffed rice and nuts. Shape into 1-inch balls and cool. Makes 2½ dozen.

Carob Sesame Balls

½ cup honey
½ cup soft butter
1 teaspoon natural vanilla extract
¾ cup noninstant nonfat dry milk
¼ cup carob powder
½ cup hulled raw sesame seeds

Cream the honey and butter together and add the vanilla. Combine the nonfat dry milk and carob powder. Add to the butter and honey mixture. Blend well. Shape into ½-inch balls and roll in sesame seeds. Chill. Makes 2 dozen balls.

Popcorn

Contrary to popular belief, you *can* make popcorn without oil, butter, or salt — and, thus, make it a healthful snack for children or grown-ups.

You can make it in a regular popcorn popper (the kind that looks like two tin pans are pressed against each other) as long as you keep over stove or fire shaking gently. You can also use hot air popcorn machine. In both methods, use only dry popcorn without any fat.

Tahini-Banana Snack

½ cup sesame Tahini
1 medium banana, mashed
1 tablespoon honey
¼ cup noninstant nonfat dry milk
¼ cup freshly grated coconut

Combine the Tahini, honey, banana, and nonfat dry milk and mix well. Shape into 1-inch balls and roll in the grated coconut. Makes 1 dozen balls.

Honey Wheat Crackers

Whole Wheat Pie Crust (see Index)
honey
cinnamon

Prepare the whole wheat pie crust dough. Roll out on the back side of a cookie sheet. Spread a thin layer of honey over the dough. Sprinkle with cinnamon. Prick with a fork, cut into squares and bake at 425°F for 10-12 minutes.

Dried Fruit Mix

½ pound pitted dates
¼ pound dried apricots
¼ pound pitted prunes
¼ pound raisins
¼ pound dried figs
½ cup hulled sesame seeds

Put the dried fruits through a food chopper, alternating fruits, to mix them. Form ½-inch balls and roll in sesame seeds. Make sure all fruits are unsulfured.

Beverages

Vegetable Broth

2 large potatoes, chopped or sliced to approximately ½-inch pieces
1 cup carrots, shredded or sliced
1 cup celery, stalks and leaves, chopped or shredded
1 medium-sized onion
2-3 cloves of garlic
1 cup any other available vegetable (optional)
Note: avoid oxalic-acid rich greens (see Formula P & L)
dash of cayenne pepper

Place all vegetables in a pot and add 1½ quarts of water. Cover and cook slowly for about 30 minutes. Let stand another 30 minutes, strain, and serve. If not used immediately, keep in refrigerator, and reheat before serving.

Vegetable broth is an alkaline, cleansing, mineral-rich drink which is used by biological clinics during juice fasting, especially in the treatment of rheumatic diseases. Lactating mothers can also use this broth to stimulate breast milk production.

Excelsior

1 cup of Vegetable Broth (see Index)
1 tablespoon whole flaxseed
1 tablespoon wheat bran

Soak flaxseed and wheat bran in Vegetable Broth overnight. Refrigerate. In the morning, warm it up, stir well, and drink — seeds and all. Do not chew the seeds, swallow them whole. Excelsior is especially beneficial for people with constipation problems. It helps to restore normal peristaltic rhythm. When used during fasting, Excelsior must be strained.

Homemade Tomato Juice

12 medium tomatoes, quartered
2 stalks celery with leaves, chopped
1 slice onion
3 sprigs parsley
½ cup water
dash of sea salt
dash of paprika

Simmer vegetables and water on low heat for 30 minutes. Strain and add sea salt and paprika. Chill and serve.

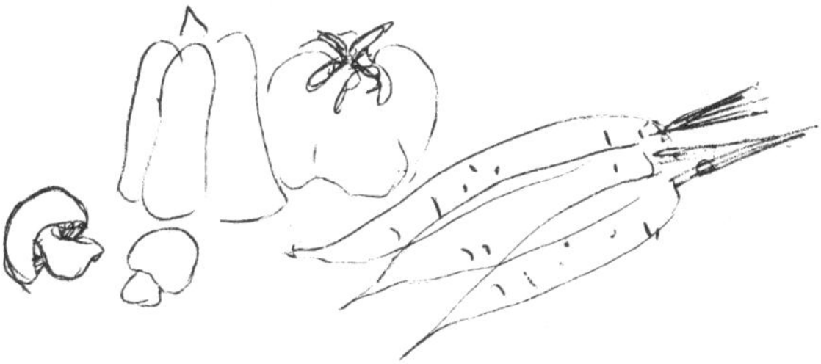

Formula P and L
(Green Juice Cocktail)

1 cup any available garden greens: parsley, lettuce, kale, turnip tops, wheat grass, alfalfa — any or all. Note: avoid such oxalic acid-rich greens as spinach and use only small quantities of cabbage-family greens, such as broccoli, Swiss chard, kale, etc., when making green juice cocktail

A small quantity of such strong-tasting greens as watercress, mint, radish tops, chives, etc., can be used. Even wild greens such as dandelion or common nettle are excellent in small quantities

2 stalks celery

1 glass freshly-made carrot and beet juice (80% carrot, 20% beet)

Pour carrot and beet juice in your electric blender and switch on low. Feed greens into the blender slowly. When all greens are in, switch on high and liquify well. You may add a pinch of kelp powder and/or other natural herbs or flavorings, if you wish.

Drink slowly; salivate well. Green juice cocktail is best taken ½ to 1 hour before lunch or dinner. Two or 3 ounces is sufficient, but a full 6-ounce glass is okay if taken 1 hour before a meal.

This is one of the most health-building juices there is; it is also an excellent supplementary drink during pregnancy and lactation. It is loaded with chlorophyll, vitamins, minerals, trace elements, enzymes, and other vital nutrients. Lactating mothers will find that it will aid in breast-milk production, especially if plenty of fresh alfalfa is used. Alfalfa is an excellent stimulant for the milk-producing glands.

Milk Shakes

Banana

1 cup milk or yogurt
2 ripe bananas

Combine the bananas and milk in a blender and blend until smooth. Serve immediately. Makes approximately 2 cups.

Banana-Berry

1 cup milk or yogurt
2 ripe bananas
1½ cups raspberries or strawberries

Combine all ingredients in a blender and blend until smooth. Makes approximately 3 cups.

Banana-Date

1 cup milk or yogurt
1 ripe banana
½ cup chopped dates

Combine all ingredients in a blender and blend until smooth. Makes approximately 2 cups.

Fortified Banana-Date

1 cup milk or yogurt
1 ripe banana
¼ cup chopped dates
1 tablespoon fresh wheat germ
1 tablespoon brewer's yeast

Combine all ingredients in a blender and blend until smooth. Makes approximately 2 cups.

Apple Juice Drink

1 quart chilled apple juice

1 quart chilled naturally carbonated water

Combine the juice and water. Serve at once.

Vegetable Juice Cocktail

½ cup fresh carrot juice
2 cups Tomato Juice (see Index)
¼ cup chopped celery
1 tablespoon chopped green onion
1 sprig parsley

Place all ingredients in the blender and blend over high speed. Serve immediately. Makes 4-6 servings.

Airola Shake

½ tablespoon brewer's yeast powder or flakes
¼ teaspoon calcium lactate or bone meal powder
1 tablespoon flax seeds, hulled sesame seeds, chia seeds, or sunflower seeds
1 tablespoon wheat bran or rice polishings, or fresh wheat germ
1 teaspoon lecithin powder or granules
1 teaspoon honey
1 teaspoon bee pollen
1½ cups certified raw milk
1 raw egg yolk (optional)
1 banana and/or 1 tablespoon carob powder

Grind sesame, flax, chia, or sunflower seeds together with bran, rice polishings, or wheat germ in an electric seed grinder. If you use wheat germ, make sure it is 100% fresh, non-rancid.

Place all ingredients in a blender, and run on high until mixture is smooth — approximately 15 seconds. Add more milk if needed. Makes 1 large glass of supernutritious and rejuvenating drink.

In my Optimum Diet, this shake can be used as a replacement for either breakfast or lunch. You can take your regular vitamin supplements with it.

For people on the go (as many are these days), a liquid breakfast may be the answer to being sure of getting adequate nutrition in spite of a busy lifestyle.

Homemade Cranberry Juice

2 cups fresh cranberries
2 cups water
¼ to 1/3 cup honey
¼ cup orange juice or 1 tablespoon lemon juice

Cook the cranberries in water till the skins pop open (about 5 minutes). Then mash, strain, bring to a boil, and add honey. Cook for two more minutes. Let cool and add orange or lemon juice. Cool thoroughly before serving.

Fresh Pineapple Juice

1 ripe pineapple

Peel and cube the pineapple. Blend on low speed for several minutes and then on high speed. Water may be added to dilute the juice. Serve immediately. Makes approximately 3 cups.

Pineapple-Banana Shake

2 cups freshly made pineapple juice (see Index)
2 ripe bananas, sliced

Combine the pineapple juice and the sliced bananas in a blender. Blend on high speed. Serve immediately with a sprig of mint. Makes approximately 3 cups.

NOTES:

Section III

Charts & Tables

Complete Vitamin Guide

Common vitamins, their functions, deficiency symptoms, and natural sources.

VITAMIN A

Known as Anti-Ophthalmic Vitamin. Usually measured in USP units, or International Units (IU), which for vitamin A are identical.

FUNCTIONS

Builds resistance to all kinds of infections. It is a "membrane conditioner" — it keeps mucous linings and membranes of the body in healthy condition. Prevents eye diseases, counteracts night blindness and weak eyesight by helping in formation of visual purple in the eye. Plays vital role in nourishing skin and hair. Essential during pregnancy and lactation. Helps to maintain testicular tissue in a healthy state. Promotes growth and vitality. Aids in secretion of gastric juices and in digestion of proteins. By improving the stability of tissue in cell walls it helps to prevent premature aging and senility; increases life expectancy and extends youthfulness. Protects against the damaging effect of polluted air. Increases the permeability of blood capillaries contributing to better tissue oxygenation.

DEFICIENCY SYMPTOMS

Prolonged deficiency may result in eye inflammations, poor vision, nightblindness; increased susceptibility to infections, especially in the respiratory tract; frequent colds; retarded growth in children; lack of appetite and vigor; defective teeth and gums; rough, scaly and dry skin, and such skin disorders as acne, pimples, boils, premature wrinkles and psoriasis; dry, dull hair, dandruff and excessive hair loss; nails which peel or are ridged; poor senses of taste and smell.

NATURAL SOURCES

Colored fruits and vegetables, particularly carrots, green leafy vegetables (such as kale, parsley, turnip greens, and spinach), melon, squash, apricots, yams, tomatoes, eggs, summer butter, fertile eggs, liver, and whole milk. The richest natural source is fish liver oils.

VITAMIN B_1

Thiamine, Thiamine Chloride, Thiamine HCl. Measured in milligrams (mg).

FUNCTIONS

Known as anti-beriberi, anti-neuritic and anti-aging vitamin. Essential for effective protein metabolism. Promotes growth, protects heart muscle, stimulates brain action. Indispensable for the health of the entire nervous system. Aids in digestion and metabolism of carbohydrates. Improves peristaltis and helps prevent constipation. Helps maintain normal red blood count. Protects against the damaging effect of lead poisoning. Prevents edema, or fluid retention, in connection with heart condition. Improves circulation. Prevents fatigue and increases stamina. Helps prevent premature aging.

DEFICIENCY SYMPTOMS

Deficiency may lead to loss of appetite; muscular weakness; slow heart beat; irritability; defective hydrochloric acid production in the stomach with accompanied digestive disorders; chronic constipation; loss of weight; diabetes; mental depression and nervous exhaustion. Prolonged, gross deficiency can cause beriberi, neuritis, edema. Deficiency can be induced by excess of alcohol and dietary sugar, and the excess of processed and refined foods.

NATURAL SOURCES

Brewer's yeast; wheat germ and wheat bran; rice polishings; most whole-grain cereals, especially millet, oats and buckwheat; all seeds, especially sunflower seeds, and nuts, and nut butters; beans, especially soybeans; milk and milk products; and such vegetables as beets, potatoes and leafy green vegetables.

VITAMIN B_2

Riboflavin, Vitamin G. Measured in milligrams (mg).

FUNCTIONS

Essential for growth and general health. Essential for healthy eyes, skin, nails and hair. May help in prevention of some types of cataracts.

DEFICIENCY SYMPTOMS

Deficiency may result in bloodshot eyes; abnormal sensitivity to light; itching and burning of the eyes; inflammations in the mouth; sore, burning tongue (magenta-colored tongue); cracks on the lips and in the corners of the mouth; dull hair (or oily hair); oily skin; premature wrinkles on face and arms; eczema; split nails; and such aging symptoms as "disappearing" upper lip. Can be a contributing cause to such disorders as seborrhea, anemia, vaginal itching, cataracts and ulcers.

NATURAL SOURCES

Milk, cheese, whole grains, brewer's yeast, torula yeast, wheat germ, millet, almonds, sunflower seeds, liver, cooked leafy vegetables, fruit.

VITAMIN B_3

Niacin, Nicotinic Acid, Niacinamide, Niacin Amide, Nicotinamide. Measured in milligrams (mg). Niacinamide is similar in effect and therapeutic value to niacin, but does not cause burning, flushing and itching of the skin that usually occurs when the isolated form of niacin is taken.

FUNCTIONS

Anti-pellagra vitamin. Important for proper circulation and for healthy functioning of the nervous system. Maintains normal functions of gastro-intestinal tract. Essential for proper protein and carbohydrate metabolism. Helps maintain healthy skin. May prevent migraine headaches. Dilates blood vessels and increases the flow of blood to the peripheral capillary system. Often prescribed in cases of cold feet and hands. In mega-doses (massive doses), niacin has been successfully used in the treatment of schizophrenia.

DEFICIENCY SYMPTOMS

Mild deficiency may cause coated tongue, canker sores, irritability, nervousness, skin lesions, diarrhea, forgetfulness, insomnia, chronic headaches, digestive disorders, anemia. Severe, prolonged deficiency may cause pellagra, neurasthenia, mental disturbances, depression, mental dullness, disorientation and mental disease.

NATURAL SOURCES

Brewer's yeast, torula yeast, wheat germ, rice bran and rice polishings, nuts, sunflower seeds, peanuts, whole wheat products, brown rice, green vegetables, liver, eggs.

VITAMIN B_6

Pyridoxine, Pyridoxine HCl. Measured in milligrams (mg).

FUNCTIONS

Aids in food assimilation and in protein and fat metabolism, particularly in metabolism of essential fatty acids. Activates many enzymes and enzyme systems. Involved in the production of antibodies which protect against bacterial invasions. Essential for synthesis and proper action of DNA and RNA. Helps in the healthy function of the nervous system and brain. Important for normal reproductive processes and healthy pregnancies. Prevents nervous and skin disorders, such as acne. Protects against degenerative diseases, such as elevated cholesterol, some types of heart disease and diabetes. Prevents tooth decay. Has been used as natural diuretic. Some studies show that it can prevent or lessen epileptic seizures. Helps prevent and relieve premenstrual edema; also effective in overweight problems caused by water retention. Vitamin B_6 regulates the balance between the minerals sodium and potassium in the body, which is of tremendous importance for vital body functions. Cases of Parkinson's Disease have responded to B_6 injections (in combination with magnesium). B_6 is required for the absorption of vitamin B_{12} and for the production of hydrochloric acid.

DEFICIENCY SYMPTOMS

Deficiency of B_6 may cause anemia, edema, mental depression, skin disorders, sore mouth and lips, halitosis, nervousness, eczema, kidney stones, inflammation of the colon, insomnia, tooth decay, irritability, loss of muscular control, migraine headaches, diseases of old age and premature senility.

NATURAL SOURCES

Brewer's yeast, bananas, avocados, wheat germ, wheat bran, buckwheat, soybeans, garbanzos, walnuts, blackstrap molasses, cantaloupe, cabbage, milk, egg yolks, liver, green leafy vegetables, green peppers, carrots and peanuts. Raw foods contain more B_6 than cooked foods. Cooking and food processing destroys vitamin B_6.

BIOTIN

Vitamin H. Measured in micrograms (mcg).

FUNCTIONS

Involved in metabolism of proteins and fats. Related to hair growth and healthy hair. Prevents hair loss. Antiseptic. It has been used in treatment of malaria.

DEFICIENCY SYMPTOMS

Deficiency may cause eczema, dandruff, hair loss, seborrhea, skin disorders, such as pallor, heart abnormalities, lung infections, anemia, loss of appetite, extreme fatigue, confusion, mental depression, drowsiness and hallucinations.

NATURAL SOURCES

Best and richest natural source is brewer's yeast. Also: walnuts, pecans, almonds, oatmeal, barley, unpolished rice, soybeans, liver, kidneys. Biotin is also normally produced in the intestines if there is sufficient amount of healthy intestinal flora.

FOLIC ACID

Vitamin B_9. Pteroylglutamic acid. Folate. Measured in milligrams (mg).

FUNCTIONS

As a co-worker with vitamin B_{12}, folic acid is essential for the formation of red blood cells. Necessary for the growth and division of all body cells and for the production of RNA and DNA, the nucleic acids that carry the hereditary patterns. Aids in protein metabolism and contributes to normal growth. Essential for healing processes. Helps build antibodies to prevent and heal infections. Essential for the health of skin and hair. Helps prevent premature graying of the hair. Its need is indicated in diarrhea, dropsy, stomach ulcers and menstrual problems. It has been used in treatment of atherosclerosis, circulation problems, anemia, radiation injuries and burns, and in treatment of sprue, a tropical nutritional deficiency disease, whose symptoms are anemia and acute diarrhea.

DEFICIENCY SYMPTOMS

Deficiency of folic acid may cause nutritional megaloblastic anemia of pregnancy, serious skin disorders, loss of hair, impaired circulation, a grayish-brown skin pigmentation, fatigue, mental depression, reproductive disorders, such as spontaneous abortions, difficult labor, high infant death rate. Also, loss of libido in males.

NATURAL SOURCES

Deep green leafy vegetables, broccoli, asparagus, lima beans, blackeyed peas, all beans, Irish potatoes, spinach, lettuce, brewer's yeast, wheat germ, mushrooms, nuts, peanuts, liver.

PABA

Para-amino-benzoic acid, Vitamin B_x. Measured in milligrams (mg).

FUNCTIONS

A growth promoting factor. Stimulates metabolism and all vital life processes, possibly in conjunction with folic acid. Prevents skin changes due to aging. Prevents graying of the hair. Has been used, in combination with pantothenic acid, choline and folic acid, in treatment of gray hair, with some success. Essential for healthy skin. Soothes the pain of burns and sunburns. When added to a salve and applied to the skin, may protect against sunburn, and even prevent skin cancer. Helpful in a variety of skin disorders, including eczemas and lupus erythematosus.

DEFICIENCY SYMPTOMS

Deficiency may cause extreme fatigue, eczema, anemia, gray hair, reproductive disorders, infertility, vitiligo and loss of libido.

NATURAL SOURCES

Brewer's yeast, mushrooms, bran, whole grain products, milk, eggs, yogurt, sunflower seeds, wheat germ, molasses and liver. PABA is also synthesized by friendly bacteria in the healthy intestines.

PANTOTHENIC ACID

Vitamin B_5, Calcium Pantothenate. Measured in milligrams (mg).

FUNCTIONS

Involved in all vital functions of the body. Stimulates adrenal glands and increases production of cortisone and other adrenal hormones. Primarily used as an anti-stress factor. Protects against most physical and mental stresses and toxins. Increases vitality. Wards off infections and speeds recovery from ill health. Helps in maintaining normal growth and development of the central nervous system. Can help prevent premature aging, especially wrinkles and other signs of aging. Can help protect against damage caused by excessive radiation.

DEFICIENCY SYMPTOMS

Deficiency can cause chronic fatigue, increased tendency for infections, graying and loss of hair, mental depression, irritability, dizziness, muscular weakness, stomach distress and constipation. May lead to skin disorders, retarded growth, painful and burning feet, insomnia, muscle cramps, adrenal exhaustion, low blood sugar (hypoglycemia) and low blood pressure. Considered to be one of the causes of allergies and asthma.

NATURAL SOURCES

Brewer's yeast, wheat germ, wheat bran, royal jelly, whole-grain breads and cereals, green vegetables, peas and beans, peanuts, crude molasses, liver, egg yolk, mushrooms, salmon, pollen.

CHOLINE

A member of the vitamin B-complex. One of the "Lipotropic Factors." Measured in milligrams (mg).

FUNCTIONS

The most important function of choline is in its teamwork with inositol as a part of lecithin. Essential for proper fat metabolism. Lecithin helps to digest, absorb and carry in the blood fats and fat-soluble vitamins: A, D, E and K. Necessary for the synthesis of nucleic acids, DNA and RNA. Minimizes excessive deposits of fat and cholesterol in the liver and arteries. Essential for the health of myelin sheaths of the nerves. Regulates and improves liver and gallbladder function. Necessary for the manufacture of a substance in the blood called phospholipid. Choline is useful in treatment of nephritis. Can prevent formation of gallstones. Useful in reducing high blood pressure. Has been used to treat atherosclerosis, kidney damage, glaucoma and myasthenia gravis.

DEFICIENCY SYMPTOMS

Prolonged deficiency may cause high blood pressure, cirrhosis and the fatty degeneration of the liver, atherosclerosis and hardening of arteries.

NATURAL SOURCES

Granular or liquid lecithin (made from soybeans), brewer's yeast, wheat germ, egg yolk, liver, green leafy vegetables and most whole grains, beans and peas.

Choline can also be manufactured in the body of healthy individuals receiving optimum nutrition, particularly adequate amounts of vitamins B_6 and B_{12}, magnesium, folic acid and methionine (an amino acid).

INOSITOL

A member of B-complex vitamin family. Measured in milligrams (mg).

FUNCTIONS

Vital for hair growth and can prevent thinning hair and baldness. As a part of lecithin, participates in all of its activity. Important for healthy heart muscle. Can help reduce blood cholesterol. Has been used in the treatment of obesity and schizophrenia (as part of brain cell nutrition).

DEFICIENCY SYMPTOMS

Deficiency may contribute to hair loss, constipation, eczema (dermatitis) eye abnormalities and high blood cholesterol.

NATURAL SOURCES

Brewer's yeast, wheat germ, lecithin, unprocessed whole grains, especially oatmeal, wheat and corn, nuts, milk, crude unrefined molasses, citrus fruits and most beans and peas.

VITAMIN B_{12}

Cobalamin, Cyanocobalamin. Also known as the "Red-Vitamin." Usually measured in micrograms (mcg).

FUNCTIONS

Essential for the production and regeneration of red blood cells. Prevents anemia. Promotes growth in children. Involved in many vital metabolic and enzymatic processes, facilitates iron absorption.

DEFICIENCY SYMPTOMS

Deficiency may cause nutritional and particularly pernicious anemia, poor appetite and growth in children, chronic fatigue, sore mouth, feelings of numbness or stiffness, loss of mental energy, difficulty in concentrating, mental depression.

NATURAL SOURCES

Milk, eggs, most natural cheeses, whey, liver, fish, fortified brewer's yeast, sunflower seeds, comfrey leaves, kelp, bananas, peanuts, concord grapes, raw wheat germ, pollen, spirulina.

Since B_{12} is present in vegetable foods only in small amounts, vegetarians are advised to use milk and/or fortified brewer's yeast, or take vitamin B_{12} in a tablet form as a supplement. B_{12} is also produced in the intestines of healthy individuals.

VITAMIN B_{13}

Orotic Acid.

FUNCTIONS

Essential for the biosynthesis of nucleic acid. Vital for the regenerative processes in cells. Considered to be of special value in the treatment of multiple sclerosis.

DEFICIENCY SYMPTOMS

Deficiencies are not known, but it is believed that they may lead to liver disorders and cell degeneration and premature aging; also overall degeneration as in multiple sclerosis.

NATURAL SOURCES

Present in whey portion of milk, particularly in soured milk.

VITAMIN B_{15}

Pangamic acid, Calcium Pangamate, N.N-Dimethylglyeine (DMG). Measured in milligrams (mg).

FUNCTIONS

Increases the body's tolerance to hypoxia, or insufficient oxygen supply to the tissues and cells. Helps to regulate fat metabolism, stimulates the glandular and nervous systems and is helpful in the treatment of heart disease, angina, elevated blood cholesterol, impaired circulation and premature aging. Can help protect against the damaging effect of carbon monoxide poisoning. B_{15} is also a good detoxicant.

DEFICIENCY SYMPTOMS

May cause diminished oxygenation of cells, hypoxia, heart disease, glandular and nervous disorders.

NATURAL SOURCES

Whole grains, seeds, nuts, wheat germ, sunflower seeds, whole brown rice, yeast, corn grits, pumpkin seeds, oats.

VITAMIN C

Ascorbic acid, Sodium aseorbate, Cevitamin acid. Usually measured in milligrams (mg). In Europe, occasionally in Units: 1 mg. equals 20 Units.

FUNCTIONS

Essential for the healthy condition of collagen, "intercellular cement". Involved in all the vital functions of all glands and organs. Necessary for healthy teeth, gums and bones. Strengthens all connective tissues. Essential for proper functioning of adrenal and thyroid glands. *Promotes healing in every condition of ill health.* Helps prevent and cure the common cold. Protects against all forms of stress: physical and mental. Protects against harmful effects of toxic chemicals in environment, food, water and air. Counteracts the toxic effect of drugs. Has been used successfully in rattlesnake bite, and as a general natural antibiotic. Specific against fever, all sorts of infections and gastro-intestinal disorders. General detoxicant. Specific protector against toxic effects of cadmium.

DEFICIENCY SYMPTOMS

Deficiency may lead to tooth decay, soft gums (pyorrhea), skin hemorrhages, capillary weakness, deterioration in collagen, anemia, slow healing of sores and wounds, premature aging, thyroid insufficiency, lowered resistance to all infections and toxic effect of drugs and environmental poisons. Prolonged efficiency may cause scurvy.

NATURAL SOURCES

All fresh fruits and vegetables. Particularly rich sources: rose hips, citrus fruits, black currants, strawberries, apples, persimmons, guavas, acerola cherries, potatoes, cabbage, broccoli, tomatoes, turnip greens and green bell peppers.

VITAMIN D

Ergosterol, Viosterol, Calciferol. Known as the "Sunshine Vitamin." Measured in USP Units.

FUNCTION

Assists in assimilation of calcium, phosphorus and other minerals from the digestive tract. Necessary for the healthy function of parathyroid glands, which regulate the calcium level in the blood. Essential for the health of thyroid gland. Very important in infancy and adolescence for the proper formation of teeth and bones. Prevents rickets. Helps prevent tooth decay and pyorrhea. Some scientists feel that vitamin D is a hormone rather than a vitamin, as its functions parallel those of hormones.

DEFICIENCY SYMPTOMS

Prolonged deficiency may lead to rickets, tooth decay, pyorrhea, osteomalacia, osteoporosis, retarded growth and poor bone formation in children, muscular weakness, lack of vigor, deficient assimilation of minerals and premature aging.

NATURAL SOURCES

Fish liver oils, egg yolks, milk, butter, sprouted seeds, mushrooms, sunflower seeds. Vitamin D is produced by sunlight on the oily skin and absorbed by the body through the skin.

VITAMIN E

Tocopherol, d-alpha tocopherol or tocopheryl, dl-tocopherol, Mixed tocopherols. For most therapeutic purposes, only ***d-alpha tocopherol*** **is used. Usually measured in International Units (IU); occasionally in milligrams (mg). One IU equals 1 mg.**

FUNCTIONS

Oxygenates the tissues and markedly reduces the need for oxygen intake. Prevents unsaturated fatty acids, sex hormones and fat soluble vitamins from being destroyed in the body by oxygen. Prevents rancidity when added to other substances. An effective vasodilator — dilates blood vessels and improves circulation. Prevents scar tissue formation in burns and sores. An effective anti-thrombin and natural anti-coagulant — prevents death through thrombosis or blood clot. Can improve circulation in tiniest capillaries. Protects lungs and other tissues from damage by polluted air. Retards the aging process. Essential for healthy function of reproductive organs. Indispensable for the prevention and treatment of heart disease, asthma, phlebitis, arthritis, burns (speeds healing and prevents scar-building), angina pectoris, emphysema, leg ulcers, "restless" legs, varicose veins, hypoglycemia, and many other conditions. Improves glycogen storage in the muscles. Has been used successfully in the prevention and treatment of reproductive disorders, miscarriages, male and female infertility, stillbirths, and menopausal and menstrual disorders.

DEFICIENCY SYMPTOMS

Deficiency may lead to degenerative developments in coronary system, pulmonary embolism, strokes and heart disease. May cause degeneration of the epithelial and germinal cells of the testicles and lead to loss of sexual potency. Prolonged deficiency may cause reproductive disorders, abortions, miscarriages, male or female sterility, muscular disorders and increased fragility of red blood cells.

NATURAL SOURCES

Unrefined, cold-pressed, crude vegetable oils, particularly wheat germ oil and sunflower seed oil. All whole raw or sprouted seeds, nuts and grains — especially oats and whole wheat. Fresh wheat germ (must be absolutely fresh, less than a week old; rancid wheat germ does *not* contain vitamin E). Green leafy vegetables, eggs, butter. *Known antagonists* (which interfere with or destroy vitamin E in the body): inorganic iron, estrogen (synthetic estrogen taken as drugs), chlorine, or chlorinated water.

BIOFLAVONOIDS

Vitamin P, Bioflavonoid complex: citrin, hesperidin, quercitin, Rutin. Considered to be a part of the vitamin C-complex. Measured in milligrams (mg).

FUNCTIONS

Strengthens capillary walls and prevents or corrects capillary fragility. Prevents capillary hemorrhaging and acts as an anti-coagulant. May prevent strokes. Protects vitamin C from destruction in the body by oxidation. Vitamin C synergist — enhances its property. Beneficial in hypertension, respiratory infections, hemorrhoids, varicose veins, hemorrhaging, bleeding gums, eczema, psoriasis, cirrhosis of the liver, retinal hemorrhages, radiation sickness, coronary thrombosis, arteriosclerosis.

DEFICIENCY SYMPTOMS

Causes capillary fragility. Appearance of purplish or blue spots on the skin. Diminished vitamin C activity. Susceptibility to above-mentioned conditions.

NATURAL SOURCES

Fresh fruits and vegetables; buckwheat; citrus fruits, especially the pulp; green peppers; grapes, apricots, strawberries, black currants, cherries, prunes. Cooking largely destroys bioflavonoids.

VITAMIN F

Essential fatty acids, linoleic and linolenic being considered the most important fatty acids. Measured in grams or milligrams (mg).

FUNCTIONS

Considered to be important in lowering blood cholesterol in atherosclerosis and, thus, preventing heart disease. Essential for normal glandular activity — especially the adrenal glands. Necessary to healthy skin and all mucous membranes. A growth-promoting factor. Needed for many metabolic processes. Promotes the availability of calcium and phosphorus to the cells. Can protect from damage by excessive radiation.

DEFICIENCY SYMPTOMS

Deficiency may lead to skin disorders, such as eczema, acne and dry skin, gallstones, falling hair, retarded growth, impairment in reproductive functions, kidney disorders, prostate disorders, menstrual disturbances.

NATURAL SOURCES

Unprocessed and unrefined vegetable oils, especially soybean oil, corn oil, flaxseed oil, safflower oil and sunflower oil.

VITAMIN K

Menadione. Measured in milligrams (mg).

FUNCTION

Essential for the production of prothrombin, a substance which aids in blood clotting. Important for normal liver function. An "anti-hemorrhaging" vitamin. An important vitality and longevity factor. Involved in energy-producing activities of the tissues, particularly the nervous system.

DEFICIENCY SYMPTOMS

May cause hemorrhages anywhere in the body due to prolonged blood-clotting time, such as nosebleeds, bleeding ulcers, etc. Lowered vitality. Premature aging.

NATURAL SOURCES

Kelp, alfalfa, turnip greens and other green plants, soybean oil, safflower oil, egg yolks, cow's milk, cheese, liver. Also manufactured by the normal bacteria in the healthy intestines.

VITAMIN T

Sesame seed factor, known to be present, but unidentified, often referred to as vitamin T.

FUNCTION

Re-establishes platelet integrity in the blood. Useful in correcting nutritional anemia. Promotes the formation of blood platelets and combats anemia and hemophilia. Useful in improving fading memory.

NATURAL SOURCES

Hulled sesame seeds, "Tahini," raw sesame butter, egg yolks and some vegetable oils.

VITAMIN U

Vitamin-like factor found in some vegetables, notably cabbage.

FUNCTION

Promotes healing activity in peptic ulcers, particularly in duodenal ulcers.

NATURAL SOURCES

Raw cabbage juice, fresh cabbage, homemade sauerkraut.

IMPORTANT NOTE ON VITAMINS

The deficiency symptoms listed in this *Vitamin Guide* could occur only after a prolonged inadequate dietary intake or the body's chronic inability to assimilate dietary vitamins. The symptoms listed do not alone prove an existing nutritional deficiency, as similar symptoms may be caused by a great number of conditions or functional disorders. If, after an adequate vitamin supplementation, these symptoms persist, they may indicate a condition other than a vitamin or nutritional deficiency.

When suffering from serious diseases, it is unwise to attempt self-treatment, with vitamins, minerals or any other way, but it is advisable to consult a doctor, preferably one who is nutritionally oriented, and to abide by his expert advice on the choice of suitable therapy.

Complete Mineral Guide

Common minerals and trace elements, their functions, deficiency symptoms, and natural sources.

CALCIUM (Ca)

FUNCTIONS

Essential for all vital functions of the body. Needed to build bones and teeth, and for normal growth. Essential for heart action and all muscle activity. High calcium dietary intake can protect against radioactive strontium 90. Needed for normal clotting of the blood, and in many enzyme functions. Is of extreme importance in pregnancy and lactation. Speeds all healing processes. Helps to maintain balance between Na, K and Mg. Essential for proper utilization of phosphorus and vitamins D, A and C.

DEFICIENCY SYMPTOMS

Deficiency may cause osteomalacia and osteoporosis (porous and fragile bones), retarded growth, tooth decay, rickets, nervousness, mental depression, heart palpitations, muscle cramps and spasms, insomnia and irritability.

NATURAL SOURCES

Milk and cheese; kelp, dulse; most raw vegetables, especially dark leafy vegetables such as endive, lettuce, watercress, kale, cabbage, dandelion greens, Brussels sprouts and broccoli. Sesame seeds and sunflower seeds are excellent sources. Other good sources are oats, navy beans, almonds, walnuts, Brazil nuts, buckwheat, wheat germ, tortillas.

PHOSPHORUS (P)

FUNCTION

Phosphorus is a mineral colleague of calcium. They work together and must be present in proper balance to be effective. Needed for building bones and teeth. It is an important factor in carbohydrate metabolism and in maintaining an acid-alkaline balance in the blood and tissues. Needed for healthy nerves and for efficient mental activity.

DEFICIENCY SYMPTOMS

May result in poor mineralization of bones, in retarded growth, rickets, deficient nerve and brain function, reduced sexual power, general weakness.

NATURAL SOURCES

Whole grains, seeds and nuts, wheat germ, legumes, brewer's yeast, dairy products, egg yolks, fish, dried fruits, corn.

MAGNESIUM (Mg)

FUNCTIONS

Improtant catalyst in many enzyme reactions, especially those involved in energy production. Helps in utilization of vitamins B and E, fats, calcium and other minerals. Needed for healthy muscle tone, healthy bones and for efficient synthesis of proteins. Essential for heart health. Regulates acid-alkaline balance in the system. Involved in lecithin production. A natural tranquilizer. Prevents building up of cholesterol and consequent atherosclerosis.

DEFICIENCY SYMPTOMS

Continuous deficiency will cause a loss of calcium and potassium from the body, with consequent deficiencies of those minerals. Deficiency can lead to kidney damage and kidney stones, muscle cramps, atherosclerosis, heart attack, epileptic seizures, nervous irritability, marked depression and confusion, impaired protein metabolism and premature wrinkles.

NATURAL SOURCES

Kelp, nuts, soybeans, brewer's yeast, buckwheat, millet, rye, raw and cooked green leafy vegetables, particularly kale, endive, chard, celery, beet tops, alfalfa, figs, apples, lemons, peaches, almonds, sunflower seeds, brown rice and sesame seeds.

POTASSIUM (K)

FUNCTIONS

Important as an alkalizing agent in keeping proper acid-alkaline balance in the blood and tissues. Prevents over-acidity. Essential for muscle contraction, therefore it is important for proper heart function, especially for normal heart beat. Promotes the secretion of hormones. Helps the kidneys in detoxification of blood. Prevents female disorders by stimulating the endocrine hormone production. Involved in proper function of the nervous system.

DEFICIENCY SYMPTOMS

Severe deficiency may cause excessive accumulation of sodium (salt) in the tissues, with severe consequences of sodium poisoning, edema, high blood pressure and heart failure. May damage the heart muscle and lead to heart attacks. Prolonged deficiency causes constipation, nervous disorders, extreme fatigue, muscular weakness and low blood sugar (hypoglycemia).

NATURAL SOURCES

All vegetables, especially green leafy vegetables, dulse, kelp, oranges, whole grains, sunflower seeds, nuts and milk. Potatoes, especially potato peelings, and bananas are especially good sources.

SODIUM (Na)

FUNCTIONS

Sodium is closely associated with potassium and chlorine in many vital functions in the body. These three minerals are known to maintain proper electrolyte balance by changing into electrically charged ions which carry nerve impulse conduction and transportation. They control and maintain osmotic pressure, which is responsible for the transportatior of nutrients from the intestines into the blood. They are involved in keeping the body fluid at normal levels. Sodium is necessary for hydrochloric acid production in the stomach, and plays a part in many other glandular secretions.

DEFICIENCY SYMPTOMS

Deficiencies are rare, and may be caused by excessive sweating, prolonged use of diuretics or chronic diarrhea. Deficiency may cause nausea, muscular weakness, heat exhaustion, mental apathy, respiratory failure. Oversupply of sodium is a more common problem because of overuse of dietary sodium chloride (common salt). Too much sodium may lead to water retention, high blood pressure, stomach ulcers, stomach cancer, hardening of arteries and heart disease.

NATURAL SOURCES

Kelp, celery, romaine lettuce, Swiss chard, watermelon, watercress, asparagus, sea water supplement, sea salt.

CHLORINE (Cl)

FUNCTIONS

Essential for the production of hydrochloric acid in the stomach, which is needed for proper protein digestion and for mineral assimilation. Helps liver in its detoxifying activity. Involved in the maintenance of proper fluid and electrolyte balance in the system.

DEFICIENCY SYMPTOMS

Impaired digestion of foods. Derangement of fluid levels in the body.

NATURAL SOURCES

Seaweed (kelp), watercress, avocado, chard, tomatoes, cabbage, endive, kale, turnip, celery, cucumber, asparagus, pineapple, oats, salt water fish.

SULFUR (S)

FUNCTIONS

"The beauty mineral." Vital for healthy hair, skin and nails. Involved in oxidation-reduction processes.

DEFICIENCY SYMPTOMS

Brittle nails and hair. Skin disorders: eczema, rashes, blemishes.

NATURAL SOURCES

Radish, turnip, onions, celery, horseradish, string beans, watercress, kale, soybeans, fish, meat.

IRON (Fe)

FUNCTIONS

Essential for the formation of hemoglobin, which carries the oxygen from the lungs to every cell of the body. Builds up the quality of the blood and increases resistance to stress and disease.

DEFICIENCY SYMPTOMS

Deficiency of dietary iron may cause nutritional anemia, lowered resistance to disease, a general run-down feeling, shortness of breath during exercise, headaches, pale complexion and low interest in sex. Deficiencies are common among young girls and pregnant women.

NATURAL SOURCES

Apricots, peaches, bananas, blackstrap molasses, prunes, raisins, brewer's yeast, whole grain cereals, especially millet, turnip greens, spinach, beet tops, alfalfa, beets, parsley, sunflower seeds, walnuts, sesame seeds, whole rye, dry beans, lentils, kelp, dulse, liver, wheat germ, pumpkin seeds, almonds.

A sufficient amount of gastric enzymes, especially of hydrochloric acid, is needed for proper assimilation of iron. Older people are often anemic in spite of plentiful iron in the diet, because they lack sufficient hydrochloric acid in their stomachs. For these reasons, the iron-containing fruits, which contain their own enzymes and acids needed for iron digestion and assimilation, are the most reliable sources of dietary iron. Vitamin C (up to 500 mg. daily) also aids in the absorption of dietary and supplementary iron. *NOTE:* Coffee and tea interfere with iron absorption.

COPPER (Cu)

FUNCTIONS

Similar to those of iron. Iron cannot be absorbed without copper. Necessary for production of RNA. Involved in protein metabolism, in healing processes and in keeping the natural color of the hair. Aids development of bones, brain, nerves and connective tissues.

DEFICIENCY SYMPTOMS

Deficiency of copper may cause anemia, loss of hair, impaired respiration, digestive disturbances, graying of hair, heart damage.

NATURAL SOURCES

Foods rich in copper are generally those rich in iron. Especially good sources: almonds, beans, peas, green leafy vegetables, whole grain products, prunes, raisins, pomegranates, liver, soy lecithin, Brazil nuts, buckwheat, rye, olive oil.

IODINE (I)

FUNCTIONS

Essential for formation of *thyroxin* — the thyroid hormone which regulates much of physical and mental activity. Regulates the rate of metabolism, energy production, and body weight. Helps to prevent rough and wrinkled skin. Plentiful dietary iodine can prevent poisoning by radioactive iodine 131. Essential for the health of thyroid gland.

DEFICIENCY SYMPTOMS

Deficiency may cause goiter and enlargement of the thyroid gland, or exophthalmic goiter. Prolonged deficiency may result in cretinism. Dietary lack may lead to anemia, fatigue, lethargy, loss of interest in sex, slowed pulse, low blood pressure and a tendency toward obesity. A serious deficiency may result in thyroid cancer, high blood cholesterol and heart disease.

NATURAL SOURCES

The best dietary sources of iodine are kelp, dulse and other seaweed (available in tablet form). Other good sources are: swiss chard, turnip greens, garlic, watercress, pineapples, pears, artichokes, citrus fruits, egg yolks, and, of course, seafoods and fish liver oils.

MANGANESE (Mn)

FUNCTIONS

Important component of several enzymes which are involved in the metabolism of carbohydrates, fats and proteins. Combined with choline, helps in fat digestion and utilization. Helps to nourish the nerves and brain and assists in the proper coordinative action between brain, nerves and muscles in every part of the body. Involved in normal reproduction and the function of mammary glands.

DEFICIENCY SYMPTOMS

Deficiency may cause retarded growth, digestive disturbances, abnormal bone development and deformities, male and female sterility, impotence in men, poor equilibrium, asthma and myasthenia gravis.

NATURAL SOURCES

Green leafy vegetables, spinach, beets, Brussels sprouts, blueberries, oranges, grapefruit, apricots, the outer coating of nuts and grains (bran), peas, kelp, raw egg yolk and fresh wheat germ.

ZINC (Zn)

FUNCTIONS

Essential for the formation of RNA and DNA and for the synthesis of body protein. Involved in many enzymatic processes and hormone activities, especially in reproductive hormones. Affects tissue respiration and normal growth processes. Needed in the construction of insulin molecule. As a constituent of insulin, involved in carbohydrate and energy metabolism. Essential for normal growth and development of sex organs and for the normal function of prostate gland. Helps the body to get rid of toxic carbon dioxide. Increases the rate of healing of burns and wounds. Needed for proper metabolism of vitamin A. Essential for bone formation.

DEFICIENCY SYMPTOMS

Retarded growth, birth defects, hypogonadism or underdeveloped gonads (sex organs), enlargement of prostate gland and impaired sexual functions, loss of fertility, lowered resistance to infections, slow healing of wounds and skin diseases, white spots on finger and toe nails, poor sense of taste and smell. Deficiency may cause lethargy, apathy, hair loss, dandruff and loss of interest in learning. Zinc deficiency is also associated with atherosclerosis, epilepsy and osteoporosis.

NATURAL SOURCES

Wheat bran and fresh wheat germ, whole grains, beans and most nuts, pumpkin seeds, sunflower seeds, brewer's yeast, milk, eggs, onions, oysters, herring, green leafy vegetables.

SILICON (Si)

FUNCTIONS

Essential for building strong bones and for normal growth of hair, nails and teeth. Beneficial in all healing processes and protects body against many diseases, such as tuberculosis, irritations in mucous membranes and skin disorders.

DEFICIENCY SYMPTOMS

Soft brittle nails, aging symptoms of skin such as wrinkles, thinning or loss of hair, poor bone development, insomnia, osteoporosis.

NATURAL SOURCES

Young green plants, such as horsetail, common nettle and alfalfa; kelp, flaxseed, steel-cut oats, apples, strawberries, grapes, beets, onions, parsnips, almonds, peanuts, sunflower seeds.

FLUORINE (F)

FUNCTIONS

Essential for bone and tooth building. Protects against infections. Acts as an internal antiseptic. Excessive fluorine, especially in form of sodium fluoride (as in fluoridated water) causes mottled teeth and can be toxic.

DEFICIENCY SYMPTOMS

Unknown.

NATURAL SOURCES

Organic fluorine is found in steel-cut oats, sunflower seeds, milk and cheese, carrots, garlic, beet tops, green vegetables and almonds. Also, normally present in sea water and naturally hard water.

CHROMIUM (Cr)

FUNCTIONS

Integral part of many enzymes and hormones. Co-factor with insulin to remove glucose from the blood into cells. Important in cholesterol metabolism. Essential for proper utilization of sugar. Involved in the synthesis of heart protein. Contains so-called Glucose Tolerance Factor.

DEFICIENCY SYMPTOMS

Severe deficiency may be a contributing cause of diabetes, high or low blood sugar, hardening of arteries and heart disease.

NATURAL SOURCES

Normally present in natural waters, particularly in hard (highly mineralized) water. The natural complex of the chromium, the Glucose Tolerance Factor, is present in whole grain bread, mushrooms, liver, brewer's yeast, raw sugar and cane juice.

MOLYBDENUM (Mo)

FUNCTIONS

Integral part of certain enzymes, particularly those involved in oxidation processes. Considered to be an antagonist to copper, thus may have protective action in copper poisoning. Involved with proper carbohydrate metabolism.

DEFICIENCY SYMPTOMS

Unknown.

NATURAL SOURCES

Whole cereals, especially brown rice, millet and buckwheat, wheat germ, lentils, peas, green beans, brewer's yeast, naturally hard water.

COBALT (Co)

FUNCTIONS

Integral component of vitamin B_{12} and necessary for the synthesis of this vitamin. If cobalt is present in the system in needed amounts, vitamin B_{12} can be synthesized in the system. Aids in hemoglobin formation.

DEFICIENCY SYMPTOMS

May lead to development of pernicious anemia.

NATURAL SOURCES

Liver. All green, leafy vegetables.

SELENIUM (Se)

FUNCTIONS

Antioxidant; its biological activity closely related to vitamin E. Has a "sparing" effect on the body's uses of vitamin E. Prevents the hemoglobin in red blood cells from being damaged by oxidation. Can help in regeneration of the liver after damage, especially by cirrhosis. May slow down the aging processes by an inhibiting action on formation of free radicals. Protects body from toxic damage by mercury poisoning. Is essential for the function of the enzyme glutathione peroxidase.

DEFICIENCY SYMPTOMS

Liver damage, muscle degeneration, premature aging. Prolonged, severe deficiency may lead to development of cancer, especially in digestive and eliminative tract.

NATURAL SOURCES

Brewer's yeast (not primary grown yeast), sea water, kelp, garlic, mushrooms, organically grown foods, seafoods, milk, eggs, butter, cereals, wheat germ and most vegetables.

IMPORTANT NOTES ON TRACE MINERALS

There are a few other trace minerals, or micronutrients, which are considered to be important in human nutrition, such as *boron, lithium, strontium, nickel, bromine*, and *vanadium*, to name a few. They have been found in the human body in minute quantities (traces), but whether they are important for the body processes or not, has not been determined, as deficiency symptoms have not been observed.

We wish to caution those who attempt to supplement their diets with the trace elements discussed in this section that although microscopic amounts of these substances are required for nutritional welfare, these micronutrients can be extremely toxic if taken in too large amounts. Therefore, great care should be exercised when considering supplementation of the diet with any isolated minerals, but particularly with trace minerals, so that the body's delicate chemistry will not be upset and possible harmful effects will be avoided. The best way to avoid toxicity and imbalances, is to use multi-mineral-trace element supplementation, especially in such natural forms as sea water, mined minerals, mineral waters, bone meal, kelp, raw vegetable and fruit juices, and natural foods mentioned in this *Mineral Guide*. Re: therapeutic uses of vitamins and minerals, see Dr. Airola's book, *How To Get Well.*

RECOMMENDED DAIL

(Designed for the maintenance of good nutritic

BASED ON TABLES PUBLISHED BY FOOD AND NUTRITIO
RESEARCH COUNCI

	AGE From up to years	WEIGHT kg.	WEIGHT lb.	HEIGHT cm.	HEIGHT in.	PROTEIN GM	FAT-SOLUBLE VITAMINS: VITAMIN A ACTIVITY I.U.	VITAMIN D I.U.	VITAMIN E ACTIVITY I.U.
INFANTS	0.0-0.5	6	13	60	24	kg. x 2.2	2,520	400	3
	0.5-1.0	9	20	71	28	kg. x 2.0	2,400	400	4
CHILDREN	1-3	13	29	90	35	23	2,400	400	5
	4-6	20	44	112	44	30	3,000	400	6
	7-10	28	62	132	52	34	4,200	400	7
MALES	11-14	45	99	157	62	45	6,000	400	8
	15-18	66	145	176	69	56	6,000	400	10
	19-22	70	154	177	70	56	6,000	300	10
	23-50	70	154	178	70	56	6,000	200	10
	51+	70	154	178	70	56	6,000	200	10
FEMALES	11-14	46	101	157	62	46	4,800	400	8
	15-18	55	120	163	64	46	4,800	400	8
	19-22	55	120	163	64	44	4,800	300	8
	23-50	55	120	163	64	44	4,800	200	8
	51+	55	120	163	64	44	4,800	200	8
	Pregnant					+30	+1,200	+200	+2
	Lactating					+20	+2,400	+200	+3

DIETARY ALLOWANCES

of practically all healthy people in the U.S.A.)

BOARD, NATIONAL ACADEMY OF SCIENCE, NATIONAL

Revised 1979

WATER-SOLUBLE VITAMINS							MINERALS					
VITAMIN C mg.	FOLACIN mcg.	NIACIN mg.	B_2 mg.	B_1 mg.	B_6 mg.	B_{12} mcg.	CALCIUM mg.	PHOSPHORUS mg.	IODINE mcg.	IRON mg.	MAGNESIUM mg.	ZINC mg.
35	30	6	0.4	0.3	0.3	0.5	360	240	40	10	50	3
35	45	8	0.6	0.5	0.6	1.5	540	360	50	15	70	5
45	100	9	0.8	0.7	0.9	2.0	800	800	70	15	150	10
45	200	11	1.0	0.9	1.3	2.5	800	800	90	10	200	10
45	300	16	1.4	1.2	1.6	3.0	800	800	120	10	250	10
50	400	18	1.6	1.4	1.8	3.0	1,200	1,200	150	18	350	15
60	400	18	1.7	1.4	2.0	3.0	1,200	1,200	150	18	400	15
60	400	19	1.7	1.5	2.2	3.0	800	800	150	10	350	15
60	400	18	1.6	1.4	2.2	3.0	800	800	150	10	350	15
60	400	16	1.4	1.2	2.2	3.0	800	800	150	10	350	15
50	400	15	1.3	1.1	1.8	3.0	1.200	1,200	150	18	300	15
60	400	14	1.3	1.1	2.0	3.0	1,200	1,200	150	18	300	15
60	400	14	1.3	1.1	2.0	3.0	800	800	150	18	300	15
60	400	13	1.2	1.0	2.0	3.0	800	800	150	18	300	15
60	400	13	1.2	1.0	2.0	3.0	800	800	150	10	300	15
+20	800	+2	+0.3	+0.4	+0.6	+1.0	+400	+400	+25	+30-60	450	20
+20	500	+5	+0.5	+0.5	+0.5	+1.0	+400	+400	+50	18	450	25

COMPOSITION OF FOODS
100 grams, edible portion

(dash (—) denotes lack of reliable data for a constituent believed to be present in measurable amount)

FOOD	CALORIES	PROTEINS grams	FATS grams	CARBOHYDRATES grams	CALCIUM mg.	PHOSPHORUS mg.	MAGNESIUM mg.	IRON mg.	SODIUM mg.	POTASSIUM mg.	VITAMIN A VALUE IU	B_1 mg.	B_2 mg.	NIACIN mg.	VITAMIN C mg.
ACEROLA cherry, raw	28	.4	.3	6.8	12	11	—	.2	8	83	—	.02	.06	0.4	1,300
ACEROLA JUICE, raw	23	.4	.3	4.8	10	9	—	.5	3	—	—	.02	.06	.4	1,600
ALMONDS, dried	598	18.6	54.2	19.5	234	504	270	4.7	4	773	0	.24	.92	3.5	trace
APPLES, freshly harvested	58	.2	.6	14.5	7	10	8	.3	1	110	90	.03	.02	.4	7-20
APPLE JUICE, canned or bottled	47	.1	trace	11.9	6	9	4	.6	1	101	—	.01	.02	.1	1
APRICOTS, raw	51	1.0	.2	12.8	17	23	12	.5	1	281	2,700	0.3	.04	.6	10
APRICOTS, dried, uncooked	260	5.0	.5	66.5	67	108	62	5.5	26	979	10,900	.01	.16	3.3	12
ARTICHOKES, globe or French, raw	9-47	2.9	0.2	10.6	51	88	—	1.3	43	430	160	.08	.05	1.0	12
cooked	8-44	2.8	.2	9.6	51	68	—	1.1	30	301	150	.07	.04	.7	8
ARTICHOKES, Jerusalem, raw	7-75	2.3	.1	16.7	14	78	11	3.4	—	—	20	.2	.06	1.3	4
ASPARAGUS, raw spears	26	2.5	.2	5.0	22	62	20	1.0	2	278	900	.18	.20	1.5	33
cooked spears	20	2.2	.2	3.6	21	50	14	.6	1	183	900	.16	.18	1.4	26
AVOCADOS, raw	167	2.1	16.4	6.3	10	42	45	.6	4	604	290	.11	.20	1.6	14
BANANAS, common, raw	85	1.1	.2	22.2	8	26	33	.7	1	370	190	.05	.06	.7	10
BARLEY, pearled, light	349	8.2	1.0	78.8	16	189	37	2.0	3	160	0	.12	.05	3.1	0

BEANS, common white, cooked	118	7.8	.6	21.2	50	148	37	2.7	7	416	0	.14	.07	.7	0
red, cooked	347	7.8	.5	21.4	38	140	—	2.7	3	340	trace	.11	.06	.7	—
pinto, raw	349	22.9	1.2	63.7	135	457	—	6.4	10	984	—	.84	.21	2.2	—
lima, immature cooked	123	8.4	.5	22.1	52	142	46	2.8	2	650	290	.24	.12	1.4	29
lima, mature, cooked	138	8.2	.6	25.6	29	154	48	3.1	2	612	—	.13	.06	.7	—
mung, sprouted, raw	38	3.8	.2	6.6	19	64	—	1.3	5	223	20	.13	.13	.8	19
green, raw	32	1.9	.2	7.1	56	44	32	.8	7	243	600	.8	.11	.5	19
green, cooked	25	1.6	.2	5.4	50	37	21	.6	4	151	540	.07	.09	.5	12
BEETS, red, raw	43	1.6	.1	9.9	16	33	25	.7	60	335	20	.03	.05	.4	10
red, cooked	32	1.1	.1	7.2	14	23	15	.5	43	208	20	.03	.04	.3	6
BEET GREENS, raw	24	2.2	.3	4.6	119	40	106	3.3	130	570	6,100	.10	.22	.4	30
cooked	18	1.7	.2	3.3	99	25	—	1.9	76	332	5,000	.07	.15	.3	15
BLACKBERRIES, raw	58	1.2	.9	12.9	32	19	30	.9	1	170	200	.03	.04	.4	21
BLUEBERRIES, raw	62	.7	.5	15.3	15	13	6	1.0	1	81	100	.03	.06	.5	14
BRAZIL NUTS, raw	654	14.3	66.9	10.9	186	693	225	3.4	1	715	trace	.96	.12	1.6	—
BROCCOLI, raw spears	32	3.6	.3	5.9	103	78	24	1.1	15	382	2,500	.10	.23	.9	113
cooked	26	3.1	.3	4.5	88	62	21	.8	10	267	2,500	.09	.20	.8	90
BRUSSELS SPROUTS, raw	45	4.9	.4	8.3	36	80	29	1.5	14	390	550	.10	.16	.9	102
cooked	36	4.2	.4	6.4	32	72	21	1.1	10	273	520	.08	.14	.8	87
BUCKWHEAT, whole grain	335	11.7	2.4	72.9	114	282	229	3.1	—	448	0	.60	—	4.4	0
BUTTER, salted	716	.6	81.	.4	20	16	2	0	987	23	3,300	—	—	—	0
unsalted	720	.6	82.	.4	20	16	—	0	8	9	3,35	—	—	—	0
BUTTERMILK, cultured, from skim milk	36	3.6	.1	5.1	121	95	14	trace	130	140	trace	0.4	.18	.1	1
CABBAGE, white, raw	24	1.3	.2	5.4	49	29	13	.4	20	233	130	.05	.05	.3	47
red, raw	31	2.0	.2	6.9	42	35	—	.8	26	268	40	.09	.06	.4	61
savoy, raw	24	2.4	.2	4.6	67	54	—	.9	22	269	200	.05	.08	.3	55
CAROB FLOUR	180	4.5	1.4	80.7	352	81	—	—	—	—	—	—	—	—	—
CARROTS, raw	42	1.1	.2	9.7	37	36	23	.7	47	341	11,000	.06	.05	.6	8
CASHEW NUTS	561	17.2	45.7	29.3	38	373	267	3.8	15	464	100	.43	.25	1.8	—
CALIFLOWER, raw	27	2.7	.2	5.2	25	56	24	1.1	13	295	60	.11	.10	.7	78
cooked	22	2.3	.2	4.1	21	42	—	.7	9	206	60	.09	.08	.6	55
CELERY, raw	17	.9	.1	3.9	39	28	22	.3	126	341	240	.03	.03	.3	9
CHARD, Swiss, raw	25	2.4	0.3	4.6	88	39	65	3.2	147	550	6,500	.06	.17	.5	32
cooked	18	1.8	.2	3.3	73	24		1.8	86	321	5,400	.04	.11	.4	16

FOOD	CALORIES	PROTEINS grams	FATS grams	CARBOHYDRATES grams	CALCIUM mg.	PHOSPHORUS mg.	MAGNESIUM mg.	IRON mg.	SODIUM mg.	POTASSIUM mg.	VITAMIN A VALUE IU	B_1 mg.	B_2 mg.	NIACIN mg.	VITAMIN C mg.
CHEESE, Blue or Roquefort	368	21.5	30.5	2.0	315	339	48	.5			1,240	.03	.61	1.2	
Cheddar	398	25.0	32.2	2.1	750	478	45	1.0	700	82	1,310	.03	.46	.1	
Cottage, creamed	106	13.6	4.2	2.9	94	152	—	.3	229	85	170	.03	.25	.1	
Cottage, uncreamed	86	17.0	.3	2.7	90	175	—	.4	290	72	10	.03	.28	.1	
Swiss	370	27.5	28.0	1.7	925	563	—	.9	710	104	1,140	.01	.40	.1	
Brick	370	22.2	30.5	1.9	730	455	—	.9	—	—	1,240	—	.45	.1	
CHERRIES, sour, red, raw	58	1.2	.3	14.3	29	19	14	.4	2	191	1,000	.05	.06	.4	10
sweet, raw	70	1.3	.3	17.4	22	19	9	.4	2	191	110	.05	.06	.4	10
frozen, sour, red	55	1.0	.4	13.4	13	22	10	.7	2	188	1,000	.04	.07	.3	5
CHESTNUTS, fresh	194	2.9	1.5	42.1	27	88	41	1.7	6	454	—	.22	.22	.6	—
COCONUT MEAT, fresh	346	3.5	35.3	9.4	13	95	46	1.7	23	256	0	.05	.02	.5	3
dried	662	7.2	64.9	23.0	26	187	90	3.3	—	588	0	.06	.04	.6	0
COCONUT WATER, from green coconuts	22	.3	.2	4.7	20	13	28	.3	25	147	0	trace	trace	.1	2
COLLARDS, raw, leaves	45	4.8	0.8	7.5	250	82	57	1.5	—	450	9,300	0.16	.31	1.7	152
cooked	33	3.6	.7	5.1	188	52	38	.8		262	7,800	.11	.20	1.2	76
CORN, whole-grain, dried, raw	348	8.9	3.9	72.0	22	268	147	2.1	1	284	490	.37	.12	2.2	
SWEET, on-the-cob, raw	96	3.5	1.0	22.0	3	111	48	.7	trace	280	400	.15	.12	1.7	12
cooked on the cob	91	3.3	1.0	21.0	3	89	19	.6	trace	196	400	.12	.10	1.4	9
flour	368	7.8	2.6	76.8	6	164	106	1.8	1	—	340	.20	.06	1.4	
bread, whole-grain	207	7.4	7.2	29.1	120	211	—	1.1	628	157	150	.13	.19	.6	1
CRANBERRIES, raw	46	.4	.7	10.8	14	10	8	.5	2	82	40	.03	.02	.1	11
CUCUMBERS, raw	15	.9	.1	3.4	25	27	11	1.1	6	160	250	.03	.04	.2	11

CURRANTS, black, raw	54	1.7	.1	13.1	60	40	15	1.1	3	372	230	.05	.05	.3	200
DANDELION GREENS, raw	45	2.7	.7	9.2	187	66	36	3.1	76	397	14,000	.19	.26	—	35
DATES	274	2.2	.5	72.9	59	63	58	3.0	1	648	50	.09	.10	2.2	0
EGGS, whole, raw	163	12.9	11.5	.9	54	205	11	2.3	122	129	1,180	.11	.30	.1	0
yolks, raw	348	16.0	30.6	.6	141	569	16	5.5	52	98	3,400	.22	.44	.1	0
cooked, whole	163	12.9	11.5	.9	54	205	—	2.3	122	129	1,180	.09	.28	.1	0
EGGPLANT, cooked	19	1.0	.2	4.1	11	21	—	.6	1	150	10	.05	.04	.5	3
ELDERBERRIES, raw	72	2.6	.5	16.4	38	28	—	1.6	—	300	600	.07	.06	.5	36
ENDIVE, raw	20	1.7	.1	4.1	181	54	10	1.7	14	294	3,300	.07	.14	.5	10
FIGS, raw	80	1.2	.3	20.3	35	22	20	.6	2	194	80	.06	.05	.4	2
dried	274	4.3	1.3	69.1	126	77	71	3.0	34	640	80	.10	.10	.7	0
FILBERTS (hazelnuts)	634	12.6	62.4	16.7	209	337	184	3.4	2	704	—	.46	—	.9	trace
GARLIC, raw	137	6.2	.2	30.8	29	202	36	1.5	19	529	trace	.25	.08	.5	15
GOOSENBERRIES, raw	39	0.8	.2	9.7	18	15	9	0.5	1	155	290	—	—	—	33
GRAPEFRUIT, raw	41	.5	.1	10.6	16	16	12	.4	1	135	80	.04	.02	.2	38
juice	39	.5	.1	9.2	9	15	12	.2	1	162	80	.04	.02	.2	38
GRAPES, raw	69	1.3	1.0	15.7	16	12	13	.4	3	158	100	.05	.03	.3	4
juice, bottled	66	.2	trace	16.6	11	12	13	.3	2	116	—	.04	.02	.2	trace
GUAVAS, whole, raw	62	.8	.6	15.	23	42	13	.9	4	289	280	.05	.05	1.2	242
HONEY	304	.3	0	82.3	5	6	3	.5	5	51	0	trace	.04	.3	1
HORSERADISH, raw	87	3.2	.3	19.7	140	64	34	1.4	8	564	—	.07	—	—	81
KALE, leaves, raw	53	6.0	.8	9.0	249	93	37	2.7	75	378	10,000	.17	.26	2.1	186
cooked	39	4.5	.7	6.1	187	58		1.6	43	221	8,300	.10	.18	1.6	93
KELP, raw		5.0	1.1		1,093	240	740	3.7	3,007	5,273					5-140
KOHLRABI, raw	29	2.0	.1	6.6	41	51	37	.5	8	372	20	.06	.04	.3	66
KUMQUATS, raw	65	.9	.1	17.1	63	23		.4	7	236	600	.08	.10	—	36
LEMONS, peeled, raw	27	1.1	.3	8.2	26	16	10	.6	2	138	20	.04	.02	.1	53
LEMON JUICE, raw	25	.5	.2	8.0	7	10	8	.2	1	141	20	.03	.01	.1	46
LENTILS, dry, cooked	106	7.8	trace	19.3	25	119	80	2.1	—	249	20	.07	.06	.6	0
LETTUCE, raw, romaine	18	1.3	.3	3.5	68	25		1.4	9	264	1,900	.05	.08	.4	18
Iceberg, New York	13	.9	.1	2.9	20	22	11	.5	9	175	330	.06	.06	.3	6
MANGOS, raw	66	.7	.4	16.8	10	13	18	.4	7	189	4,800	.05	.05	1.1	35

FOOD	CALORIES	PROTEINS grams	FATS grams	CARBOHYDRATES grams	CALCIUM mg.	PHOSPHORUS mg.	MAGNESIUM mg.	IRON mg.	SODIUM mg.	POTASSIUM mg.	VITAMIN A VALUE IU	B_1 mg.	B_2 mg.	NIACIN mg.	VITAMIN C mg.
MILK, cow's, whole	65	3.5	3.5	4.9	118	93	13	trace	50	144	140	.03	.17	.1	1
skim	36	3.6	.1	5.1	121	95	14	trace	52	145	trace	.04	.18	.1	1
dry, whole	502	26.4	27.5	38.2	909	708	98	.5	405	1,330	1,130	.29	1.46	.7	6
dry, skim non-instant	363	35.9	.8	52.3	1,308	1,016	143	.6	532	1.745	30	.35	1.80	.9	7
MILK, goat's, raw	67	3.2	4.0	4.6	129	106	17	.1	34	180	160	.04	.11	.3	1
MILLET, whole-grain	327	9.9	2.9	72.9	20	311	162	6.8	—	430	0	.73	.38	2.3	0
MOLASSES, blackstrap	213	—	—	55	684	84	258	16.1	96	2,927	—	.11	.19	2.0	—
MUSHROOMS, cultivated, raw	28	2.7	.3	4.4	6	116	13	.8	15	414	trace	.10	.46	4.2	3
MUSKMELONS, raw, cantaloupe	30	.7	.1	7.5	14	16	16	.4	12	251	3,400	.04	.03	.6	33
honeydew	33	.8	.3	7.7	14	16		.4	12	251	40	.04	.03	.6	23
MUSTARD GREENS, raw	31	3.0	.5	5.6	183	50	27	3.0	32	377	7,000	.11	.22	.8	97
NECTARINES, raw	64	.6	trace	17.1	4	24	13	.5	6	294	1,650	—	—	—	13
OATMEAL or rolled oats, dry	390	14.2	7.2	68.2	53	405	144	4.5	2	352	0	.60	.14	1.0	0
cooked	55	2.0	1.0	9.7	9	57	21	.6	—	61	0	.08	.02	.1	0
OKRA, raw	36	2.4	.3	7.6	92	51	41	.6	3	249	520	.17	.21	1.0	31
ONIONS, mature, raw	38	1.5	.1	8.7	27	36	12	.5	10	157	40	.03	.04	.2	10
green, bulb & top	36	1.5	.2	8.2	51	39	—	1.0	5	237	2,000	.05	.05	.4	32
ORANGES, peeled, raw	49	1.0	.2	12.2	41	20	11	.4	1	200	200	.10	.04	.4	50
ORANGE JUICE, raw	45	.7	.2	10.2	11	17	11	.2	1	200	200	.09	.03	.4	50
PAPAYA, raw	39	.6	.1	10.0	20	16		.3	3	234	1,750	.04	.04	.3	56
PARSLEY, raw	44	3.6	.6	8.5	203	63	41	6.2	45	727	8,500	.12	.26	1.2	172
PARSNIPS, raw	76	1.7	.5	17.5	50	77	32	.7	12	541	30	.07	.08	.1	10
PEACHES, raw	38	.6	.1	9.7	9	19	10	.5	1	202	1,330	.02	.05	1.0	7
PEANUTS, raw, with skins	564	26.0	47.5	18.6	69	401	206	2.1	5	674	—	1.14	.13	17.2	0

PEARS, raw	61	.7	.4	15.3	8	11	7	.3	2	130	20	.02	.04	.1	4
PEAS, raw, from pods	53	3.4	.2	12.0	62	90	35	.7	—	170	680	.28	.12	—	21
green, cooked	71	5.4	.4	12.1	23	99	—	1.8	1	196	540	.28	.11	2.3	20
split, cooked	115	8.0	.3	20.8	11	89	—	1.7	13	296	40	.15	.09	.9	—
PECANS	687	9.2	71.2	14.6	73	289	142	2.4	trace	603	130	.86	.13	.9	2
PEPPERS, raw, sweet, green	22	1.2	.2	4.8	9	22	18	.7	13	213	420	.08	.08	.5	128
raw, red	31	1.4	.3	7.1	13	30	—	.6	—	—	4,450	.08	.08	.5	204
PERSIMMONS, raw	127	.8	.4	33.5	27	26	8	2.5	1	310	—	—	—	—	66
PINEAPPLE, raw	52	0.4	0.2	13.7	17	8	13	0.5	1	146	70	.09	.03	.2	17
juice, canned, unsweetened	55	.4	.1	13.5	15	9	12	.3	1	149	50	.05	.02	.2	9
PLUMS, prune-type, raw	75	.8	.2	19.7	12	18	9	.5	1	170	300	.03	.03	.5	4
POTATOES, raw	76	2.1	.1	17.1	7	53	34	.6	3	407	trace	.10	.04	1.5	20
baked in skin	93	2.6	.1	21.1	9	65	—	.7	4	503	trace	.10	.04	1.7	20
boiled in skin	76	2.1	.1	17.1	7	53	—	.6	3	407	trace	.09	.04	1.5	16
PUMPKIN, raw	26	1.0	.1	6.5	21	44	12	.8	1	340	1,600	.05	.11	.6	9
PUMPKIN SEEDS, dry	553	29.0	46.7	15.0	51	1,144	—	11.2	—	—	70	.24	.19	2.4	—
RADISHES, raw	17	1.0	.1	3.6	30	31	15	1.0	18	322	10	.03	.03	.3	26
RAISINS, natural, uncooked	289	2.5	.2	77.4	62	101	35	3.5	27	763	20	.11	.08	.5	1
RASPBERRIES, raw, black	73	1.5	1.4	15.7	30	22	30	0.9	1	199	trace	.03	.09	0.9	18
red	57	1.2	.5	13.6	22	22	20	0.9	1	168	130	.03	.09	0.9	25
RICE, brown, cooked	119	2.5	.6	25.5	12	73	29	.5	3	70	0	.09	.02	1.4	0
RICE BRAN	276	13.3	15.8	50.8	76	1,386	—	19.4	trace	1,495	0	2.26	.25	29.8	0
RICE POLISHINGS	265	12.1	12.8	57.7	69	1,106	—	16.1	trace	714	0	1.84	.18	28.2	0
RUTABAGAS, raw	46	1.1	.1	11.0	66	39	15	.4	5	239	580	.07	.07	1.1	43
cooked	35	.9	.1	8.2	59	31	—	.3	4	167	550	.06	.06	.8	26
RYE, whole-grain	334	12.1	1.7	73.4	38	376	115	3.7	1	467	0	.43	.22	1.6	0
flour, dark	327	16.3	2.6	68.1	54	536	73	4.5	1	860	0	.61	.22	2.7	0
SAUERKRAUT, solids and liquid	18	1.0	.2	4.0	36	18	—	.5	—	140	50	.03	.04	.2	14
SESAME SEEDS, dry, whole	563	18.6	49.1	21.6	1,160	616	181	10.5	60	725	30	.98	.24	5.4	0
SOYBEANS, dry, raw	403	34.1	17.7	33.5	226	554	265	8.4	5	1.677	80	1.10	.31	2.2	—
cooked	130	11.0	5.7	10.8	73	179	—	2.7	2	540	30	.21	.09	.6	0
sprouted, raw	46	6.2	1.4	5.3	48	67	—	1.0	—	—	80	.23	.20	.8	13
sprouted, cooked	38	5.3	1.4	3.7	43	50	—	.7	—	—	80	.16	.15	.7	4

SOYBEAN CURD (TOFU)	72	7.8	4.2	2.4	128	126	111	1.9	7	42	0	.06	.03	.1	—
SOYBEAN FLOUR, full-fat	421	36.7	20.3	30.4	199	558	247	8.4	1	1,660	110	.85	.31	2.1	0
SOYBEAN MILK, powder	429	41.8	20.3	28.0	278	—	300	—	—	—	—	—	—	—	—
SPINACH, raw	26	3.2	.3	4.3	93	51	88	3.1	71	470	8,100	.10	.20	.6	51
cooked	23	3.0	.3	3.6	93	38	65	2.2	50	324	8,000	.07	.14	.5	28
SQUASH, summer, all varieties, raw	19	1.1	1.1	4.2	28	29	16	0.4	1	202	410	.05	.09	1.0	22
cooked	14	.9	.1	3.1	25	25	16	0.4	1	141	370	.05	0.8	.8	10
winter, raw	50	1.4	.3	12.4	22	38	17	.6	1	369	3,700	.05	.11	.6	13
cooked (baked)	63	1.8	.4	15.4	28	48	17	.8	1	461	4,200	.05	.13	.7	13
STRAWBERRIES, raw	37	.7	.5	8.4	21	21	12	1.0	1	164	60	.03	.07	.6	59
SUNFLOWER SEED KERNELS, dry	560	24.0	47.3	19.9	120	837	38	7.1	30	920	50	1.96	.23	5.4	—
TOMATOES, ripe, raw	22	1.1	.2	4.7	13	27	14	.5	3	244	900	.06	.04	.7	23
TOMATO JUICE, canned	19	.9	.1	4.3	7	18	10	.9	200	227	800	.05	.03	.8	16
TURNIPS, raw	30	1.0	.2	6.6	39	30	20	.5	49	268	trace	.04	.07	.6	36
cooked	23	.8	.2	4.9	35	24	—	.4	34	188	trace	.04	.05	.3	22
TURNIP GREENS, raw	28	3.0	.3	5.0	246	58	58	1.8	—	—	7,600	.21	.39	.8	139
WALNUTS, black	628	20.5	59.3	14.8	trace	570	190	6.0	3	460	300	.22	.11	.7	—
English	651	14.8	64.0	15.8	99	380	131	3.1	2	450	30	.33	.13	.9	2
WATERCRESS, raw	19	2.2	.3	3.0	151	54	20	1.7	52	282	4,900	.08	.16	.9	79
WATERMELON, raw	26	.5	.2	6.4	7	10	8	.5	1	100	590	.03	.03	.2	7
WHEAT, whole-grain, spring	330	14.0	2.2	69.1	36	383	160	3.1	3	370	—	.57	.12	4.3	0
winter	330	12.3	1.8	71.7	46	354	160	3.4	3	370	—	.52	.12	4.3	0
WHEAT BRAN	213	16.0	4.6	61.9	119	1,276	490	14.9	9	1,121	0	.72	.35	21.0	0
WHEAT GERM, raw	363	26.6	10.9	46.7	72	1,118	336	9.4	3	827	0	2.01	.68	4.2	0
WHEY, powder	349	12.9	1.1	73.5	646	589	130	1.4	—	—	50	.50	2.51	.8	—
YAM, tuber, raw	101	2.1	.2	23.2	20	69	31	.6	—	600		.10	.04	.5	9
YEAST, brewer's debittered	283	38.8	1.0	38.4	210	1,753	231	17.3	121	1,894	trace	15.61	4.28	37.9	trace
torula	277	38.6	1.0	37.0	424	1,713	165	19.3	15	2,046	trace	14.01	5.06	44.4	trace
YOGURT, from whole milk	62	3.0	3.4	4.9	111	87	12	trace	47	132	140	.03	.16	.1	1
from skimmed milk	50	3.4	1.7	5.2	120	94	13	trace	51	143	70	.04	.18	.1	1

SOURCES: Agriculture Handbook No. 8., U.S. Dept. Agric. Washington, D.C.; Home and Garden Bulletin No. 72.

WEIGHTS AND MEASURES
Equivalents

a pinch or dash	= less than 1/8 teaspoon
1 teaspoon	= 1/3 tablespoon
3 teaspoons	= 1 tablespoon
2 tablespoons	= 1/8 cup or 2 fluid ounces
4 tablespoons	= 1/4 cup
5-1/3 tablespoons	= 1/3 cup
8 tablespoons	= 1/2 cup
16 tablespoons	= 1 cup or 8 ounces
2 cups	= 1 pint
4 cups	= 1 quart
4 quarts	= 1 gallon
1 pound	= 16 ounces

1 ounce	= 28 grams
1 pound	= 454 grams
1 kilogram	= 2.2 pounds

1 teaspoon	= 5 milliliters
1 tablespoon	= 15 milliliters
1 fluid ounce	= 30 milliliters
1/4 cup	= 59 milliliters
1/3 cup	= 78 milliliters
1/2 cup	= 118 milliliters
1 cup	= 236 milliliters
1 quart	= .946 liter (litre)
1 gallon	= 3.785 liters
1 liter (litre)	= 1.057 quarts

INDEX

H

J

K

L

M

N

O

P

R

S

T

V

W

X

INDEX OF RECIPES

Beverages

Breads

Desserts

Entrees

Fruits

Lactic Acid (Fermented) Foods

Salad Dressings, Relishes and Dips

Sauces

Snacks for Children

Soups

Vegetables

Prepared Vegetables (Vegetable Dishes)

Vegetable Salads

Whole Grains, Cereals & Legumes

ABOUT THE AUTHOR

Paavo Airola, Ph.D., N.D., is an internationally-recognized nutritionist, naturopathic physician, educator, and award-winning author. Raised and educated in Europe, he studied biochemistry, nutrition, and natural healing in biological medical centers of Sweden, Germany, and Switzerland. He lectures extensively world-wide, both to professionals and laymen, holding yearly educational seminars for physicians. He has been a visiting lecturer at many universities and medical schools, including the Stanford University Medical School.

Dr. Paavo Airola is the author of fourteen widely-read books, notably his two international best-sellers, ***How to Get Well***, and ***Are You Confused? How to Get Well*** is the most authoritative and practical manual on natural healing in print. It is used as a textbook in several universities and medical schools, and regarded as a reliable reference manual, the "Bible of Natural Healing," by doctors, researchers, nutritionists, and students of health and holistic healing. Dr. Airola's book, ***Hypoglycemia: A Better Approach***, has revolutionized the therapeutic concept of this insidious, complex, and devastating affliction. The American Academy of Public Affairs issued Dr. Airola the Award of Merit for his book on arthritis.

Dr. Airola's monumental work, ***Everywoman's Book***, is a great new contribution in the field of holistic medicine. It not only confirms Dr. Airola's unchallenged leadership in the field of nutrition and holistic healing, but demonstrates his genius as an original thinker, philosopher, and profound humanitarian.

The Airola Diet & Cookbook is Dr. Airola's newest book. It contains not only 300 delicious and nutritious recipes and Dr. Airola's Weight Loss Program, but also the most thorough presentation to date of the scientific basis for the Airola Optimum Diet — the world-famous diet of supernutrition for superhealth.

Dr. Airola is President of the International Academy of Biological Medicine; a member of the International Naturopathic Association; and a member of the International Society for Research on Civilization Diseases and Environment, the prestigious Forum for world-wide research founded by Dr. Albert Schweitzer. Dr. Airola is listed in the ***Directory of International Biography, The Blue Book, The Men of Achievement, Who's Who in American Art, Who's Who in the West,*** and ***Canadian Who's Who.***

WHAT CRITICS, DOCTORS, AND READERS SAY ABOUT

DR. PAAVO AIROLA'S WORK

"EVERYWOMAN'S BOOK is a massive accomplishment by a single author. Comprehensively documented. Invaluable qualities of judgement, assessment, evaluation, and selectivity, and the analytical deliberation, ethical standards, and mature wisdom distinguish Dr. Airola as a giant in the field. His book deserves to be immediately read and then used as a reference by families throughout our country. We will recognize true progress in creating a healthy American population when Benjamin Spock's influence of decades ago is replaced by Paavo Airola and his new book."

Dr. Robert S. Mendelsohn, M.D.; author; Associate Professor, University of Illinois, College of Medicine; President, National Health Federation; Chicago, IL

"HOW TO GET WELL is extremely practical and helpful for the reader, and a giant example of research and work. I will refer to it many times, giving you credit all the way . . . Many thanks, and congratulations!"

Linda Clark, M.A., author, nutritionist, Carmel, CA

"I am congratulating you for your pioneering work. It will contribute to the freedom of thought and therapeutic alternatives — and, thus, to the improvement of the health standards in the world."

Dr. L.E. Essén, M.D., Sweden

"May I thank you for your exemplar teachings in the field of Biological Medicine from which I have derived a lot of benefits as one of your many students. I frequently refer to your excellent books for helpful answers to vexing problems of my patients and friends"

Dr. Stanley F. Hansen, M.D., F.A.P.A., El Cajon, CA

"I have read all of your books and regard you as the ultimate authority on health matters. HOW TO GET WELL is my nutrition Bible."

M.H., Lantana, FL

"Dr. Airola's HOW TO GET WELL Is undoubtedly the book of the century! He is America's foremost nutritionist and is in the unique position of having his ideas received favorably by a growing number of medical doctors."

Scott Smith, Assoc. Editor, Vegetarian Times

"Your book (EVERYWOMAN'S BOOK) is a masterpiece! It should be read by every woman —preferably together with her husband!"

Dr. Abram Ber, M.D., Phoenix, AZ

"EVERYWOMAN'S BOOK answers every question any woman could ever have. My only regret is that it wasn't published sooner — many women would have been saved a lot of unnecessary suffering. Your book will be a reference for me for the rest of my life."

Rebecca Clarkes, Editor, ALIVE Magazine, Canada

"I have just read your book on cancer. It is such a beautiful work, honest, concise, and well documented. You are doing such a good work in reawakening mankind's consciousness to natural healing resources within us which can enable us to reach new heights in health and awareness."

Dr. Jeff Migdow, M.D., Summit Station, PA

"Thank you for your wonderful books. You are spreading an important message all over the world which shows suffering mankind the way to better health and happiness."

Ebba Waerland, Author, healer. Switzerland

"EVERYWOMAN'S BOOK is fantastic. I cannot relive my life but I can sure live the rest of it better and teach my children with the help of your books."

Mrs. S.K., Toronto, Canada

"I am using Dr. Airola's books as textbooks in my Honors Class on nutrition-health relationship. I know of no better author on such matters."

Dr. Louis Junker, Ph.D., Prof., Western Michigan University

"Never have I read such a fascinating, exciting, and complete health manual. EVERYWOMAN'S BOOK is the most needed book of the century! In my own practice I rely heavily on the information and proven practices advocated in Dr. Airola's books."

Dr. Mary Ann Kibler, M.D., Corry, PA

"My mother-in-law was supposed to have died of cancer two years ago. After following instructions in your book, doctors cannot find a trace of cancer in her."

S.Z., Hillsboro, CA

"HOW TO GET WELL is wonderful. No one deserves more than yourself the success you are having."

Betty Lee Morales, nutritionist; President, Cancer Control Society, Los Angeles, CA

"Without doubt, HOW TO GET WELL is the best and the most informative book on natural healing ever published. Finally we have a book that we can recommend to every one of our customers —and feel good about it."

M.H., health food store owner, Charleston, WV

"The best and most effective treatment for low blood sugar was developed by Dr. Paavo Airola and outlined in his book, HYPOGLYCEMIA: A BETTER APPROACH. Up to 80% of my patients have low blood sugar and I treat them with the Airola diet with excellent results — it is far superior to the traditional high protein diet."

Dr. Willem H. Khoe, M.D., President, Acupuncture Research Institute, Las Vegas, NV

"For years I have been impressed by your rational, independent thinking, your comprehensive approach to health and nutrition questions, and your flexible, adaptable orientation to new information and new ideas. I personally have derived great benefit from your books and am always recommending them to others."

J.D. Shapiro, Assoc. Prof., Memorial University of Newfoundland, Canada

"Your book, ARE YOU CONFUSED?, is the most important health book ever published."

Dr. R. Huckabay, N.D., D.C., Los Angeles, CA

"I feel that your fasting book is a masterpiece. I have fasted many times in the past on water, but your juice fasting method is superior. I am on my 28th day of a juice fast, and feel great!

F.C.W., Phoenix, AZ

"After having suffered for three years with severe symptoms of hypoglycemia, such as periodic loss of coordination, dizziness, and exhaustion, I found your book, HYPOGLYCEMIA: A BETTER APPROACH — and bless the day I did! Now, one month later, no more symptoms — I feel great!"

S.M., La Jolla, CA

"EVERYWOMAN'S BOOK is a book every woman should own and treasure. I certainly will! It is a remarkable achievement and certainly your best book to date."

Dr. Susan Smith Jones, Ph.D., Los Angeles, CA

"No doubt in my mind about it: you are the Number One nutritionist and the most knowledgeable health writer."

A.S., Reg. Therapist, Escondido, CA

"I am an M.D. with an open mind. I am employing your programs, described in THERE *IS* A CURE FOR ARTHRITIS and they are actually doing wonders for my patients."

Dr. T.J., M.D., Grafton, WV

"I have read widely on nutrition, but your books are, in my opinion, the most balanced in emphasis and sound in conclusions of any that I have read. I give your books to my patients and they are most appreciative of them."

Dr. J.S.J., M.D., Carmel, CA

"EVERYWOMAN'S BOOK is the best to-date by a Holistic author placing an emphasis on the integration of the Body, Mind, and Spirit."

Dr. J.H. Coyle, M.D., D.Psych., Scottsdale, AZ

"I became a follower of your approach to health a few years ago when I discovered ARE YOU CONFUSED?. I found your attitude, your sense of responsibility to the public, and your method of formulating principles very refreshing, and rare. I will always be grateful that I read EVERYWOMAN'S BOOK before starting a family. I can't say enough good about it — it is a timely and altogether wonderful book. I am glad, too, that you, who hold such a recognized position in the health field, emphasize so strongly the spiritual and moral aspects of health. This is what America needs now. Thank you for your concern for people."

J.L.S., Gig Harbor, WA

"Your book, HOW TO GET WELL, is sensational! I am impressed with the way you conceived and constructed it, with your fabulous and expert presentation of the philosophy of Biological Medicine and with the common and academic sense it makes . . . you rendered a great service to a disease-ridden mankind."

Dr. H. Rudolph Alsleben, M.D., Anaheim, CA

"I have been using your ideas in my practice for several years now with excellent results. There are people back on the job after being told by their prior physicians to retire because of disability with their arthritis. Keep up the good work."

Dr. Harvey Walker, Jr., M.D., Ph.D., Clayton, MO

"We respect you for the fact that you are not out to just make money from the public by lending your name to breads, soups, teas, herbs, vitamins, etc., etc., as so many nutritionists do, but that you are sincerely interested in better health for all people. We have all of your books and frequently loan them to friends to get them started on the Airola Diet."

R.J.M., Huntington Beach, CA

"My congratulations and heartfelt thanks on behalf of suffering humanity . . . Only through such research and writings as yours that the tide is ever going to turn from passive disease thinking to positive health thinking."

Dr. T.F., N.D., Pasadena, CA

"God bless you in your wonderful work."

Carlson Wade, renowned author, NY, NY

"Your service to mankind cannot be overestimated. You are a leader in the natural health field and your books are invaluable both for laymen and professionals. Keep up the good work!"

Dr. W.D. Currier, M.D., Pasadena, CA

"I have read through HOW TO GET WELL many times and have received both practical and philosophical information of great help to me."

Dr. L.M. Lawrence, D.M.D., Wharton, NJ

"I have been using and profitting from your books for several years. Thank you for the help and joy your books have added to the life of this one person. But even more, thank you for the information and help you so tirelessly make available to the whole human family."

Mrs. E.L., Scottsdale, AZ

"Thank you for HOW TO GET WELL. I refer to it daily for my family and clients."

Dr. Joy H. Bailey, Ed.D., George State University

"Your book, ARE YOU CONFUSED? is a masterpiece. It should be must reading for everyone who wants to achieve better health."

Robert Yaller, author, Venice, CA

"EVERYWOMAN'S BOOK is truly a treasure chest! Each chapter is a jewel and an obvious product of thorough research."

Dr. Virginia Flanagan, M.D., Assistant Clinical Professor, U.C.L.A.; Director, International College of Applied Nutrition; Sherman Oaks, CA

"If EVERYWOMAN'S BOOK was used as a major text in the curriculum of our medical schools, we would have a healthier and stronger America."

Dr. J.P. Hutchins, M.D., Fallbrook CA

"Thank God for such eye-opening knowledge about nutrition. Information in your books saved my life. A billion thanks!"

S.W., Los Angeles, CA

"You have absolutely no idea how much your book, HYPOGLYCEMIA: A BETTER APPROACH, has meant to me; it is literally a life-saver!"

G.W.K., Redding, CA

"In our clinic I have noticed a great improvement ever since we started using Dr. Airola's concepts. Before I was one of the 'Pasteurian thinkers', but Dr. Airola changed that. My sincerest thanks and compliments!"

Dr. R.T. Kennedy, Ph.D., N.D., St. Thomas, Ontario

"I wish to compliment you on your brilliant and dynamic presentations of contemporary health problems and how they can be overcome in a most logical and convincing sequence. I have received great pleasure and stimulation from reading your books and feel you have given to the people of the Western world some priceless teachings which they are so pathetically in need of."

Dr. M.O. Garten, N.D., author, naturopathic physician, San Jose, CA

"Dr. Airola is not only the most knowledgeable but also the most honest writer of them all."

Dr. Kathleen M. Power, D.C., Pasadena, CA

"Congratulations on a truly excellent and much needed book. I literally could not put it down. The material in EVERYWOMAN'S BOOK is comprehensive, well-organized, and presented with clarity."

Dr. Michael E. Rosenbaum, M.D.; Vice President, Orthomolecular Medical Society; Mill Valley, CA

"I cannot tell you in words what your wonderful book, HOW TO GET WELL, has meant to me. For ordinary people like me who are earnestly seeking information leading to better health — and there must be thousands of us — this book is a God-send answer. May the Lord bless you for this wonderful work of yours!"

I.L., Honolulu, HI

"I have read many books on nutrition but none of them have explained in such clear, concise, easy to understand terms the relationship of diet to our emotional, physical and spiritual wellbeing."

L.R., Hyattsville, MD

"Next to my Bible, HOW TO GET WELL is the best book I have ever read!"

Mrs. K.B., Dayton, OH

"Your HOW TO GET WELL book is tremendous. How I wish it had crossed my path years ago."

E.W.M., Chula Vista, CA

"Thank you for your wonderful book, HOW TO GET WELL. I had acne for 12 years. I've tried everything. Nothing really helped. So when I read your treatment for acne, I didn't have much faith in it, but decided to try it anyway. Imagine my surprise when my acne cleared up 90%!!! As long as I stay on your program my face remains clear — for the first time in years!"

J.A., Carlsbad, CA

"I have read all of your books and consider you to be the most important figure in the alternative health field."

C.M. Bryant, E.B., P.H.E.; Director, Natural Health Institute; Glendale, CA

"EVERYWOMAN'S BOOK is magnificent: It is one of your most important works. Your conclusions are well-documented by massive scientific references. I commend you for it."

Dr. Michael L. Gerber, M.D., Mill Valley, CA

"Thank you for the priceless gift of your hardwon knowledge and your generous spirit which seeks to aid and guide the sick onto alternate and safer paths to healing of body and mind."

Mrs. C.D.T., Hatboro, PA

(There are hundreds of similar unsolicited comments in publishers' files.)

NOTES

NOTES

NOTES

NOTES